THE THEORY AND PRA
DEVELOPMENT EDUCATION

Development education is much more than learning about development; it is a pedagogy for the globalised societies of the twenty-first century that incorporates discourses from critical pedagogy and postcolonialism, and a mechanism for ensuring that differing perspectives are reflected within education, particularly those from developing countries. Learning about development and global issues is now part of the school curriculum in a number of countries, and terms such as global citizenship, sustainable development and cultural understanding are commonplace in many educational contexts. Development education has been recognised as one of the educational discourses that has influenced the acceptance of these terms, for both policy-makers and practitioners.

This ground-breaking volume addresses the history, theoretical influences, practices and impact of development education in Europe, North America, Australia and Japan. Chapters include how development education evolved, the influence of theorists such as Paulo Freire, the practices of aid and development agencies and the impact of governments seeking evidence of public understanding of and engagement with development.

The Theory and Practice of Development Education provides essential reading for anyone engaged in re-thinking and reflecting upon the educational needs of a globalised society, and seeking approaches towards learning that place social justice at the heart of that practice. It will be of particular interest to academics and post-graduate students in the fields of development education, international education and globalisation.

Douglas Bourn is Director of the Development Education Research Centre at the Institute of Education, University of London, UK.

THE THEORY AND PRACTICE OF DEVELOPMENT EDUCATION

A pedagogy for global social justice

Douglas Bourn

Routledge
Taylor & Francis Group

LONDON AND NEW YORK

First published 2015
by Routledge
2 Park Square, Milton Park, Abingdon, Oxon OX14 4RN

and by Routledge
711 Third Avenue, New York, NY 10017

Routledge is an imprint of the Taylor & Francis Group, an informa business

British Library Cataloguing in Publication Data
A catalogue record for this book is available from the British Library

Library of Congress Cataloging-in-Publication Data
Bourn, Douglas.
   The theory and practice of development education : a pedagogy for global
social justice / Douglas Bourn.
      pages cm
1. Critical pedagogy. 2. Developing countries. I. Title.
LC196.B68 2014
370.11'5–dc23   2014016351

ISBN: 978-1-138-80476-0 (hbk)
ISBN: 978-1-138-80477-7 (pbk)
ISBN: 978-1-315-75273-0 (ebk)

Typeset in Bembo
by Keystroke, Station Road, Codsall, Wolverhampton

CONTENTS

ACKNOWLEDGEMENTS

This publication builds on the research undertaken by the Development Education Research Centre at the Institute of Education, University of London. Since its inception in 2006, this Centre has acted as the hub for knowledge development, raising the academic profile and building evidence of the impact of learning about development and global issues within education. The Centre established the first ever academic journal on development education, the *International Journal of Development Education and Global Learning*, articles from which are regularly referred to in this volume.

The stimulus for this volume came from discussions with students on the Masters Programme in Development Education at the Institute, who have been asking why there is so little published academic material on development education, and why it is so difficult to find articles and publications that bring together the range of debates and examples of practice. Throughout the volume, reference is made to research, dissertations and theses produced by students from the Development Education Research Centre at the Institute of Education, University of London.

I would particularly like to thank both my past and current students from the Masters Programme in Development Education, and the very talented doctoral students I have had the privilege to supervise, for continually questioning what development education is all about and producing some ground-breaking research.

To Clare Bentall, Nicole Blum and Fran Hunt from the Research Centre and other colleagues at the Institute of Education for their comments, advice and support.

Finally to Elspeth Cardy for her support and help with the final draft.

I would like to thank the *British Journal for Educational Studies* for permission to reproduce the table on categories of global citizenship from L. Oxley and P. Morris, 'Global citizenship, a typology for distinguishing its multiple conceptions', *British Journal of Educational Studies*, 2013, 1–25.

Earlier versions of Chapter 2 appeared in a chapter on 'Development education', in the *Routledge Companion to Education* edited by J. Arthur and A. Peterson, 2012.

An earlier version of Chapter 3 was presented at the European Association of Development Institutes, Development Education Working Group, in June 2012.

An earlier version of the themes outlined in Chapter 6 was first published in *The Theory and Practice of Global Learning*, DERC Research Report no. 11.

ABBREVIATIONS

DEA	Development Education Association (renamed Think Global, 2010)
DEAR	Development Education Association and Resource Centre (Japan)
DEEEP	Developing Europeans' Engagement for the Eradication of Global Poverty
DELLS	Department for Education, Lifelong Learning and Skills (Wales)
DERC	Development Education Research Centre, Institute of Education, London
DFES	Department for Education and Skills (England)
DFID	Department for International Development (UK)
EC	European Commission
ESD	Education for Sustainable Development
GENE	Global Education Network Europe
IDEA	Irish Development Education Association
NGOs	Non-governmental organisations
NORAD	Norwegian Agency for Development Co-operation
OECD	Organisation for Economic Co-operation and Development
RORG	RammeavtaleORGanisasjo (Norway)
UNESCO	United Nations Education, Scientific and Cultural Organisation
VENRO	Verband Entwicklungspolitik Deutscher Nichtregierungs Organisation e.V (Germany)

Note on terminology

In this volume, the terms 'Global North' and 'Global South' are used as metaphors to make distinctions between the richer and higher income countries and the poorer and lower income countries.

PART I

History, terminology and structures

1

INTRODUCTION

A personal journey and rationale

Personal journey

I first became aware of development education during the 1980s whilst running a national voluntary youth organisation in England. I discovered, through supporting a project that promoted learning about global and development themes, that issues were raised about power and inequality in the world; and that perspectives on people who I had regarded as 'poor and helpless' and in need of support were being challenged. The engagement in that project led me to question my assumptions, often based on 'images' of the so-called 'developing world', and to look again at how one relates to and understands people, communities and cultures very different from one's own.

This interest in development education remained with me, and in 1993 I was fortunate enough to be appointed as Director of a new educational charity, the Development Education Association in England (DEA), which brought together under one umbrella a network of organisations actively engaged in promoting learning about development issues.

What I discovered was a well respected, yet educationally marginal, movement of organisations that shared a common belief in wanting to make the world a better place, and saw the concept of development education as a major way of achieving this.

This movement of organisations, particularly the locally based Development Education Centres (DECs), had an approach to learning about global and development themes that not only resonated with my involvement in the youth organisation, but had a values base that resonated with my own philosophy. It offered an array of excellent resources that as a practising educationalist I knew were highly popular and well regarded.

During my thirteen years as Director of the DEA, I was privileged to see the growth of a network that gained increasing educational and political influence. This practice in England, which was mirrored in other European countries, gained little influence however within academic debates in education, compared with, say, environmental education. Questions began to emerge in my mind about the need for greater intellectual rigour and clarity about what underpinned this approach to learning, this distinctive pedagogy.

Dialogue with academics engaged in these debates, particularly Annette Scheunpflug in Germany and Vanessa Andreotti de Oliveria, now based in Canada, led me to a journey of re-conceptualising development education. This culminated in my decision to secure funding to establish a research centre on Development Education at the Institute of Education, University of London, offering a Masters in Development Education, establishing an academic journal, and publication of an edited volume that brought together the work of the current leading theorists in development education today (Bourn, 2008).

This volume takes my learning journey to a new level in taking forward ideas developed since 2006, influenced particularly by research in the Centre, the work of my students and colleagues, and evidence gained from dialogue with academics, researchers and practitioners around the world.

Rationale and structure

The world of the twenty-first century is a globalised world that is still dominated by great divisions of wealth and inequality. Understanding not only the details of this inequality, but why it still exists, has to be an important component of any educational practice around the world.

The practice of Development Education and its related concepts of Global Education, Global Citizenship and Global Learning have been the main vehicles through which this approach to learning about the wider world has taken place in many countries around the world.

Its roots however come from a combination of a desire by governments and non-governmental organisations to build a constituency of support and understanding of global and development issues within society, alongside a desire by radical educationalists such as Paulo Freire to promote a transformational approach to learning.

Development Education is an approach to education that is not generally well known, although it is visible in academic or research terms or as part of the vocabulary of educational practitioners in most industrialised countries. Yet periodically the term raises its head, either through the announcement of new sources of funding, or cuts in funding, or through promotion of specific initiatives on themes such as global citizenship, understanding climate change or support for United Nations Development Goal targets.

This volume is the first to cover the area of development education by more than simply reporting on current practice or summarising key debates. It aims to give a rationale for its existence, to set out its strengths and weaknesses, and to outline a new pedagogical framework. It also summarises evidence of research, particularly in relation to understanding what is meant by development and globalisation, and their relevance to living in a global society. This volume suggests that too little attention has been paid by both theorists and practitioners engaged in debates on development education to understanding different viewpoints and perspectives on development and globalisation.

Another major theme in this volume is the role that non-governmental organisations have played, both in terms of agenda setting and in terms of the impact of their approach on processes of learning and increased understanding.

Key questions posed throughout the volume are:

- Why has development education continued to exist and grow in many industrialised countries?
- What is the specific relevance and relationship of development education to debates about the learning and skills needs for a global society, being a global citizen, intercultural understanding and sustainable development?
- What are the potential theoretical justifications for a body of practice in development education, and what might these theories be?
- What has been the impact of development education in a range of industrialised countries in terms of building understanding of development, equipping learners to understand the global nature of their society, and promoting an approach to education that is radical and transformatory?
- Where has development education had an impact, particularly within formal education?
- What evidence is there that development education has led to changes in learners' perceptions about notions of social justice, charity giving, recognition of inequalities in the world, and the value of sustainable development?

To answer these questions, development education is proposed here as a pedagogy, an approach to learning which recognises that learners come to development and global issues from a wide range of starting points, perspectives and experiences.

The second chapter begins by providing an overview of the history and evolution of development education and its relationship to similar concepts such as global education, global citizenship and education for sustainable development. Chapter 3 reviews different interpretations of the concept from around the world and highlights the tensions between those who see the area as a means to secure changes in behaviour and support for campaigns, and those who are more focused on the learning process.

Chapter 4 looks at some of the reasons why development education has been perceived to be on the margins of educational practice, by highlighting the different ways in which educationalists have viewed the area, including as a social movement or a community of practice.

The volume then moves into a second part that looks at the theories seen as relevant to development education. Chapter 5 looks at the influence of two academics, Annette Scheunpflug and Vanessa Andreotti, and a range of other theories including development, globalisation, cosmopolitanism, global citizenship, postcolonialism and transformative learning. Underpinning the influences seen as relevant to development education is the work of the Brazilian educationalist, Paulo Freire. Other theorists discussed include Jack Mezirow, Amartya Sen, Edward Said, Henry Giroux and Ulrick Beck.

Chapter 6 takes these theories forward into a new pedagogic framework that brings together elements of a global outlook, the role of power and ideology, belief in social justice, and commitment to reflection, critical thinking and transformative learning. This pedagogic framework acknowledges a range of influences and takes account of recent research and practice in this area.

The third section of the volume looks at the practice of development education including development (Chapter 7), globalisation (Chapter 8), and global justice (Chapter 9) and impact. The examples are reviewed in relation to the extent to which they address themes identified in the pedagogical framework for development education outlined in Chapter 6. Research into practice that directly relates to understanding international development is reviewed through examples in school textbooks, a specific examination of international development, and the influence of personal experience through volunteering and an international school link. The chapter on globalisation looks at examples that are particularly related to understanding what living in a global society means, and reviews examples within schools, youth work, further education colleges and higher education. The third theme of global social justice is reviewed through the activities of some international NGOs, notably Save the Children, Plan International and Oxfam.

Chapter 10 concludes this section by reviewing examples of practice that specifically address the impact of projects and initiatives promoting increased learning and understanding about development and global themes. The role and influence of policy-makers is discussed particularly in relation to the possible contradictory needs of development funders and educational policy-makers. The chapter suggests that a valuable approach would be to look at research approaches that are open-ended and focus on processes of learning rather than behaviour change and outcomes.

The fourth section takes forward the pedagogical framework outlined in Chapter 6, and suggests a pedagogical approach to development education using the term global learning. Chapter 11 identifies examples that particularly embrace the elements of a global outlook, recognition of power and inequality in the world, a belief in social justice, and a commitment to reflection, dialogue and transformation. The examples chosen are those that consciously put the learning process at the heart of the project or activity. The following chapter (12) summarises the importance and potential contribution of this pedagogy of development education and its application through global learning.

The final chapter summarises the issues raised in the volume.

The pedagogical approach proposed in this volume will hopefully provoke debate and discussion. It should not be seen as the last word, nor as an approach that simply needs to be applied within formal education. There is a continuing need to encourage more reflective and critical approaches to how learning about global and development issues is undertaken within formal education.

Reference

Bourn, D. (ed.) (2008) *Development Education: Debates and Dialogues*. London: Bedford Way Papers.

2

FROM LEARNING ABOUT DEVELOPMENT TO GLOBAL LEARNING

This chapter outlines the history and traditions that have come to define and influence what is now known as development education. It makes reference to the influence of concepts around 'international development', to broader progressive educational thinking and the relationship to the global education tradition, the work of Paulo Freire, and the practice of a range of non-governmental organisations (NGOs). Finally the chapter notes that key to understanding the history and traditions around development education is the changing role of governments and publicly funded bodies.

Learning about the wider world

Learning about the wider world is nothing new. Bonnett (2008) refers to the desire of peoples to find meaning in the world from earliest human history. Probably from the Ancient Greeks and Romans onwards there has been a thirst to learn about societies and communities beyond one's own community. But as Bonnett (2008) suggests, in many societies this has been based not only on stories of the wider world, but also on the need to identify one's relationship with that world, and a sense of being at the centre, with the rest of the world being on the periphery.

As economies expanded and trade became crucial to the prosperity of many societies, understanding about other places became linked to economic growth and consequent political expansion. The growth in interest in geography, for example, often went alongside the emergence of modern industrialisation; and with the growth of colonial powers in Europe in the nineteenth century, there was a need for the social elites to be aware of people, places and customs elsewhere in the world.

Whilst other influences such as the enlightenment and religion have played a role in the growing interest in learning about the wider world, it is evident that at least in countries such as the UK, economic considerations, aligned with political influence, were the dominant drivers for the growth of subjects such as geography.

By the twentieth century, with the emergence of more democratic societies and, in Europe and North America at least, free access to education, learning about the world was seen as part of everyone's learning in schools. In the UK, for example, Fairgreave, in his *Geography in the School*, published in 1926, stated:

> The function of geography in school is to train future citizens to imagine accurately the conditions of the great world stage and so to help them to think sanely about political and social problems in the world around.
>
> *(quoted in Lambert and Balderstone, 2000: 19)*

Learning about other places or the world in general cannot however be divorced from social, cultural, economic and political motivations and lenses. In the nineteenth and most of the twentieth century, knowledge in Europe and North America about continents such as Africa was influenced by a view of the superiority of the west and subjugation of the peoples of that continent. The history of the teaching of geography in countries such as the UK, for example, has to be understood within the context of the British Empire and colonialism (Binns, 1995; Lambert and Morgan, 2010).

Whilst these perceptions dominated the teaching of geography in the UK up to and in some cases beyond the Second World War, there was evidence of traditions linked to enlightenment and modernity. For example, from the study of geography in English schools in the 1930s there is a recognition of the need to give 'pupils a picture of the lives and work of the peoples of the world' (Simon and Hubback, 1939: 237). Another example of a school curriculum of the same period states that from studying the cotton industry in Uganda, pupils will appreciate the 'lives of people in other parts of the world, and therefore develop sympathy with them, and thus . . . feelings of world citizenship' (ibid.: 258).

These examples however need to be contextualised within a period in world history where there were debates about the relationship of education to democracy and citizenship, promotion of the principles of the League of Nations, and campaigns against the rise of fascism and militarism (Bourn, 1978). It was during this period that movements such as the Council for Education in World Citizenship in the UK emerged (Harrison, 2008).

Following the end of the Second World War and the emergence of a number of international institutions including the United Nations and later UNESCO, the need for education to have a more international outlook became recognised in a large number of industrialised countries. For example the 1974 UNESCO Statement of Purpose of Worldwide Education Policy stated:

> [it should include] an international dimension at all levels of education: understanding and respect for all peoples, their cultures, values and ways of life; furthermore awareness of the interdependence between peoples' and

nations' abilities to communicate across cultures: and last but not least to 'enable the individual to acquire a critical understanding of problems at a national and international level.'

(quoted in Tye, 1999: 38)

This was however not easy in countries such as the United States where up until at least the 1970s, the dominant educational outlook was inward-looking. Also more internationally minded approaches tended to gain little favour in the period of the Cold War, when terms such as peace and international understanding were often linked to closer ties with communist states. As Andrew Smith commented: 'During the mid-1970s, educators and policymakers began to raise concerns about how well U.S. schools were preparing students for this rapidly changing world, and global education began to take shape' (2002: 38).

In Europe, the progressive educational movements that had begun to emerge during the inter-war period (Harrison, 2008; Bourn, 1978) grew, with an increased emphasis on child-centred learning and the emergence of cross-curricular thinking from a liberal and humanist perspective. This culminated in the UK, for example, in a flood of radical publications that suggested linkages between education and social change (Simon, 1991). Educationalists such as A.S. Neill, John Holt and the Brazilian educationalist Paulo Freire were major influences on people like Robin Richardson in the UK, in many respects the father figure of what at first was called 'world studies' and later 'global education' in the UK.

Robin Richardson (1990) noted two long-standing traditions that have influenced global education. The first is an approach towards education that is learner-centred, emphasising the individual's personal development in a broadly humanistic and liberal tradition. The second is concerned with challenging inequalities in society. As Richardson states, 'both traditions are concerned with wholeness and holistic thinking' (1990: 6–7).

From world studies to global education

To understand how development education emerged, there needs to be recognition of these influences on learning about the wider world, the continuing influence of colonial ideas and the emergence of progressive educational thinking under the umbrella of international understanding or global education. All of these traditions were located within modernity, enlightenment thinking and concepts of social progress.

It is in the United States of America (USA) that one sees the earliest emergence of a specific education tradition with an international and global outlook, as a conscious break from colonialist traditions. This was a response in part to the influence of international understanding traditions as exemplified by UNESCO and their Associated Schools Programme, and in part to the emergence of social studies within the curriculum. But it was also in response to a broader worldview in the 1960s and 1970s as a result of more international exchange programmes, the need to learn foreign languages, and reactions to the Vietnam War (Tye, 1990). Key figures in what became known as the global education movement, such as James Becker, Robert Hanvey, Lee Anderson and later Kenneth Tye, Jan Tucker and Merry Merryfield, became influential not only in North America but also in Europe, Australia and Japan. This global education tradition, whilst suffering from right-wing political attacks at various stages for being unpatriotic and un-American, provided a bedrock of ideas and examples of practice upon which academics, practitioners and policy-makers in a number of countries have built since the 1970s to the present day.

A number of themes can be seen within this tradition. The first, influenced by the American education system, is a conscious promotion of a worldview, of encouraging looking outwards to the wider world, not in a way that is about exporting American ideals but rather valuing and understanding different perspectives. This 'perspectives consciousness', as Hanvey (1976) called it, made an important distinction between opinion and perspective. He saw opinion as the surface layer but it was the deeper layers where racism and bias often lay. Following on from this is a recognition of cross- and inter-cultural awareness. There is also within this tradition the need to promote an in-depth understanding of global issues, and this is where the linkages to the curriculum and influences within social studies can be seen. Finally there is the recognition of changing global dynamics and the role the individual can play in securing change.

This movement around global education was led by a number of key academics in the 1970s and 1980s, with support from teachers. There was a period during the 1980s, through the creation of a number of networks and programmes in Florida, California, Mid-West and East Coast USA, of a strong movement that produced a range of educational materials, innovative projects and partnerships with key subject areas such as social studies (Tye, 1999; Kirkwood-Tucker, 2009). However, repeated right-wing attacks in the late 1980s and 1990s put the movement very much on the defensive.

The situation in the UK was slightly different in that whilst there had been elements of an international outlook within aspects of education, they were dominated by colonialist thinking or were on the margins of progressive educational practices. Even an organisation such as the Council of Education for World Citizenship, which had existed since the late 1930s and became closely linked to international organisations such as the United Nations and UNESCO, had little influence beyond private schools and the more elite aspects of the education system.

It was in the 1970s that a global or world outlook approach to education emerged in the UK, with the formation of the World Studies Project under the direction of Robin Richardson. He became very influential in developing a methodology for teaching about world issues with a particular emphasis on active learning methods (see Starkey, 1994). The work of Richardson and others such as James Henderson and later David Selby, Graham Pike and Dave Hicks was influenced by a desire to promote and provide practical materials that supported a child-centred and world-minded approach and a belief in learning for change

(Richardson, 1976). They were influenced not only by UK progressive education and influences from the inter-war period but also by American academics such as Lee Anderson and Robert Hanvey (Hicks, 2003).

This World Studies movement, or Global Education as it became known in the UK from the late 1980s, had a degree of influence amongst teachers and educationalists through a range of curriculum projects. It also however, as in the USA, suffered from political attacks in the 1980s that accused it of encouraging political indoctrination.

The World Studies Trust, as it came to be called, became the main proponent of global education in the UK, into the 1990s and the first decade of the twenty-first century. This Trust saw Global Education as a 'dimension' or 'extra filter' that runs across the curriculum and not as a subject in itself. They also saw Global Education as incorporating progressive teaching methods, being child-centred and co-operative in style. Finally they also suggested that Global Education should include an active element, not only the development of skills and attitudes 'that enabled people to take responsibility for their own lives' but also the skills to 'become active global citizens' (Hicks, 2003).

Elsewhere in Europe, notably in Scandinavia, the Netherlands and Germany, and also in Japan, there is evidence from the 1970s onwards of approaches to education that promote a more international outlook, under themes such as 'education for international understanding' or 'intercultural learning'. In some countries there was a strong influence from UNESCO, in others from the increased role of the European Commission, or in the case of Japan a conscious move from its imperial past to a more outward-looking view of the world (Harrison, 2008; Ishii, 2003; Osler, 1994).

The emergence of the adjectival educations

The emergence of the global education movement had links with other traditions that were also emerging in the 1960s and 1970s. These 'adjectival' movements (Sterling and Huckle, 1996) include environmental, peace, multi- and inter-cultural, human rights and later anti-racist education. These movements had their own origins and distinctive traditions but they had common themes around lobbying for links with societal concerns and education, and a belief that their agenda could use education to secure some form of personal and social trans-formation (Palmer, 1998; Greig et al., 1987).

These traditions grew in the 1980s, particularly in North America, Australia and Europe, with networks of organisations emerging to promote their particular approach to education. Recognising that these trends had common themes and underlying principles, a number of the proponents of the global education tradition, such as Graham Pike and David Selby, initially based in the UK but later in Canada, re-defined global education as the over-arching term to incorporate all of these adjectival educations. Lister, one of their disciples, had stated in 1986 that he welcomed these new movements because their 'twin stresses on human-centred education and global perspectives constitute a radical shift away from the dominant tradition of schooling (which is knowledge based and ethnocentric)' (Lister, 1986: 54).

A variation on this concept of global education emerged in Europe in the 1990s with closer links to development education, but aiming to bring these adjectival educations together because of their perceived interconnectedness and sense of social justice. This concept of Global Education has secured considerable political support from policy-makers as a result of the work of the Council of Europe and particularly its North-South Centre, which at the Maastricht conference in 2002 secured commitment to a strategy from governments, parliamentarians, local and regional organisations and civil society bodies. This definition of Global Education emphasises the opening of people's eyes and minds to 'the realities of the world, and awakens them to bring about a world of greater justice, equity and human rights for all'. It further makes reference to encompassing development, human rights, sustainability, citizenship, intercultural and peace education (see Osler and Vincent, 2002; O'Loughlin and Wegimont, 2005).

The emergence of the development agenda and development education

It is in recognition of these global education traditions that the emergence, growth and specific features of development education need to be understood. Before we explore in detail the specific features of development education, it should be noted that these traditions around global and the other adjectival educations had a major influence on the practices of organisations that would come to see themselves as part of a development education tradition. The emphasis on wider world viewpoints and participatory and child-centred approaches, as will be outlined, can be clearly seen within the practices of organisations such as Oxfam and Save the Children in the UK.

Up until the late 1960s, the dominant view in Europe about the 'third world' was that it was a problem and it was best left to the churches to help poor people. The dominant image was of helpless people who needed charity: 'giving money for black babies' was a common phrase. This meant that in many industrialised countries the medium through which people often learnt about the 'developing world' was via the church.

The de-colonisation approach, whilst beginning in some parts of the world in the nineteenth century, really only began to gather pace in the 1950s and 1960s. This meant for countries such as the UK, France, the Netherlands and Belgium, their relationship to the former colonies would now be based on economic, social and cultural ties. This is where development and aid came in. From the late 1960s onwards, governments followed the traditional modernist interpretation of development and economic growth. Alongside governments, non-governmental organisations emerged in the leading industrialised countries, although some had earlier origins, such as Save the Children after the First World War, and Oxfam in the UK during the Second World War.

From the late 1960s onwards in countries such as Sweden, the Netherlands, Norway, Canada and the UK, publicly funded programmes emerged to support aid. To ensure these programmes had public support, resources began to be given to ensure the public were supportive, through educational programmes, production of resources and general awareness-raising.

Ishii (2003) in reviewing the growth of development education noted that it tended to emerge in a country that had:

1) a high income and industrialised economy
2) a foreign policy for becoming a politically important country by means other than military power
3) an emphasis on welfare, human rights, and the equality of the distribution of national wealth in domestic policy
4) links with developing countries
5) the existence of racial minorities from developing countries, who place new demands on the social system.

(ibid.: 156)

What needs to be added to this list is the influence of the drive for public support for aid, from both governments and voluntary organisations. The need for legitimacy in spending increasingly large sums of taxpayers' money on people and communities thousands of miles away required some degree of public endorsement.

There is evidence that a factor in a number of countries' support for development and aid was their own social, cultural and political relationship to international systems such as the United Nations and associated bodies. In countries such as Sweden, the Netherlands and Canada, for example, from where some of the leading international figures such as Olaf Palme emerged, there was a strong internationalist outlook.

But even in Sweden, development education in the 1960s and 1970s was seen in relation to the dominant discourses of the time, of modernisation, economic growth and concern about population growth (Knutsson, 2011).

This link between an international outlook and the growth of development assistance programmes became an influence not only on policy-makers but also on non-governmental organisations. In the UK for example the work of Oxfam, the development and aid agency, provides a typical example of how and why an NGO supported and became engaged in work with schools. These activities are well documented by Harrison (2008), who suggests that the motivation was 'a desire to open up hearts and minds, as well as the purses, to the problem of poverty in countries overseas' (Black, 1992: 102).

Much of this practice, as Hammond (2002) has commented, was located within an approach that served to educate for support a 'largely ignorant or disinterested public' through education based on delivering information within an uncritical view of development and economic growth. This approach of providing information and resources about third world problems became a feature of development education practice in many countries (Starkey, 1994).

In reviewing the evolution of development education, McCollum (1996) notes that it is essentially a 'by-product of colonialism' and, quoting Foubert, states: 'Could it be that the present concept of development education still remains too entangled in its rather questionable roots in fundraising appeals and a semi-colonial and paternalistic vision of the Third World?' (Foubert, 1984: 122).

Pradervand's report on trends in seven western European countries in the 1980s reinforced these paternalistic perceptions and noted particularly the dominance of middle-class viewpoints, the influence of the church, agendas of the state and the dominant influence of NGOs (Pradervand, 1982).

The emergence of a more critical stance and a movement for radical change

During the 1970s however there was an emergence within development education practice of more critical approaches (Lemaresquier, 1987). Practitioners were beginning to question the aid industry and, often as a result of personal experience and volunteering, people saw the need for a more social justice-based approach (Harrison, 2008). Jorgen Lissner was also posing major questions about the relationship of NGOs to development and development education, and recognising the need to bring in debates around social justice, equity and solidarity (Lissner, 1977).

It was perhaps in Sweden that the first emergence of this more radical approach could be seen within policy materials and examples of practice. There were references to international solidarity and social justice, and to exploitation and powerlessness (Knutsson, 2011: 173).

A more political agenda emerged, influenced in part by continued struggles against Portuguese continued colonisation in Africa but also by hearing about radical educational approaches, notably the work of Paulo Freire (1972). In Canada, for example, people who had been working in NGOs in Latin America recognised the power of Freire's pedagogy to transform society and brought its principles back to Canada, where they adapted them to Canadian culture and reality (Cronkhite, 2000: 152).

Similar observations can be found in Germany and Austria where a Freirean critique of the 'banking method of education' emerged alongside more participatory forms of learning about development (Hartmeyer, 2008: 36). Osler (1994) in her study on development education noted during the 1980s the increasingly radical tone of much of the practice, influenced particularly by Freire but also by leading third world figures of the time, such as Julius Nyerere, and the linking of ideas to action for change.

John Fien, a leading Australian academic in this field, stated in 1991:

> the whole purpose of development education is to promote social justice, to change the world, through understanding, empathy and solidarity with the patterns of life experienced by societies different from our own. In particular

it is concerned with the lives and future well-being of the oppressed, the people who live in the Third World countries of the South or under Third World conditions in the North.

(Fien, 1991, quoted in Starkey, 1994: 28)

By the 1990s in countries such as the UK, Canada, Germany, the Netherlands and Japan there were movements of educationalists, mainly working within NGOs but with some support from teachers and academics, promoting an approach primarily influenced by critical perspectives on development, combined with the pedagogy of Freire and progressive classroom practices (Kirby, 1994; Walkington, 2000; McCollum, 1996). As Regan and Sinclair, two leading figures within the development education tradition, commented:

there has been a general movement from seeing development education as a matter of information, to make up an information deficit in the 'west', to seeing education as the very fuel for the engine of development both in the 'west' and in the 'Third World'.

(Regan and Sinclair, 2006: 109)

Networks emerged that brought these traditions and perspectives together in countries such as the UK, Canada, Australia and Japan. In England a network of local Development Education Centres that had existed since the 1980s joined forces with a number of leading international organisations to form the Development Education Association (DEA) in 1993. For the DEA, development education was much more than learning about development. The definition the Association used at its launch built on practices in the UK and elsewhere in Europe. It emphasised the links between peoples around the world, the importance of increasing understanding of the forces that shape their lives, and the promotion of a more 'just and sustainable world' (Kirby, 1994; Bourn, 2008).

But as McCollum commented in her research on the state of development education practice in England, even in the mid-1990s:

development education had evolved largely through the efforts of individual practitioners who with minimal guidance and few resources have through trial and error gradually developed their own working practices . . . the development education debate thus remains at a superficial level precisely because there is little discussion of the theory implicit in the practice.

(McCollum, 1996: 22)

Whilst it could be argued that the work of the World Studies Trust and the thinking of Richardson in particular had a theoretical framework, there had been little academic-based literature on development education. The literature that did exist tended to focus on changing political influences, with references to examples of practice (Arnold, 1988; Osler, 1994). There was no clear reference point that

70's strong emergence/articulation ⤳ dev.ed. as critical form of ed.
80's wane in UK/US due to conser. gov'ts
90's rise due to EC & public interest → rise of term 'global'
2000s cut due to wane in interest + global economic crisis.

From learning about development to global learning **17**

demonstrated the educational rationale or evidence of the value of development education to educational needs and goals. This meant that the movement was an easy prey to attacks from both political and educational forces that questioned the approach.

Political support and legitimacy for aid

The apparent superficiality suggested by McCollum was in many countries a result of the agendas and priorities of governments and the leading international development agencies. Support for development education emerged as a result of the perceived need for public support for development, and legitimacy for aid. In terms of government support for development education, there was a view that the public needed to understand the development agenda, and therefore funding and resources needed to be given to educational programmes. As a result, in most countries that had a donor aid programme, funding and programmes emerged from the late 1970s onwards to support the work of NGOs, particularly in schools.

However such resourcing of programmes tended to be linked to an awareness of development from political parties that recognised a social justice approach. Where governments were more conservative, support for development education was less evident or was consciously cut, as in the UK and USA in the 1980s and Canada and Australia in the 1990s.

Throughout the 1980s, development education was perceived as being closely allied to social democratic politics and an overtly political agenda. The typical conservative view was that money should go to overseas aid work and not to supporting domestic needs. Funding became related to the political outlook of the government of the day. Development education, world studies and global education agendas came under political attack (McCollum, 1996; Marshall, 2005; Cronkhite, 2000) and it was only in countries such as Sweden and the Netherlands, with strong political support, that national-based funding grew (Osler, 1994). The European Commission's support did however grow, to the extent that by 1990 nearly 10 per cent of their NGO funding for development-related projects was spent on development education.

There was also a conscious decision in some countries, notably Canada, to re-brand educational programmes on development themes as 'global', for political reasons. A consequence of this re-branding was a stronger curriculum focus. However the political support from the government-funded international develop-ment agency (CIDA) in Canada in the 1980s was cut again in 1996 (Cronkhite, 2000) and only began to recover on a limited basis in the first decade of the twenty-first century.

Support for development education from the late 1990s onwards grew in many industrialised countries, in part due to increased public interest in development, the growth of NGOs, and increased interest from bodies such as the European Commission. Development education became politically important within the European Commission: with the major expansion of the Union to countries that had not traditionally been donor aid countries, support and understanding of development was needed in order to justify expenditure in this area. A range of resolutions and policy statements were agreed within European structures in the first decade of the twenty-first century, from a resolution of the Committee of Development Ministers in 2001 through to a policy statement in 2005 which stated that the Union would give particular attention to development education. This led in 2005 to the European Consensus document on development education which called on member states to increase funding and reminded all stakeholders of internationally agreed support for development (EU Multi-Stakeholder Forum, 2005).

This growth was combined with support from the Council of Europe at its 2002 Maastricht Congress on Global Education, which called on all member states to give funding and lobby educational bodies to promote learning about global issues (Osler and Vincent, 2002).

Although there was less political controversy in the first decade of the twenty-first century, in part due to governmental and international desire to secure support for the United Nations Millennium Development Goals, funding for development education started to suffer as aid budgets became squeezed in the economic recession of 2008 and 2009. For example, in 2009 major cuts in funding occurred in Ireland, Sweden and the Netherlands, in part because of the economic crisis but also because there appeared to be questions about its value and impact.

The changing role of the media and emergence of a campaigning focus

Earlier in this chapter it was suggested that development education first emerged related to raising awareness and support for aid and development, but that it gradually began to take a more critical stance. At various times since the 1970s, this critical stance has been challenged and in some cases diverted by media campaigns on development issues, often generated by crises such as famine or other disasters. This has meant that whilst development education has striven to promote appropriate and positive images of people on continents such as Africa, media images have reinforced traditional stereotypes or reduced issues to simple messages that might have helped NGOs and governments, but not necessarily educationalists (Burnell, 1998).

An example of this in the UK was Live Aid in 1985, which based its approach on the public's perceptions, rather than the causes of famine and the issues. Whilst there is some evidence that raising the profile of the Ethiopian famine did result in increased public concern for the poor of the world, development education organisations thereafter found themselves having to put all their energies into promoting resources and materials that challenged the dominant perceptions that still existed for adults and young people, of helplessness and need for aid (Arnold, 1988; McCollum, 1996).

There has been a considerable amount of literature on the media and development (Dogra, 2012; Orgad, 2012; Chouliaraki, 2013) and there have been attempts in a number of countries to lobby for and promote campaigns aimed at the media, to encourage a range of perspectives about what is happening in developing countries. An example of this in the UK was the formation of an organisation, later called the International Broadcasting Trust (IBT), supported by a coalition of NGOs, churches, trade unions and educational bodies, which became a leading influence, producing its own programmes for television but also lobbying broadcasting bodies.

The need to challenge dominant and negative views about the developing world following Live Aid became a major concern of development and development education organisations. VSO (2002) noted in its report on public perceptions of development that the Live Aid legacy was still very prevalent in UK society. NGOs in many countries had throughout the 1990s continued to put a lot of their energies into resources for schools consisting of photo packs looking at different images of communities and peoples in developing countries. Alongside the production of these materials, there was an increased emphasis in both NGOs and government-funded programmes on 'public education and awareness-raising' strategies.

Terms such as 'development awareness' became commonplace in Europe, including in the UK in 1997, with a new Labour government which, although committed to development education, put equal emphasis on communications and media engagement with development (DFID, 1998).

These trends, and a growing desire by NGOs to encourage greater active involvement in development, culminated in the Make Poverty History initiative of 2005. Despite an apparent 'radical' perception about promotion of the need to combat global poverty and the desire for global justice, the key themes and messages from most NGOs were based on accepting the dominant paradigms on develop-ment. As academic debates took increasing notice of critiques of development, from such as Escobar, or postcolonialists such as Spivak or Said (see Andreotti, 2006), mainstream promoters of awareness-raising of development, such as the leading NGOs, were promoting the Millennium Development Goals, fair trade or climate change.

It was outside of development discourses that new thinking began to challenge, and propose new approaches within development education.

Growing influence of globalisation and learning in a global society

During the 1990s the term 'global' came to be seen in some countries and amongst some academics as a more appropriate term than 'development'. Programmes, projects, resources and initiatives in countries such as the UK, Canada, Germany, Australia and Finland began to refer to global rather than development. This was in part for tactical reasons: people no longer understood, if they ever did, what development education actually meant.

There was also an increasing use of the term global in response to recognition by policy-makers and practitioners of the increasing influence of globalisation. So around the world, networks and initiatives emerged that particularly used this term.

In Germany, for example, Klaus Seitz in 1991 used the term 'global learning' in response to globalisation and the needs of a global society. Learning for the future, he said, should be seen as global learning. At a conference in 1990, Seitz argued against the 'third world' being added to the curriculum. There was a need, he said, for a wider horizon for the promotion of a world that had global connections (see Hartmeyer, 2008: 45).

Annette Scheunpflug, whose ideas are explored later, challenged the value of the term development education. She stated that with the moves towards a more global society, development no longer had a subject. There were still power centres in the world, but their location was less and less defined. The increasing complexity of societies challenged the lines of thinking that promoted modernisation. To her, a more appropriate term was 'global learning', which she defined as the pedagogical reaction to a world society with social justice at its heart. She also questioned the traditions within development education of promoting individual action for social change (see Hartmeyer, 2008).

In a number of countries, such as the USA, Canada, Australia, Finland, Sweden, Germany, Austria, Switzerland and the Netherlands, the term global education or global learning was, by the first decade of the twenty-first century, the dominant term within which discourses around learning and understanding about international development could be found. In some cases, as in Central Europe, this was due to a combination of the influences of the views of Seitz and Scheunpflug; but also to the work of the Council of Europe and its recommendations of closer linkages between development, human rights, environment and intercultural learning. In North America and Australia it was also related to leading influences coming from academic discourses, particularly the influence of Selby and Pike, rather than political influences.

In the UK, the response to debates on terminology was in part tactical: the term global was more accessible than development. But it was also due to the need to re-think the whole tradition of development education within the context of globalisation. Thus, in a range of publications by the Development Education Association and local Development Education Centres, and in regional strategies in support of schools, 'learning in a global society' became a common phrase.

This questioning of the term 'development' in England took a new turn in the DEA however, in 2008, when it decided effectively to drop the term 'development education', and replace it with the term 'global learning'. Whilst this was initially a tactical decision, moving on from a term that was increasingly unfashionable, it provided the space for the Association to re-conceptualise the whole tradition. The DEA defined global learning as education that puts learning in a global context, including an understanding of global issues, critical and creative thinking, and promoting a sense of optimism for a better world (DEA, 2008).

In 2013 a new strategic development education initiative was launched in England, with funding from the DFID for schools – but called the Global Learning Programme (GLP), as this was deemed a more user-friendly concept for schools and teachers.[1]

These evolving debates around terminology were increasingly influenced by closer proximity, in both thinking and practice, to similar traditions in the adjectival educations already mentioned; but there was a new coming together of these movements, around sustainable development and global citizenship.

The new adjectivals: sustainable development and global citizenship

Sustainable development as a term emerged in the 1990s and early twenty-first century following the Brandt Commission and the UN summit in Rio in 2001. Learning and understanding about sustainable development had been a feature of educational programmes in a number of countries prior to the launch of the UN Decade on Education for Sustainable Development in 2005. The roots of this area of learning go back to the Brundtland Report in 1987 and the recommendations made at the UN Rio Summit on Sustainable Development in 1992 (see Scott and Gough, 2003).

Research and evaluation on sustainable development education from 1992 onwards have, in the main, suggested that initiatives in this area have been little more than an extension of environmental education (Reid, 2002; Bourn, 2009). Yet in defining education for sustainable development in 1992, there was a recognition that it was based on bringing together both environmental and development education (Sterling, 1992).

Rost has commented from a German perspective that:

> Education for sustainability is to a greater extent a concept that stems from an expression of (international) political will. It could be understood as a kind of mission from the political arena, given to education professionals and academics, to design an educational concept that correctly deals with the necessary requirements for sustainable development in our world.
>
> *(Rost, 2004: 6–8)*

Reviewing the history of Education for Sustainable Development (ESD) in the UK for example, there is considerable evidence to support this notion, although the will came during the 1990s primarily from NGOs rather than from politicians.

There was also the view from UK academics such as Sterling and Huckle (1996) that ESD provided the opportunity for a new and more radical and transformative approach to education that built on some of the best of the adjectival educations. Sterling for example talked about the need for a 'reorientation' of education towards the concept of 'sustainable education' (Sterling, 2004). He posed that sustainability implies a change of purpose to education, with the emphasis on 'systemic learning' as the basis for change in order to understand and engage with the world. Huckle (2010) sought to combine critical social theories of the environment and education with critical pedagogy. To Huckle, there is a close relationship between sustainability and global democracy.

These views on ESD need to be seen alongside much of the writing and practice, not only in the UK but elsewhere in the world, which places a strong emphasis on the urgency of education for sustainability, the threat of climate change and the need for the public to be actively engaged. The UN Decade on Education for Sustainable Development from 2005 to 2014 provided a new political impetus for sustainability as the over-arching concept.

Linked particularly to the growing influence of ESD was the return to one of the rationales for the 'adjectival educations' which was that education had become a vehicle by which to secure behavioural change − in this case to have more environmentally aware and responsible citizens and young people who could be more ethical in terms of their purchases, through fair trade, and their lifestyle, by recycling and monitoring their carbon footprint.

These changes were also helped by the usage of a relatively new term from the 1990s onwards, that of 'global citizenship'. At a similar time to the emergence of ESD, the term global citizenship began to emerge as a way of demonstrating a personal commitment to learning about global and development issues, but also because of the need to recognise the changing nature of power blocs in the world and shifting patterns regarding identity. Miriam Steiner in the UK appears to have been one of the first to use the term in her book in 1996 on the 'Global Teacher', in which she stated: 'The apparent dissolution of ideological and geographical power blocs and the growth of transnational economic trading communities have created a sense that frontiers and borders are of less importance and significance' (Steiner, 1996: xv).

Steiner also notes the increased interest in a number of industrialised countries in the concept of citizenship and the need to re-conceptualise this in relation to the global domain. Throughout the 1990s and into the first decade of the twenty-first century, a sudden wealth of literature emerged that took these debates further. The term 'global citizenship' came in some circles to be related to global communications, travel, use of different languages (Falk, 1994); or in others as related to personal and social action, influenced by a growing anti-globalisation movement (Mayo, 2005). But it is from the development education movement, notably Oxfam in the UK, that the term global citizenship became a way of interpreting personal and social responsibility and engagement in global and development issues, with a nod to educational agendas around identity and political citizenship (Oxfam, 2006). Oxfam's framework of global citizenship, first published in 1996, demonstrates the influences of both the action-orientated elements of development education and early Oxfam figures such as Og Thomas (Harrison, 2008), and the global education movement as elaborated by Selby, Pike and Hicks.

Policy-makers and practitioners in Wales attempted to bring these two new adjectival educations together. The strategy in Wales started from the need for a holistic approach towards education and recognition of the complex and inter-related nature of the world. The strategy is located within a learning framework, recognising that a key element of the programme should be to 'build the skills that will enable learners to think critically, think laterally, link ideas and concepts and make informed decisions' (DELLS, 2006). Since the launch of the programme in 2005 there have been a range of initiatives developed across all sectors of education that aim to take this thinking forward (Norcliffe and Bennell, 2011).

In 2007, perhaps partially influenced by the Welsh model but also in recognition that the dominant environmental agendas were global, i.e. climate change which necessitated greater public engagement, the English school curriculum authority (QCA) produced new guidelines for schools aiming to bring these different agendas together, as one of a number of new cross-curricular themes. However these guidelines became sidelined in 2010 as the UK Coalition government began a process of promoting a more knowledge- and subject-based core curriculum.

Moving from the margins to the mainstream

Regardless of the discussions around terminology, what cannot be denied is that the first decade of the twenty-first century witnessed the biggest ever expansion of support, interest and engagement with learning about global and development issues in the leading industrialised countries. There were a number of reasons for this.

At a policy level, the launch of the Millennium Development Goals in 2000 placed an onus on governments to demonstrate impact and influence. The support of the public for these goals and major advances in development made them a political priority for many countries. Secondly, the drive for support for development goals was given a major boost by the 2005 campaign Make Poverty History. Thirdly, the wider world and developing countries in particular seemed in the North to be no longer far away. Globalisation, instant communications, the impact of climate change and support for campaigns around fair trade, for example, made learning about global issues a part of everyday learning. There was no longer questioning within education of learning about wider world issues. The challenge was much more around equipping the educational community with the skills and knowledge to respond to the needs of learners.

Policy-makers and practitioners were beginning to be able to demonstrate the value of learning about development issues, not only in terms of public support for development, but also in educational terms. In a number of countries, such as Finland, Germany, Austria, England and Portugal, strategies emerged under the label of development awareness, global learning or global education that were owned not only by ministries responsible for aid, but also those responsible for education, and with the engagement of civil society bodies.

Educational institutions, whether schools, colleges or universities, were beginning to refer to the need to equip their learners for living and working in a global society. Universities in North America, the Far East and Europe talked about equipping their students to be global citizens. Schools referred to learning about global issues, using links with schools in developing countries as part of creating a global mindset. Academics increasingly wrote about education and globalisation not only in terms of the impact of economic forces, but in terms of the need for new skills and a different world outlook.

Conclusion

This evolution of development education and its relationship to broader themes such as global education, global citizenship and education for sustainable development could at one level be seen as a maturing of a pedagogical movement. Manuela Mesa refers to the evolution of development education in terms of five generations, from a charitable and assistance-based approach through to a more solidarity-based approach to human and sustainable development, and finally to global citizenship education (Mesa, 2011a). But in reflecting on these generational models, Mesa notes the importance of recognising that there is no single or exclusive definition of development education, and that there is a relationship between these models and broader social and political traditions (Mesa, 2011b).

Whilst this framework has some value and will be referred to again in the next chapter on definitions of development education, there is a danger of seeing this model as some form of evolutionary process. In practice, the history of development education has been far from linear, with progress and setbacks throughout its history. If there is one emerging theme, however, it is that the concept and tradition around development education has had greatest impact where it has been subsumed or metamorphosed into broader movements in education for sustainable development, global citizenship or global learning.

As this volume will outline, behind the growth of development education there has been a distinctive pedagogical approach that needs to be recognised for what it is, a pedagogy for global social justice. Whilst elements of its practice have had an impact on educational policies and practices, its underlying radicalism has perhaps at a number of times and in a number of countries become too diluted. It is the connection to critical pedagogy, transformative learning and postcolonial theories that opens the possibilities for a new radical development education, based on a distinctive approach towards learning.

Note

1   www.globaldimension.org.uk/glp-e

References

Andreotti, V. (2006) 'Soft versus critical global citizenship education', *Development Education, Policy and Practice*, 3(1): 40–51.

Arnold, S. (1988) 'Constrained crusaders? British charities and development education', *Development Policy Review*, 6 (Summer): 183–209.

Binns, T. (1995) 'Geography in development', *Geography*, 8(4): 303–322.

Black, M. (1992) *A Cause for Our Times: Oxfam, the First 50 Years*. Oxford: Oxfam.

Bonnett, A. (2008) *What Is Geography?* London: Sage.

Bourn, D. (1978) 'The development of Labour Party ideas on education', unpublished PhD thesis, University of Keele.

Bourn, D. (ed.) (2008) *Development Education: Debates and Dialogue*. London: Institute of Education.

Bourn, D. (2009) 'Education for sustainable development and global citizenship – the UK perspective', in B. Chalkey, M. Haigh and D. Higgitt (eds) *Education for Sustainable Development: Papers in Honour of the United Nations Decade of Education for Sustainable Development (2005–2014)*. Abingdon: Routledge, pp. 233–238.

Burnell, P. (1998) 'Britain's new Government: new White Paper, new aid? Eliminating world poverty: a challenge for the 21st century', *Third World Quarterly*, 19(4): 787–802.

Chouliaraki, L. (2013) *The Ironic Spectator: Solidarity in the Age of Post-Humanitarianism*. Cambridge: Polity.

Cronkhite, L. (2000) 'Development education: making connections North and South', in D. Selby and T. Goldstein (eds) *Weaving Connections*. Toronto: Sumach Press, pp. 146–167.

DEA (2008) *Global Matters Learning - Case Studies*. London: DEA.

DELLS (2006) *Education for Sustainable Development and Global Citizenship: A Strategy for Action, DELLS Information Document No: -17-06*. Cardiff: Welsh Assembly Government.

Department for International Development (DFID) (1998) *Building Support for Development*. London: DFID.

Dogra, N. (2012) *Representations of Global Poverty: Aid, Development and International NGOs*. London: I.B. Taurus.

EU Multi-Stakeholder Forum (2005) *The European Consensus on Development: The Contribution of Development Education and Awareness Raising*. Brussels: DEEEP.

Falk, R. (1994) 'The making of global citizenship', in B. Van Steenbergen (ed.) *The Condition of Citizenship*. London: Sage, pp. 127–140.

Fien, J. (1991) 'Commitment to justice, a defence of a rationale for development education', *Peace, Environment and Education*, 2(4) (Peace Education Commission, Sweden).

Foubert, C.H. (1984) *Working in Partnership with the Third World, Development Education: The State of the Art*. Geneva: NGLS.

Freire, P. (1972) *Pedagogy of the Oppressed*. London: Penguin.

Greig, S., Pike, G. and Selby, D. (1987) *Earthrights*. London, Kogan Page/World Wide Fund for Nature.

Hammond, B. (2002) 'DFID's invisible hand: a challenge to development education?' unpublished dissertation for MA, UEA.

Hanvey, R. (1976) *An Attainable Global Perspective*. Denver: Center for Teaching International Relations.

Hartmeyer, H. (2008) *Experiencing the World Global Learning in Austria: Developing, Reaching Out, Crossing Borders*. Munster: Waxmann.

Harrison, D. (2008) 'Oxfam and the rise of development education in England from 1959 to 1979', unpublished PhD, Institute of Education, University of London.

Hicks, D. (2003) 'Thirty years of global education', *Education Review*, 55(3): 265–275.

Huckle, J. (2010) 'ESD and the current crisis of capitalism: teaching beyond Green New Deals', *Journal of Education for Sustainable Development*, 4(1): 135–142.

Ishii, Y. (2003) *Development Education in Japan*. New York and London: Routledge.

Kirby, B. (ed.) (1994) *Education for Change: Grassroots Development Education in Europe*. London: DEA.

Kirkwood-Tucker, T.F. (ed.) (2009) *Visions in Global Education*. New York: Peter Lang.

Knutsson, B. (2011) *Curriculum in the Era of Global Development, Gothenburg Studies in Education Science, 315*, Gothenburg, Sweden: Gothenburg University.

Lambert, D. and Balderstone, D. (2000) *Learning to Teach Geography in the Secondary School*. London: Routledge.

Lambert, D. and Morgan, J. (2010) *Teaching Geography 11–18*. Oxford: Oxford University Press.

Lemaresquier, T. (1987) 'Prospects for development education, some strategic issues facing European NGOs', *World Development*, 15(Supplement): 189–200.

Lissner, J. (1977) *Politics of Altruism, Study of the Political Behaviour of Voluntary Development Agencies*. Geneva: Lutheran World Federation.

Lister, I. (1986) 'Global and international approaches to political education', in C. Harber (ed.) *Political Education in Britain*. Lewes: Falmer Press, pp. 47–62.

Marshall, H. (2005) 'Developing the Global Gaze in citizenship education: exploring the perspectives of global education NGO workers in England, *International Journal of Citizenship and Teacher Education*, 1(2): 76–92.

Mayo, M. (2005) *Global Citizens: Social Movements and the Challenge of Globalisation*. London: Zed Books.

McCollum, A. (1996) 'On the margins? An analysis of the theory and practice of development education in the 1900s', PhD thesis, Open University.

Mesa, M. (2011a) 'Evolution and future challenges of development education', *Educacion Research Global*, 0: 141–160.

Mesa, M. (2011b) 'Reflections on the five generation model of development education', *Educacion Research Global*, 0: 161–167.

Norcliffe, D. and Bennell, S. (2011) 'Analysis of views on the development of education for sustainable development and global citizenship policy in Wales', *International Journal of Development Education and Global Learning*, 3(1): 39–58.

Ogra, S. (2012) *Media Representation and the Global Imagination*. Cambridge: Polity.

O'Loughlin, E. and Wegimont, L. (2005) *Global Education in the Netherlands: The European Global Education Peer Review Process*. Lisbon: North-South Centre.

Orgad, S. (2012) *Media Representation and the Global Imagination*. Cambridge: Polity Press.

Osler, A. (1994) *Development Education*. London: Cassell.

Osler, A. and Vincent, K. (2002) *Citizenship and the Challenge of Global Education*. Stoke-on-Trent: Trentham Books.

Oxfam (2006) *Education for Global Citizenship*. Oxford: Oxfam.

Palmer, J. (1998) *Environmental Education in the 21st Century*. London: Routledge.

Pike, G. and Selby, D. (1988) *Global Teacher, Global Learner*. Sevenoaks: Hodder & Stoughton.

Pradervand, P. (1982) 'Would you please empty your teacup? Epistemological and conceptual aspects of development education', *International Review of Education* 28(1): 449–455.

Qualification and Curriculum Authority (QCA) (2008) *The Global Dimension in Action*. London: QCA.

Regan, C. and Sinclair, S. (2006) 'Engaging development – learning for a better future? The world view of development education', in C. Regan (ed.) *80:20 Development in an Unequal World*, 5th edn. Bray: 80:20 Educating and Acting for a Better World, pp. 107–120.

Reid, A. (2002) 'Discussion on the possibility of education for sustainable development', *Environment Education Research*, 8(1): 5–8.

Richardson, R. (1976) *Learning for Change in World Society*. London: World Studies Project.

Richardson, R. (1990) *Daring to be a Teacher*. Stoke-on-Trent: Trentham Books.

Rost, J. (2004) 'Competencies for global learning', *Development Education Journal*, 11(1): 6–8.

Scott, W. and Gough, S.R. (2003) *Sustainable Development and Learning: Framing the Issues*. London: Routledge/Falmer.

Simon, B. (1991) *Education and the Social Order*. London: Lawrence & Wishart.

Simon, E. and Hubback, E. (eds) (1939) *Education for Citizenship in Elementary Schools*. Oxford: Oxford University Press.

Smith, A. (2002) 'How global is the curriculum?' *Education Leadership*, 60(2): 38–41.

Starkey, H. (1994) 'Development education and human rights education', in A. Osler (ed.) *Development Education*. London: Cassells, pp. 11–31.

Steiner, M. (ed.) (1996) *Developing the Global Teacher*. Stoke-on-Trent: Trentham Books.

Sterling, S. (1992) *Good Earth-Keeping, Education, Training and Awareness for a Sustainable Future*. London: UNEP-UK.

Sterling, S. (2004) 'Higher education, sustainability and the role of systemic learning', in P. Corcoran and A. Wals (eds) *Higher Education and the Challenge of Sustainability: Contestation, Critique, Practice, and Promise*. Dordrecht: Kluwer, pp. 47–70.

Sterling, S. and Huckle, J. (eds) (1996) *Education for Sustainability*. London: Earthscan.

Tye, K. (ed.) (1990) *Global Education: From Thought to Action*. Alexandria: ASCD.

Tye, K. (1999) *Global Education: A Worldwide Movement*. Orange, CA: Interdependence Press.

VSO (2002) *The Live Aid Legacy*. London: VSO.

Walkington, H. (2000) 'The educational methodology of Paulo Freire: to what extent is it reflected in development education in the UK classroom', *Development Education Journal*, 7(1): 15–17.

3

WHAT IS MEANT BY DEVELOPMENT EDUCATION?

Development education as a term has a number of different meanings and inter-pretations, from awareness raising about global poverty to learning about devel-opment issues to a framework for broader learning that has an active, change com-ponent. This chapter summarises the main components of development education in terms of the different definitions that exist today, and suggests a possible typology as to how the term could be interpreted. It covers the perspectives of both NGOs and policy-makers; and viewpoints from both donor aid countries and the Global South. It also suggests that a number of interpretations of development education have become subsumed within broader themes such as Global Education or mainstream educational programmes.

Consensus and common themes and principles

In reviewing the ways in which the term 'development education' is interpreted it is noticeable that despite the variations in terminology and approach outlined later, there are some common themes running across the views of NGOs and policy-makers. This is particularly the case in Europe where from 2001 to 2010 a number of initiatives led by NGOs or policy-makers, or a combination of these groupings with academics and researchers, culminated in what became the 'European Consensus on Development: The Contribution of Development Education and Awareness Raising'.

This Consensus document, agreed in 2005, identified the following common aim:

> The aim of development education and awareness raising is to enable every person in Europe to have life-long access to opportunities to be aware of and understand global development concerns and the local and personal relevance of those concerns, and to enact their rights and responsibilities as inhabitants

of an interdependent and changing world by effecting change for a just and sustainable world.

(EU Multi-Stakeholder Forum on Development Education, 2005: 5)

This document had the support and involvement of foreign affairs and aid ministries, NGOs and networks across Europe. The Consensus document, whilst recognising that organisations had different objectives and values bases, noted the importance of working in partnership between funder and recipient, educator and learner, and actors in the Global North and Global South. Within these common principles, a key theme is the recognition of the value of a 'rich variety of voices and perspectives', particularly giving voice to those who 'are marginalised from or adversely affected by global development' (ibid.: 6).

Giving space to the voices of the Global South has been a component of development education, as mentioned in the previous chapter. The review of funding from the European Commission for development education and awareness projects in 2010 (Rajacic et al., 2010a) makes reference to the importance given by both funders and NGOs to 'active Southern involvement' in projects. The involvement of Southern partners via direct exchanges of peoples between the Global North and the Global South or the engagement of minority communities within Northern projects has been a feature of European development education practice for a number of years (Pardinaz-Solis, 2006; Ohri, 1997).

Another key feature of the Consensus document is the recognition of the linkages between globalisation and development, the 'interconnectedness of people's lives and needs', and the 'commonality of development processes and interests throughout the world by engaging the public in experiences and creative responses that highlight the relevance of global development to local situations' (EU Multi-Stakeholder Forum on Development Education, 2005: 6). This theme links closely to definitions and approaches undertaken by bodies such as the DEA in England, which in its definition of Development Education up to 2006 referred to 'enabling people to understand the links between their own lives and those of people throughout the world' (DEA, 2005).

Implicit in the Consensus document, but also mentioned in other European-focused material (Rajacic et al., 2010a, 2010b; Krause, 2010), is the importance of a multi-stakeholder approach. This means securing ownership and engagement in strategies and delivery of programmes of a range of bodies covering government at local, regional and national level, NGOs, educational bodies, universities, media, business, trade unions and Southern partners.

Another strand in the same European material is the emphasis on participatory learning methodologies and the promotion of critical thinking. Rajacic et al. (2010a) make reference to good practice in development education, including the notion that the learner takes on responsibility for learning, to enable autonomous choices and support confidence building.

The Consensus document also emphasised the importance of working with and through existing systems and processes, particularly mainstream education such as the school curriculum. It suggests the need to develop common agendas with the other adjectival educations, i.e. human rights, peace, environment and inter-culturalism. This again built on well-established practices by both NGOs and policy-makers, seeing the value of working through established practices and bodies rather than establishing separate and distinct programmes.

Finally the Consensus document referred to what development education was not, which was not public relations or simply encouraging public support for development or to raise money. This continues the long tradition of development education practice that distinguishes itself from public communications pro-grammes.

The Consensus document has continued to be supported by organisations across Europe since 2005 and has been influential in the development of national strategies, particularly in Portugal, the Czech Republic and Poland (O'Loughlin, 2008; IPAD, 2010; Luczak, 2010). It provides an important baseline for under-standing what are seen as the common features of development education. However, as will be outlined below, consensus material can sometimes hide differing interpretations and practices.

Role of education and learning as opposed to campaigning

Before one looks at specific typologies it is important to note the views held by networks and policy-makers in a number of countries on the distinction between education/learning and campaigning. In Austria for example the development education working group of NGOs stated that 'global learning' is about an open-ended educational process which does not and cannot have predetermined results or campaigns with a clear output goal or focus on the mobilisation of people and political change (Rajacic et al., 2010a).

This recognition of the primacy of education and learning is often in con-tradiction with the goals and objectives of NGOs who, as outlined in the previous chapter, have historically seen their role as securing public support for and engagement with their campaigns and viewpoints.

These tensions between an education and campaign focus have been noted by Chasaide (2009) in reviewing practices in these areas in Ireland, where at a conference in 2008 the need was noted to 'protect and strengthen open learning spaces, with no pre-determined outcomes to participation. This reflected the NGO community's desire to guard against instructive approaches to identifying political solutions and routes to political action' (Chasaide, 2009: 29).

These debates are not unique to development education and have been commented upon by Gearon (2006) with regard to human rights, Vare and Scott (2008) with regard to the environment, and Marshall (2005) with regard to global themes.

What is noticeable is that due in part to the increased influence of results-based approaches within development and education, and the specific impact of the Make Poverty History campaign in 2005, there has been a tendency in a number of

European countries (particularly the UK, the Netherlands, Germany, Italy and Sweden) to place increased emphasis on seeking engagement within education systems as a means of promoting specific campaigns. This is an important element of the landscape of development education practice but it is important to clarify the distinction between education and campaigning before looking in more detail at different perspectives.

There is a view, as expressed by Rajacic et al. (2010a), that the term 'Global Citizenship Education for Change' should be used to cover both global learning, which is to do with the development of the competencies of the learner, and campaigning and advocacy, being concerned with changes in individual behaviour or institutional/corporate policies. These authors in the Final Report for the European Commission on the review of funding for development education and awareness raising (Rajacic et al., 2010b) make a distinction between a 'Global Learning approach' that aims to enhance the 'competences of the learner' with a focus on dialogue and experiential methodologies, and differing perspectives within a 'Campaigning/Advocacy approach that aims at concrete changes in individual behaviour or institutional/corporate policies' (ibid.: 11). This distinction is similar to that outlined by Vare and Scott (2008) who, in reviewing education for sustainable development, refer to two types, one with a focus on open-ended learning and one with a focus on clear goals and objectives.

What is important to note here is that the introduction of the terms 'global citizenship' and 'global citizenship education' has in some quarters been used to cover both a learning and activist focus. For example, Oxfam UK in the promotion of their work with schools states:

> Oxfam works in education policy and practice to empower young people to be active Global Citizens. We promote education that helps young people understand the global issues that affect their lives and take action towards a more just and sustainable world.[1]

The relationship between education, learning and advocacy and the value of the concept of global citizenship will be explored in greater depth in later chapters. A recurring theme within the debates on development education practice across Europe has been the relationship between learning for its own sake and as a means towards preferred goals and objectives. To understand these debates, the differing approaches by NGOs need to be reviewed.

NGO perspectives

As indicated in the previous chapter, development education has evolved through a number of different interpretations that have often been determined by funders, whether governments or NGOs. Reference was made in the previous chapter to the five generations model outlined by Mesa (2011). Regardless of various definitions and interpretations, there has been recognition, at least within European

NGOs, of a number of common elements, as can be summarised from a survey undertaken in 2010:

- to inform and raise awareness of development issues
- to change attitudes and behaviours
- to enable understanding of causes and effects of global issues
- to mobilise citizens through informed action (Krause, 2010).

These elements are close to the definition of the Development Awareness Raising and Education (DARE) Forum. It sees the term as:

> an active learning process, founded on values of solidarity, equality, inclusion and co-operation. It enables people to move from basic awareness of international development priorities and sustainable human development, through understanding of the causes and effects of global issues to personal involvement and informed actions.

> Development education fosters the full participation of all citizens in influencing more just and sustainable economic, social, environmental, and human rights based national and international policies.[2]

What is distinctive about the approach of NGOs from say the European Consensus document is the linkage between awareness-raising learning and informed action, with an emphasis on empowerment and democratic engagement to secure global social change. The perspectives of NGOs also tend to be based on a strong values base around equity and social justice.

Throughout Europe one can find variations on this definition, with in some countries a closer relationship to sustainable development, in others to intercultural understanding or a focus on action for change. For example in Ireland, the network of development-based NGOs, DOCHAS, sees development education as not just about 'increasing people's awareness and understanding of global issues and of the inter-dependence of different countries', but also what is needed to secure more 'equal development'. It also sees the concept as about an 'education based on reflection, analysis and action at local and global level'.[3]

In a number of countries there is a close linkage between development and global and intercultural understanding. The Danish NGO MS for example refers to all Danish people accomplishing 'a competence in dealing with, mixing with and respecting other cultures', as well as 'a competence in understanding, and self involvement and taking responsibility in society and world affairs, no matter whether local or global'.[4]

Within the UK, there is a network of local Development Education Centres and a typical definition used by them is as follows:

> Development Education aims to raise awareness and understanding of how global issues affect the everyday lives of individuals, communities and

societies. It is about teaching and learning awareness of issues related to development, the environment and sustainability and understanding the personal, local, national and global significance of these issues.

Development Education raises questions about our role and responsibilities in an increasingly unequal world where millions of people are denied their basic rights.[5]

For most NGOs there would be an underlying values base to their practice. This might be religion-based, as in the case of Catholic organisations around Europe such as CAFOD in the UK, which refers to the values of compassion, solidarity, stewardship and hope as central to its ethos and identity. Another example is HIVOS from the Netherlands, a humanist-based organisation which emphasises global social justice.[6] UNICEF takes a more particular standpoint related to its educational work around the UN Convention on the Rights of the Child.[7]

Plan International related its development education activity to its long-term commitment to empowering communities in the South, with the focus on child-centred basic programmes. The job of development education in Plan in the UK was:

not only to build a better world to pass on to our young people, but to instil the values and abilities in our young people that we believe will allow them to change the world for themselves, throughout their lives.

(Plan UK, 2010)

In reviewing and reflecting upon these definitions and approaches there have been a number of observations from academics engaged in these debates. Marshall (2007) has commented that too often NGOs have promoted the affective to the detriment of the cognitive domain. Scheunpflug and Asbrand (2006) have criticised NGOs for their lack of attention to the importance of competencies and the links between knowledge and skills, and their overemphasis on individual action and change.

In the review of funding for development education for the European Commission by Rajacic et al. (2010a), an emphasis on 'challenging global injustice and poverty' was identified as the ultimate goal, with challenging misinformation and stereotypes, encouragement of active participation, understanding globalisation and engagement of civil society as the means to achieve this (ibid.: 118). This suggests that action and change are central to the perspectives of many NGOs.

In conclusion, the key characteristics of NGO perspectives could be summarised as:

* understanding the globalised world including links between our own lives and those of people throughout the world;
* ethical foundations and goals including social justice, human rights and respect for others;

- participatory and transformative learning processes with the emphasis on dialogue and experience;
- developing competencies of critical self-reflection;
- supportive active engagement;
- coming together as active global citizens (Rajacic et al., 2010a: 121).

Foreign affairs and aid ministries interpretations

As has been indicated in the previous chapter, a strong influence on development education practice has been the role, support and policy objectives of government ministries with responsibility for aid and international development.

Within many policy statements of international bodies such as the OECD or the European Commission or specific national governments, there have been references to communication about development policies and programmes with a specific educational focus. For example the OECD saw development education in terms of an approach to learning that opens people's eyes and minds to the realities of the world with a focus on justice, equity and human rights (OECD Development Centre, 2009).

The European Commission however would place greater emphasis on raising awareness and changing attitudes in order to anchor development policy in European societies and also to mobilise greater public support for action against poverty and fairer relations between developed and developing countries; and to change attitudes to the issues and difficulties facing developing countries and their peoples.

The level of understanding and engagement with international development varies from country to country, according to their historical role as a donor aid country and the extent of their cultural and societal ties with the Global South. For example the role of national foreign affairs and aid ministries is likely to be very different in countries such as Norway and Poland. The former has a strong tradition of engaging in development and aid, with a strong civil society movement (Nygaard, 2009); the latter has a relatively recent role as a donor aid country (Luczak, 2010).

Donor aid countries in seeking public support for their programmes are likely to put resources towards using the media and other communication mechanisms as a way of building awareness of development. This has been a feature of what some governments would call development education and awareness raising since the 1990s (Winter, 1996). What has been a feature of debates at national (DFID, 1998), European (Rajacic et al., 2010a, 2010b) and global levels (OECD Development Centre (2009), has been the relative importance of communicating messages, building awareness and investing in long-term educational programmes. The Rajacic et al. review notes that at a European Union level there are two alternative visions:

- A means of informing the public or sections of the public about overseas development efforts by the European Union and its Member States with the purpose of increasing public support for official policies.

- Critical engagement of European citizens with a broader concept of 'development', including not only overseas aid but also the relationship between their own local society and global events and processes.

(Rajacic et al., 2010a: 15)

The Rajacic et al. review notes that in reviewing policies across member states in the European Union, the majority of actors see the second vision as the most popular and common (2010a: 15–16).

Linked to this second vision is the viewpoint of seeing development education as not only about deepening understanding of global poverty, but also about encouraging the involvement of citizens and civil society organisations or, as in Ireland, encouraging people towards action for a more just and equal world (Irish Aid, 2007). Strategies and viewpoints across Europe from governments tending to support this perspective have put most of their funding resources into some form of grant programme aimed at NGOs.

This was, for example, the viewpoint of the UK Labour government from 1997 to 2010 through its DFID-led development awareness programme. Central to the strategy was the creation of a development awareness fund, which mirrored the Department's overall goals to support activities that promoted:

- knowledge and understanding of the major challenges and prospects of development, in particular the poverty reduction agenda, but also of the developing countries themselves;
- understanding of our global interdependence and in particular that failure to reduce global poverty levels will have serious consequences for all of us;
- understanding of and support for international efforts to reduce poverty and promote development including the international development targets;
- understanding of the role that individuals can play – enabling them to make informed choices (DFID, 1998).

In reviewing the progress and impact of this strategy, Verulam Associates (2009) noted that DFID appeared to have two broad purposes for its strategy, one political and one moral. The political was to increase legitimacy and support for development and the target of 0.7 per cent of GDP for aid. The moral purpose, with the focus on children and schools and making connections to subjects such as citizenship, was to 'build a better society' by shaping the values of the young.

Verulam Associates also noted that the strategy and the funding programme did not define development and left 'building support for development' and 'development awareness' open to interpretation.

In Norway, Nygaard in reviewing the growth of the NGOs in this area noted the importance of securing government support for an approach that valued and recognised different interpretations:

> The NGOs have had a breakthrough in stressing the role of civil society not just as service providers in the South, but as 'watch dogs' as well as 'lead dogs'

in the North, achieving political consensus in parliament for the basic principle that the state should fund its own critics. This has opened up and stimulated, with the strong participation of NGOs, a lively and critical debate on global development issues and policies. This has been crucial for mobilizing a critical civil society in a country where the alternative to state-funding has been and is fund-raising.

(Nygaard, 2009: 27)

This approach of encouraging and promoting different interpretations of development education, whilst recognised in a number of European countries through funding programmes for non-governmental organisations, did however leave the area open to criticism over lack of evidence of impact.[8] These criticisms have been most evident when the national government has become more conservative or has been faced with the threat of major cuts in funding. Examples of these changes can be found in the UK, Sweden, the Netherlands, Germany and Denmark.

What these strategies suggest is a complex and in some cases contradictory range of programmes. There is recognition of the value of learning and understanding about development and global issues, to encourage a values base around equity and justice, but at the same time there is the bottom line of needing political support for development and aid programmes. It is the extent to which policy-makers are prepared to see linkages between building support for aid and development and wider societal themes such as social justice and equity that has determined the extent to which development education has been seen as more than just learning about development.

One initiative that has consciously tried to address these linkages has been the Global Learning Programme in England, funded by DFID. This programme, through the encouragement of a network of schools, aims to commit their pupils to 'make a positive contribution to a globalised world by helping their teachers to deliver effective teaching and learning about development and global issues'.[9]

Development within the global

In implementing these different interpretations and definitions, a common feature of the thinking of a number of NGOs and policy-makers has been the re-conceptualisation of the term 'development education' within the broader umbrella term of 'global education'. Within Europe, the Global Education Network Europe (GENE) has played a major role in this, building on the practices and perspectives developed in the Netherlands, Austria, Germany and Finland and Sweden. This term is also the dominant one used in North America, Australia and New Zealand by both policy-makers and NGOs.

In reviewing these different interpretations and re-conceptualisations, the question that needs to be posed is: to what extent are they a conscious re-configuring of the debates and issues, responding to external influences; or a conscious break with how development education was perceived?

Within Europe, the view often taken about why the use of the term 'global education' came about is because, as Scheunpflug and Seitz (see Hartmeyer, 2008) have stated, development is an outmoded concept, and linkages to broader global themes ensure the primacy of learning goals and objectives. The Austrian Development Agency for example differentiates between 'global learning' and 'development education'. The former term is now dominant in Austria, influenced by the thinking of Scheunpflug and her approach of promoting 'competencies to leading a fulfilling life in the twenty-first century'. These competencies include: to 'understand and critically reflect global interdependencies, own values and attitudes, develop own positions and perspectives, see options, capability to make choices, and to participate in communication and decisions within a global context' (Rajacic et al., 2010a: 107). In reviewing the emergence of global learning in Austria, Forghani-Arani and Hartmeyer (2011) note the influence of a number of conceptual roots including civics, peace, human rights and environmental education, stating their close affinity with the development education field.

In a number of countries the use of the term 'global education' or 'global learning' has been an indicator that the government ministry responsible for development and the leading NGOs recognise the value of connections between development and broader societal agendas, particularly in relation to cultural understanding, issues of immigration, the impact of globalisation and of 9/11. An example of this is Finland where the government strategy document recognises the changing nature of civil society: 'the task of global education [is] to enhance intercultural understanding, on the one hand; and to foster awareness of one's prejudices and change attitudes, on the other' (Ministry of Education, Finland, 2007: 9).

Finland's global education strategy, based on a partnership between foreign affairs and education ministries with the starting point of the Millennium Development Goals, defined global education in this broader societal context. It is seen as an activity that includes global responsibility, embracing recognition of human rights, the need to economise the earth's resources and understand the impact of globalisation and its 'cultural ramifications'; and that promotes intercultural dialogue.

Alasuutari (2011) in reviewing the evolution of this strategy in Finland notes the need for a more critical development education pedagogy, particularly critical literacy and ethical intercultural learning.

Rajacic et al. (2010a) in their review of funding and support for development education across Europe in 2010 make reference to the point that a feature of a lot of national development education strategies is the link to other adjectival educations.

An example of both NGOs and policy-makers taking a conscious decision to use the term global education rather than development education could be seen in New Zealand. The leading NGO in the country, Global Focus, re-branded its area of practice as global education to enable links to be made to broader societal and global concerns.

Global Focus started from the following definition:

> Global Education raises awareness and understanding of how global issues affect the everyday lives of individuals, communities and societies, and how all of us can and do influence the global situation to create a safe and just world.[10]

For Global Focus, global education had a strong social justice, equity and human rights focus, but also incorporating many dimensions and concepts including: multicultural studies, diversity, human rights, environment and sustainability education, peace and conflict studies, development education, citizenship, and futures education.

What made Global Focus rather different from some of the traditional approaches to both development and global education in Europe was the emphasis put on developing critical thinking skills, recognising and valuing different viewpoints, and the following:

- Communication: the ability to listen, and the ability to describe and explain one's ideas and decisions in a variety of ways and with a variety of other people.
- Decision making and problem solving: weighing up the relevance, validity and implications of alternative solutions to issues or problems.
- Social skills: expressing one's views and feelings clearly and considerately to others, to authorities and to members of cultures other than one's own.

This central focus on learning, voices and perspectives reflects also the influence of Andreotti, who was based in New Zealand from 2007 to 2010. The emphasis given to analysis positioned Global Focus closer to a more critical pedagogical position. For example they stated:

> Analysing a global issue can be complex because there are often various and competing perspectives. It is not always possible to say what is right or wrong in association with a global issue, and therefore the ability to research and analyse are critical. Some issues can also be controversial and contentious.

The fragile nature of development education practice in many countries can be evidenced by the closure of Global Focus in 2012.

Canada is another country where you cannot divorce the history of development education from the growth of global education, with the influence particularly of Pike and Selby, and more recently Shultz (2010) and Mundy (2007). Canada is unusual internationally in that it is one of the few countries where academic influence has had a strong impact within development education. Combined with the provincial educational structure, the strength of NGOs such as UNICEF and the related influence of themes such as human rights and citizenship education have meant that there are a number of common themes. These, as Mundy suggests, are:

- view of the world as one system – and of human life as shaped by a history of global interdependence;
- commitment to the idea that there are basic human rights and that these include social and economic equality as well as basic freedoms;
- commitment to the notion of the value of cultural diversity and the importance of intercultural understanding and tolerance for differences of opinion;
- belief in the efficacy of individual action;
- commitment to child-centred or progressive pedagogy;
- environmental awareness and a commitment to planetary sustainability (Mundy, 2007: 9).

What is noticeable about these 'orientations' is the absence of specific reference to international development. This has resulted in a wider range of actors being involved in the pursuit of broad goals and objectives. A specific consequence has been the development of province-based curriculum initiatives and the emergence of some independent academic discourses around themes such as global citizenship and human rights (Abdi and Shultz, 2008).

Similar traditions can be seen in the United States where, with minimal support from the Federal government, development education has in reality become subsumed within global education, led by networks of academics and teachers with the engagement of a small number of NGOs (see Kirkwood-Tucker, 2008). The practice of global education in the United States builds on the long established activities of the American Forum for Global Education, and the work of academics such as Merry Merryfield. The focus of global education practices in the United States has tended to be through the social studies school curriculum, with an emphasis on knowledge and understanding about world affairs.

Partnerships with education policy-makers and broader societal agendas

A feature of practices and policy statements on development education in the first decade of the twenty-first century has been the engagement with education policy-makers, which has led to new definitions, or the subsuming of development education within broader programmes. A goal of NGOs and foreign affairs/development ministries in most countries has been to secure the engagement of educational policy-making bodies.

Since 2000, there have been numerous examples of this starting to take place and they can be summarised into four main themes. These have tended to follow one of the following:

- use of the term global learning;
- linkage with international education;
- linkage to education for sustainable development;
- specific curriculum focus around key subjects such as geography, social studies, history.

Underpinning these examples is the desire by both NGOs and foreign affairs or development ministries to see the impact of their programmes within the context of broader learning goals or wider social policies. In some cases this is for pragmatic reasons but in many countries there is a common theme that development education will only have any impact when it is seen as an integral component of mainstream learning, particularly in relation to the school curriculum.

This can be seen in a number of countries that have developed strategies on development education. In Ireland for example the strategic aim is:

> To ensure that development education reaches a wide audience in Ireland by increasing the provision of high-quality programmes to teachers and others involved in development education and by working with the education sector, NGOs and civil society partners.
>
> *(Irish Aid, 2007: 8)*

In Poland, it has been noted that due to the involvement of NGOs and the education ministry, 'global education materials have been incorporated into the reformed core curriculum' (Luczak, 2010).

In England under the Labour government from 1997 to 2010 themes such as learning in a global society, global citizenship and sustainable development were reflected in a range of curriculum initiatives and policy statements by the education ministry. For example in 2005 the education ministry published its strategy for international education, entitled 'Putting the World into World Class Education' (DfES, 2005a). Within this strategy were a number of objectives related to promoting English education overseas and encouraging international partnerships. The 'global dimension' was recognised as one element of this. At around the same time, the same education ministry published a strategy on education for sustainable development, the 'Sustainable Development Action Plan', which again made a small reference to the global dimension (DfES, 2005b). From 2000, with the promotion of a new curriculum subject of Citizenship, the ministry had already encouraged the concept of 'global citizenship' both within this subject and as a theme in other subjects such as geography.

There are also examples from a range of countries where development education or its related terms have been seen as educational approaches to tackle domestic issues of racism and cultural understanding, or themes such as global terrorism and fundamentalism. This can be seen in the USA, for example, through a number of educational programmes that arose in response to 9/11 (Merryfield, 2002), or in Europe where economic migration was giving rise to new tensions within communities, for example in Ireland, Sweden and Germany.

Another linkage has been the level of support and resources given to broader initiatives such as Education for International Understanding, building on the tradition outlined in the previous chapter, from UNESCO. This can be seen for example in a relatively new donor aid country such as South Korea (Kim, 1997) and in China in reviewing the role and purpose of their education in the context of globalisation (Bau-cun, 2010).

The UN Decade on Education for Sustainable Development (ESD) has also resulted in a number of countries looking at how their development or global education programmes contribute to these broader goals. In a number of industrialised countries such as Japan, Germany (Scheunpflug and Asbrand, 2006), the Netherlands and the UK, most notably Wales, the principal driver for learning about global and development issues has become education for sustainable development (Norcliffe and Bennell, 2011). With the possible exception of Wales, where the sustainable development agenda has been developed in partnership with a framework for global citizenship, the influence of development education on these strategies has been minimal (Bourn, 2008).

Development education in the Global South

Up until now, there has been little reference to whether or where the term development education is used in the Global South. This is because the term has historically been constructed by Northern-based organisations for their own constituency, to develop learning and understanding about the South.

Where the term development education is used, it is predominantly seen in relation to 'personal and community through the maximum harnessing of available human and natural resources' (Abdi, 2003: 1). Concepts and terms such as 'global citizenship' have in the main not been used, in part because they are perceived as western constructions or because, as in the case of Malawi, notions of 'citizenship' per se are still problematic, with related notions of national identity and the challenges of creating democratic societies.

Southern theorists and practitioners have however, as already suggested in this volume, played a major role in the discourses around development education. Throughout this publication reference will be made to the work and influence of not only Paulo Freire but also more recently academics such as Vanessa Andreotti, originally from Brazil, Catherine Odora Hoppers from South Africa, and Ajay Kumar, based in India. Behind these academics lie three interpretations of development education that go beyond and, in some cases, question development education in relation to human development.

Three traditions from the Global South could be identified as having a connection to or using the term development education:

- Freirean and Popular Education as seen in Latin America;
- Development Education as outlined in South Africa;
- Development Education in South Asia.

The first tradition, one that has emerged from within Latin America, is the use of terms such as 'popular education', seen as an approach towards the educational dimension of participatory community development (Kane, 2010). This tradition, inspired by the work of Freire, has an influence around the world, particularly in adult education, by promoting participatory techniques and empowering communities to secure social and political change. In Brazil there is evidence of the influence of Freire through educational programmes that make connections between human rights, global issues and social change. Centro de Criacao de Imagem Popular (CECIP) for example is a civil society organisation that seeks to 'democratise the access by all layers of the Brazilian Society to quality information on their basic rights, thus fostering a conscientious, active and participative citizenry'.

The second tradition, whilst taking 'development as a pedagogical field and human development as a goal', poses the forms of transformative action that need to take place in Africa for these goals to be achieved. This approach is central to the interpretation of development education offered by Catherine Odora Hoppers, Professor of Development Education at the University of South Africa. Central to her perspective is knowledge development, especially indigenous knowledge systems and the anchoring and articulation of the African perspective within disciplines and the curriculum. She argues that the knowledge society of today requires a recognition that knowledge production can no longer be confined to the silos of formal education, and that non-formal learning is only mentioned as an add-on. Her approach is about much more than challenging dominant western ideologies within education; it also recognises the 'multiplicity of worlds and forms of life' (Odora Hoppers, 2008). This diversity of knowledge means that development education should be more inclusive, responsive and dialogic, to expose learners to different experiences and approaches. Hoppers argues that the focus of development education should not be the competency to adapt to current globalisation, but rather to destabilise the homogenisation of other forms of knowledge.

The third tradition has its origins in India, and brings together notions of human development with concepts of dialogical learning and critical humanism, merging, as Ajay Kumar (2008) has stated, the influence of Freire and Gandhi. Kumar states that development education must be concerned with:

> how learning, knowledge and education can be used to assist individuals and groups to overcome educational disadvantage, combat social exclusion and discrimination, and challenge economic and political inequalities – with a view to securing their own emancipation and promoting progressive social change.
>
> *(Kumar, 2008: 41)*

Kumar goes on to suggest that development education is a kind of 'emancipatory and dialogical learning based on critical humanist pedagogy'. Dialogic education, he suggests, is where learners together pose problems, enquire and seek solutions. It builds on Freire's notions of teachers and students being co-investigators in an open and ongoing enquiry, combined with Gandhian notions of an education that liberates us from servitude and builds mutual respect and trust.

However these perspectives are often at variance with the dominant messages in the Global South about education and development, where the focus has been more on access to education than on quality and pedagogy. As Liddy (2013) notes, where development education has been used as a concept, for example in Liberia, the focus has been much more on community development approaches. As Liddy also notes, the pressure in countries such as Liberia has been to focus on skills development; but themes that may appear within education such as gender, conflict and the environment are global issues which require an understanding of different perspectives and critical reflection. At present, however, development education debates, policies and practices have remained focused primarily in the Global North.

Concepts that have emerged out of the development education tradition from the Global North are being discussed, debated and in some cases applied in many countries in the Global South. Global citizenship for example is now referred to within UNESCO documents, although the focus appears to be more on equipping learners to have skills to engage in a global economy and to have some understanding of sustainable development, rather than linking to Freirean traditions or the practices of NGOs.

The UN Global Citizenship initiative provides a potential opportunity to demonstrate the relevance of a more critical reflective and transformative approach towards learning. It states:

> The world faces global challenges, which require global solutions. These interconnected global challenges call for far-reaching changes in how we think and act for the dignity of fellow human beings. It is not enough for education to produce individuals who can read, write and count. Education must be transformative and bring shared values to life. It must cultivate an active care for the world and for those with whom we share it. Education must also be relevant in answering the big questions of the day. Technological solutions, political regulation or financial instruments alone cannot achieve sustainable development. It requires transforming the way people think and act. Education must fully assume its central role in helping people to forge more just, peaceful, tolerant and inclusive societies. It must give people the understanding, skills and values they need to cooperate in resolving the interconnected challenges of the 21st century.[11]

The UNESCO Global Monitoring Report for 2014 also makes reference to these themes by stating that 'Global citizenship education requires transferable skills, such as critical thinking, communication, problem solving and conflict resolution' (UNESCO, 2014: 296). The evidence suggests, however, that despite the increasing use of concepts such as global citizenship, the themes implicit within development education do not appear to have been recognised or incorporated (Pasha, 2014).

Research by MacCallum (2014) on sustainable livelihoods and global learning and Zanzibar demonstrates that an educational approach that is global in outlook, and participatory in approach, encouraging learning from differing perspectives, can be not only empowering to communities but make a positive contribution to social change. Her research showed that if a pedagogical approach is taken towards global learning, then it can have relevance and value both in the Global North and the Global South. She summarised these common and transferable features as:

- Globally aware and informed communities are more likely to make more sustainable choices;
- Unless an individual can relate to the issue at hand they will not understand it or see its relevance to them, so relevance was key to social change;
- Understanding and building on perceived strengths was an empowering process rather than an outcome;
- Being exposed to different perspectives strengthened ability to set priorities and agendas;
- Experiential, hands on, peer led social learning approaches develop awareness and new knowledge.

(MacCallum, 2014: 330)

The issue of the relevance of the pedagogy of development education and global learning to education in the Global South is a very important one, but due to the lack of research and evidence to date, it is difficult to draw any general conclusions. Therefore the focus of this volume is primarily concerned with theory and practice in the Global North.

Development education, global learning and critical pedagogy

Since the late 1970s development education has shown elements of a more transformative and critical learning approach. This has its roots in the ideas of Paulo Freire but also incorporates elements of postcolonialism and transformative learning. Whilst this approach will be explored in more depth in later chapters, it is appropriate to make reference to it here, particularly in the context of the influence of the work of Vanessa Andreotti, perspectives from such bodies as Think Global, the Development Education Association in England, and debates in journals such as *Policy and Practice* in Ireland, the *Critical Literacy Journal* and the *International Journal of Development Education and Global Learning*.

The work of Vanessa Andreotti is particularly important; a Brazilian educator who has built on the thinking of Freire, postcolonialism and postmodernism to pose approaches to learning about global and development issues that recognise different interpretations and encourage critical dialogue but also that re-conceptualise knowledge, identities and culture within education (Andreottti, 2010).[12] Her work has been influential in Canada, New Zealand and Europe particularly through the creation of two practice-focused web-based materials for educators, Through Other Eyes and Open Space for Dialogue and Enquiry

(OSDE). These web-based materials provide examples of how to encourage dialogue and debate within educational environments, to recognise different voices but also to move from just understanding these perspectives to their implications for yourself and others in how you interpret the world.

Elements of the influence of Andreotti's work can be seen in the practice of a number of development education organisations in the UK, and in the recent re-conceptualisation of development education into global learning by the Development Education Association (DEA), now Think Global.

Shah and Brown (2010) from the DEA, in reviewing critical thinking for global learning, identified six elements that need to be considered:

- making connections within and between systems particularly in terms of social, economic and environmental dimensions;
- awareness that many terms such as sustainability are contested;
- the need to respond to complexity and change;
- understanding the significance of power relations;
- the importance of self-reflection;
- the promotion of values-based literacy.

They make reference to the work of Andreotti and the OSDE methodology and also a similar approach entitled Philosophy for Children that has been developed by a number of development education providers in the UK and North America. Philosophy for Children (P4C) is a methodology that encourages learning through enquiry and dialogue. P4C aims to 'improve children's critical, creative and rigorous thinking' and 'develop higher order thinking skills, improve communication skills and help children learn to co-operate with others'.[13]

Within the UK, a number of Development Education Centres have used P4C as a training tool for teachers around global issues. It is seen as an approach that encourages critical thinking, open-mindedness, respect, co-operation and empathy and helps children develop their own opinions from a range of viewpoints about global issues.

Behind these approaches is recognition of the need to include a more critical and creative approach to learning about the wider world. The impact and influence of these traditions are discussed in later chapters.

Towards a typology of development education practices and identification of common principles

There have been numerous attempts to summarise these different interpretations of development education and related concepts. Arnold (1988) referred to different pedagogies around information, critical skills and mobilisation with three visions: charity, interdependence and empowerment. Krause (2010), in identifying typologies for development education in Europe, identified the following different approaches:

- development education as public relations for development aid;
- development education as Awareness Raising – public dissemination of information;
- development education as Global Education – focusing on local-global interdependence;
- development education as enhancement of life skills – focusing on the learning process and critical thinking.

Whilst these typologies have some value, they tend to hide the complexities of the influences and ways in which development education is perceived and interpreted. Some interpretations of development education would view the different perspectives along some form of continuum, from awareness and information about development at one end, to action and change at the other. This approach however ignores the influences related to moving beyond development to the global, and also the relationships to mainstream educational provision. The increasing use of the term global citizenship education comes from a number of different influences and has a number of different meanings. There is also the influence of actors from the Global South who, whilst having a number of different interpretations, would link development education in some way to their own broader goals of education in general, with a more personal and human approach to education.

Different pedagogical approaches need to be seen in relation to the various sectors of education. For example, activities and programmes within formal education settings have in the main tended to be more focused on knowledge and skills, compared with, say, work with adults. A number of the more informal educational programmes such as global youth work have more of an action orientation. The relationship of the different interpretations to different practices and approaches to learning will be explored later on.

Despite these varying interpretations, in concluding this overview it is valuable to return to some common themes and practices. Whilst not necessarily seen as the 'consensus' outlined in the European document, or necessarily the viewpoint of all policy-makers and practitioners, the following underlying themes are suggested here as the basis for a pedagogy of development education.

First, within most of the development education policies and practices there is recognition of the promotion of the interdependent and interconnected nature of our lives, the similarities as well as the differences between communities and peoples around the world (Regan and Sinclair, 2006).

A second theme is about ensuring that the voices and perspectives of the peoples of the Global South are promoted, understood and reflected upon, along with perspectives from the Global North. This means going beyond a relativist notion of different voices to one that recognises the importance of spaces for the voices of the oppressed and dispossessed.

Thirdly, underpinning practice in many countries is the encouragement of a more values-based approach to learning, with an emphasis on social justice, human rights, fairness and the desire for a more equal world (Abdi and Shultz, 2008).

Finally, many NGOs would wish to see development education as incorporating linkages between learning, moral outrage and concern about global poverty, and a desire to take action to secure change (Oxfam, 2006).

Many aspects of these approaches are summarised in the work of 80/20, an Irish-based development and development education organisation. To 80/20, development education:

- is an educational response to issues of development, human rights, justice and world citizenship;
- presents an international development and human rights perspective within education here and in other parts of the world;
- promotes the voices and viewpoints of those who are excluded from an equal share in the benefits of human development internationally;
- is an opportunity to link and compare development issues and challenges here with those elsewhere throughout the world;
- provides opportunities for people to reflect on their international roles and responsibilities with regard to issues of equality and justice in human development;
- is an opportunity to be active in writing a new story for human development.

(Regan and Sinclair, 2006: 109)

Development education in schools

If you went into a school classroom in many European countries, at some stage during a school year there would be examples of learning about development issues or some form of activity or project about global issues. What would first distinguish this activity as a 'development education' activity would be the extent to which it moved beyond a traditional view of seeing the Global South as 'just about poor people' who were helpless and needed aid and charity. Positive examples would be where there was learning that questioned, challenged assumptions and stereotypes, and located poverty within an understanding of the causes of inequality, recognising what people were doing for themselves.

This move from a 'charity mentality' to one of social justice remains an underlying theme of development education in practice in schools. A development education perspective would question the emphasis a school might give to raising money for charitable purposes, unless it was located within broader learning. It would also mean that central to learning would be the promotion of positive images, often through the use of well-chosen photographs and personal stories.

Secondly, development education practice in schools would often include giving space to the stories and perspectives of people from the Global South. This would lead on to looking at issues through different lenses. Examples of this are the Open Space for Dialogue and Enquiry and Through Other Eyes projects referred to in Chapter 11.

Thirdly, development education learning would, as Oxfam (2006) has suggested, encourage 'a sense of moral outrage', of wanting to take the learning forward through some form of follow-up activity that might well include taking part in some form of campaign on areas such as climate change, fair trade or the Millennium Development Goals.

Linked to this, fourthly, is a sense of empowerment, a sense that engagement in society enriches and strengthens democracy and leads to a feeling of global social responsibility (Rajacic et al., 2010b).

Fifthly, central to all development education practice would be the encouragement of participatory learning methodologies, with clear echoes of the influence of Freire and other radical educationalists from the 1970s and 1980s.

Finally, development education also enhances the competences of the learners, enabling them to reflect on their sense of place in a globalised world.

This chapter has provided an overview of the various ways in which development education is interpreted, its links to broader themes, and the role of NGOs and policy-makers. Although development education may still have a marginal influence within education in most industrialised countries, there is evidence of a growing maturity as to its practices and relationship to broader societal and educational goals. There may still be a lot of rhetoric from a number of NGOs about development education as a vehicle for social change. However there is evidence through the policy statements of governments, the increasing engagement of academics, and the impact within schools, of an emerging body of practice that locates development education as a pedagogy for global social justice.

Notes

1 www.oxfam.org.uk/education/global-citizenship
2 www.deeep.org
3 www.dochas.ie
4 www.actionaid.dk
5 www.decsy.org.uk/about-us/what-is-development-education
6 www.hivos.nl
7 www.unicef.org.uk/education
8 See Chapter 10.
9 http://globaldimension.org.uk/glp
10 www.globalfocus.org.nz
11 www.globaleducationfirst.org/220.htm
12 The work and influence of Andreotti is discussed in more detail in Chapters 5, 6 and 11.
13 What is Philosophy for Children, www.philosophy4children.co.uk/home/p4c

References

Abdi, A.A. (2003) 'Searching for development education in Africa: select perspectives on Somalia, South Africa and Nigeria', *International Education Journal*, 4(3): 192–200.

Abdi, A. and Shultz, L. (eds) (2008) *Educating for Human Rights and Global Citizenship*. Albany: State University of New York Press.

Alasuutari, H. (2011) 'Conditions for mutuality and reciprocity in development education policy and pedagogy', *International Journal of Development Education and Global Learning*, 3(3): 65–78.

Andreotti, V. (2010) 'Global education in the 21st century: two different perspectives on the post of postmodernism', *International Journal of Development Education and Global Learning*, 2(2): 5–22.

Arnold, S. (1988) 'Constrained crusaders? British charities and development education', *Development Policy Review*, 6(Summer): 183–209.

Bau-cun, L. (2010) 'Education for international understanding for cosmopolitan citizenship in a globalised world', paper presented at Education and Citizenship in a Globalising World conference, 19–20 November 2010, London, available at www.ioe.ac.uk/about/ 37498.html

Bourn, D. (2008) 'Education for sustainable development and global citizenship', *Theory and Research in Education*, 6(2): 193–206.

Chasaide, N. (2009) 'Development education and campaigning linkages', *Policy and Practice: A Development Education Review*, 8(Spring): 28–34.

DEA (2005) *Annual Report*. London: DEA.

DfES (2005a) *Putting the World into World Class Education*. London: DfES.

DfES (2005b) *Sustainable Development Action Plan*. London: DfES.

DFID (1998) *Building Support for Development*. London: DFID.

EU Multi-Stakeholder Forum (2005) *The European Consensus on Development: The Contribution of Development Education and Awareness Raising*. Brussels: DEEEP.

Forghani-Arani, N. and Hartmeyer, H. (2011) 'Global learning in Austria', *International Journal of Development Education and Global Learning*, 2(2): 45–58.

Gearon, L. (2006) 'NGDOs and education: some tentative considerations', *Reflecting Education*, 2(2), available online at http://reflectingeducation.net.

Hartmeyer, H. (2008) *Experiencing the World Global Learning in Austria: Developing, Reaching Out, Crossing Borders*. Munster: Waxmann.

Instituto Portugues de Apolo ao Desenvolvimento (IPAD) (2010) *National Strategy for Development Education*. Lisbon: IPAD.

Irish Aid (2007) *Development Education Strategy Plan 2007–2011*. Dublin/Limerick.

Kane, L. (2010) 'Community development: learning from popular education in Latin America', *Community Development Journal*, 45(3), 276–286.

Kim, H. (1997) 'Global understanding and global education in Korea', *ACSD Global Connection*, 5(2): 8–12.

Kirkwood-Tucker, T.F. (ed.) (2008) *Visions in Global Education*. New York: Peter Lang.

Krause, J. (2010) *The European Development Education Monitoring Report – Development Education Watch*. Brussels: DEEEP.

Kumar, A. (2008) 'Development education and dialogical learning in the 21st century', *International Journal of Development Education and Global Learning*, 1(1): 37–48.

Liddy, M. (2013) 'Education about, for, as development', *Policy and Practice: Development Education Review*, 17: 27–45.

Luczak, R. (2010) *The Present State and Future Perspectives of International Development Co-operation Research and Education in Poland*. Warsaw: Warsaw School of Social Sciences and Humanities/Norwegian Institute of International Affairs/Global Development Research Group.

MacCallum, C. (2014) 'Sustainable livelihoods to adaptive capabilities: a global learning journey in a small state, Zanzibar', unpublished PhD thesis, Institute of Education, University of London.

Marshall, H. (2005) 'Developing the global gaze in citizenship education: exploring the perspectives of global education NGO workers in England', *The International Journal of Citizenship and Teacher Education*, 1(2): 76–92.

Marshall, H. (2007) 'Global education in perspective: fostering a global dimension in an English secondary school', *Cambridge Journal of Education*, 37(3): 355–374.

Merryfield, M. (2002) 'The difference a global educator can make', *Educational Leadership*, 60(2): 18–21.

Mesa, M. (2011) 'Evolution and future challenges of development education', *Educacion Research Global*, 0: 141–160.

Ministry of Education, Finland (2007) *Global Education 2010*. Helsinki: Ministry of Education International Relations.

Mundy, K. (2007) *Charting Global Education in Canada's Elementary Schools*. Toronto: Ontario Institute for Studies in Education (OISE)/UNICEF.

Norcliffe, D. and Bennell, S. (2011) 'Analysis of views on the development of Education for Sustainable Development and Global Citizenship policy in Wales', *International Journal of Development Education and Global Learning* , 3(1): 39–58.

Nygaard, A. (2009) 'The discourse of results in the funding of NGO development education and awareness raising: an experiment in retrospective baseline reflection in the Norwegian context', *International Journal of Development Education and Global Learning*, 2(1): 19–30.

Odora Hoppers, C. (2008) *South African Research Chair in Development Education – Framework and Strategy*. Pretoria: University of South Africa.

OECD Development Centre (2009) *Communication and Development – Practices, Policies and Priorities in OECD Countries*. Paris: OECD.

Ohri, A. (1997) *The World in Our Neighbourhood*. London: DEA.

O'Loughlin, E. (ed.) (2008) *Global Learning in the Czech Republic: The European Global Education Peer Review Process, National Report on the Czech Republic*. Lisbon: North-South Centre of the Council of Europe.

Oxfam (2006) *A Curriculum for Education for Global Citizenship*. Oxford: Oxfam.

Pardinaz-Solis, R. (2006) 'A single voice from the South in the turbulent waters of the North', *Development Education Journal*, 12(3): 4–6.

Pasha, A. (2014) 'Global citizenship and Pakistan', unpublished Masters dissertation, Institute of Education.

Plan UK (2010) 'Draft development education strategy', unpublished paper.

Rajacic, A., Surian, A., Fricke, H.-J., Krause, J. and Davis, P. (2010a) *Study on the Experience and Actions of the Main European Actors Active in the Field of Development Education and Awareness Raising – Interim Report*. Brussels: European Commission.

Rajacic, A., Surian, A., Fricke, H.-J., Krause, J. and Davis, P. (2010b) *DEAR in Europe – Recommendations for Future Interventions by the European Commission: Final Report of the Study on the Experience and Actions of the Main European Actors Active in the Field of Development Education and Awareness Raising*. Brussels: European Commission.

Regan, C. and Sinclair, S. (2006) 'Engaging development – learning for a better future? The world view of development education', in C. Regan (ed.) *Development in an Unequal World*. Dublin: 80:20, pp. 107–120.

Scheunpflug, A. and Asbrand, B. (2006) 'Global education and education for sustainability', *Environmental Education Research*, 12(1): 33–46.

Shah, H. and Brown, K. (2010) 'Critical thinking in the context of global learning', in T.L.K. Wiseley, I.M. Barr, A. Britton and B. King (eds) *Education in a Global Space*. Edinburgh: IDEAS, pp. 37–42.

Shultz, L. (2010) 'What do we ask of global citizenship education? A study of global citizenship education in a Canadian university', *International Journal of Development Education and Global Learning*, 3(1): 5–22.

UNESCO (2014) *Teaching and Learning: Achieving Quality for All, Global Monitoring Report for 2014*. Paris: UNESCO.

Vare, P. and Scott, W. (2008) 'Education for sustainable development: two sides and an edge', DEA Thinkpiece, available at www.tidec.org/Visuals/Bill%20Scott%20 Challenge/dea_thinkpiece_vare_scott.pdf

Verulam Associates (2009) *Review of Building Support for Development*. London: DFID.

Winter, A. (1996) *Is Anyone Listening? Communicating Development in Donor Countries*. Geneva: UN – Non-Governmental Liaison Service (NGLS).

4

A NETWORK, A COMMUNITY OF PRACTICE OR A MOVEMENT FOR EDUCATIONAL CHANGE?

As the previous two chapters have outlined, the evolution of development education has been closely allied to the practices of a range of non-governmental organisations and to a form of distinctive identity that was seen as evolving outside of mainstream educational traditions. One criticism raised about development education has been its marginality from mainstream education, and that all too often those organisations that have promoted themselves under the banner of development education have just talked among themselves (McCollum, 1996).

Whilst there is clear evidence that development education has some commonly agreed underlying themes, what has been less clear is the extent to which it has been more than simply a collection of organisations with common themes and focus. The focus and themes that underpin development education practice are important because they help to clarify if there is a distinctive pedagogical approach, and also the extent to which this approach is open, transparent and clear to the broader educational community. This chapter aims to address these questions by reviewing the literature on communities of practice, social movements and network organisations, and assessing their relevance to the practices of development education.

All reviews of development education have tended to summarise the area of practice in terms of groupings of organisations. Arnold (1987), in his influential text on development education in the UK in the late 1980s, summarised the landscape in terms of a number of organisations with a common vision of the rejection of a 'charitable mentality' towards the third world. A review of development education across Europe in the early 1990s also emphasised the lead role of NGOs, often with a grouping of visionary and hard-working individuals (Kirby, 1994). Peer reviews of global education through the Global Education Network Europe (GENE) process across Europe also show similar traditions, although the influence of voluntary organisations has been smaller within Central Europe

(North-South Centre, 2005, 2006a; O'Loughlin, 2010). What is less clear from the existing literature is the extent to which being part of a network, a broader movement or identifiable community of practice has been a positive or negative contribution to development education. McCollum's research suggests that in the 1990s in the UK, being part of a broad movement was having a negative impact for development education. However it is clear, as will be shown later in this chapter, that development education has often had its biggest impact within main-stream education where there has been some element of coherence, coordination and clear focus to the practice.

Voluntary networks

A distinctive feature of the history of development education in many countries has been the extent to which organisations have come together in the pursuit of common goals and agendas. This is a natural part of any form of social and educational activity that seeks change; but it is also a feature of societies where organisations feel a need to come together and work collaboratively almost as a defence mechanism. Organisations also come together to lobby, often for greater recognition of their area of practice and to secure funding.

This coming together is often through the creation of voluntary networks. These tend to be self-organising groups with a coherent set of actions and some sense of common identity and values base. Such networks are particularly common in education whether practitioner- or teacher-led or as coalitions of organisations who are trying to influence practice within education.

The organisation may have its own *raison d'être* or reason for existence but may share, either completely or in part, some common aspirations; and to further its cause, may recognise the value of collaboration and shared goals. This can lead to a number of types of co-operation such as:

- filtering, processing and managing knowledge for its constituents;
- promoting dialogue, exchange and learning;
- shaping the agenda by clarifying little known or understood ideas for the public;
- convening organisations or people;
- facilitating action by members;
- building communities by promoting and sustaining the values and standards of the group of individuals within it (Wilson-Grau and Nunez, 2006).

Wilson-Grau and Nunez note that individuals or organisations may well have a range of reasons for joining networks. 'Some may be more interested in receiving information or the tools it generates while others join for the political spaces and relationships a network offers' (ibid.: 315).

There is considerable evidence of such networks around the world that label themselves as development education networks, or use such related banners as global learning, global education or global citizenship education. They tend to fall into three distinct groupings:

- networks with a strong coordinating body that tend in practice to be more of an umbrella association or membership organisation than a flat network;
- networks of NGOs and other civil society organisations that exist to act as a platform to influence national or international structures with funding and influence over policy in development education and related fields;
- specialist networks related to a specific area of practice, such as research or work with young people, or groupings of individuals such as teachers.

The first type of network or coordinating body can be seen in the UK through distinct bodies in England, Scotland and Wales; and in Ireland, Norway, Lithuania, Finland and Japan. What is distinctive about all of these bodies is that whilst they have networking functions of providing information, sharing ideas and offering forums for debate and dialogue, their existence has been supported by the major policy and funding bodies for development education in their country. Such networks or bodies provide the opportunity for the policy-making body to have dialogue and consultation with one organisation and use it as the conduit of information.

There are however differences between these networks, due in part to historical traditions and the relative scope and influence of development education within each country. Most of these networks – IDEAS in Scotland, DEAR in Japan, RORG in Norway and Cyfanfyd in Wales – have been run by a small team of full-time staff, usually of between one and four people. Most of these networks see their role as primarily about raising awareness of development education and influencing policy. For example, the International Development Education Association of Scotland (IDEAS) promoted itself as 'a network of organisations and individuals involved in Development Education and Education for Global Citizenship across Scotland'. Its website states that:

> By raising awareness of global concerns and illustrating the potential for change, the IDEAS network aims to influence those in all sectors of formal and informal education and life long learning including teachers, policy makers, youth and adult education.[1]

The network in Japan, DEAR, has seen its role as to:

- communicate with the government and give suggestions on its policy;
- develop networks and exchange information with related organisations in the world;
- research Development Education;
- gather information on Development Education in both Japan and the world and share the information;
- help to provide learning opportunities in communities and schools.[2]

The network in Norway, RORG, has a more formal role in relation to dialogue with the Norwegian Foreign Affairs and Development Ministry, NORAD. In Ireland, the network IDEA has put a lot of its energy into the promotion of dialogue for members, with an open space forum and opportunities to share ideas and experiences.

The network in Finland, KEPA, coordinates 'a global education network comprising over 160 organisations'. Like some of the other networks it provides training and encourages co-operation between its members.

LITDEA is the Lithuanian development education and co-operation network (association) of non-governmental institutions. It is an example of a network that has moved from an informal role to a more formal role as a result of interest and support from national governmental bodies. LITDEA was established as a distinct formal organisation in 2010.

The network in England, formerly the Development Education Association, now called Think Global, has a history of many of these activities and approaches but today puts more of its emphasis on producing support, resources and materials directly for teachers, rather than through intermediary bodies such as NGOs or Development Education Centres.

A feature of some of these bodies is that they have networks within the network. For example Cyfanfyd has networks of teachers and educators in schools, lifelong learning and youth work. Think Global has also had a distinct teachers' network. In reality, all of these networks could be said to be, in practice, as much umbrella and membership bodies, in that they have a coordinating function and aim to act on behalf of and support the work of their members.

A similar function could be said to operate at a European level through the Development Awareness Raising and Education (DARE) Forum. This Forum is a representative body of NGO networks around Europe but it does fulfil many of the tasks of a network. Its objectives for example include the following:

- To increase the European public's critical knowledge and understanding of the causes of global poverty and inequity and our global interdependence.
- To embed development education and awareness-raising in relevant national and EU policies, and in formal, non formal and informal education systems.
- To undertake development education and awareness-raising activities in a coherent and coordinated fashion, including promoting coherence between the different stakeholders, and between the national and EU levels.
- To ensure that there is the participation of civil society and that their perspectives are considered in every stage of the policy development, programming and evaluation processes, and that there are structured and transparent mechanisms for effective dialogue between NGOs and public institutions.[3]

The strength of these networking organisations appears to depend on two main factors: the commitment and support of NGOs to work collaboratively; and external, usually national government, support and funding. There is however considerable evidence to suggest that by having some form of strong and well-organised coordinating body, development education can have a higher profile and be more effective. This for example can be seen in the work of the secretariat that has supported the Development Awareness Raising and Education Forum, the DEEEP project. This secretariat has, for example, played a central role in securing the European Consensus document on development education and has secured a significantly higher profile for the practice within the European Union.

The second type of development education network is more informal, often with no coordinating structure and operating usually as a forum to influence policy-makers, as a common voice to government or to international bodies such as the European Union. In most European countries these are usually called the NGO Platforms, who act as the link body with DARE and national development NGO networks (Krause, 2010).

These networks, whilst often acting as the communication mechanism between government bodies and NGOs, tend to have minimal resources and are often part of broader organisational groupings related to international development. For example in Germany, within the development networking organisation VENRO, there is a working group on global learning of thirty NGOs. But as Krause's study on development education noted, in countries such as France, Italy, Estonia, Cyprus, Bulgaria and Slovenia, these networks are relatively weak. Only where there is some form of national strategy, as for example in Spain or Portugal, do the networks appear to have some strength (Krause, 2010).

One network which, whilst having a small secretariat, acts more as an informal body is Global Education Network Europe (GENE). This network brings together ministries, agencies and other bodies that develop national policy and provide funding for Global Education in European countries. Started in 2001 with six national institutions from six countries, GENE has now grown to facilitate the sharing of policy learning between thirty-one ministries and agencies and other bodies from twenty-one countries, through the regular GENE roundtables and networking mechanisms. It is more of an informal network because, given its structure of national governments and coordinating bodies, it is difficult in practice to have a distinctive viewpoint or position. The purpose of GENE is to support national structures in their work of improving the quality and increasing the provision of Global Education in Europe. Since its inception, GENE could be described as having three main aims:

- to share experience and strategies among existing and emerging national structures, in order to inform best practice nationally and provide mutual support and learning;
- to disseminate learning from other countries in Europe, so that structures subsequently emerging will learn from this experience, and so that,

eventually, all countries in Europe might have national coordinating structures for the increase and improvement of Global Education;

- to develop and pursue a common European agenda on strengthening Global and Development Education.[4]

Such networks can be a stepping stone towards more formal structures, but as in the case of GENE, this rather loose network enables sharing of experiences without restricting national voices. However tensions have been known to exist within these more informal development education networks, between those organisations that are stronger and more powerful and those that are weaker and have less influence.

The third type of network is one that is more specific to particular educational groupings and clearly more closely related to the use of social networking and internet forms of communication and dialogue. Examples of this type of network include the London Global Teachers Network, the Global Education Conference, coordinated in the USA, and the Global Education Network in Canada. These networks are also examples of initiatives that are clearly located within specific professional educational groupings.

The London Global Teachers Network, for example, although initiated by development education NGOs, has become an independent network for and led by teachers. It provides an opportunity for teachers to share experience, opinions and resources around global learning – online and through meetings and events hosted at various London venues.[5]

Led by educationalists in the United States, the Global Education Conference is a collaborative, worldwide community initiative involving students, educators, and organisations at all levels. 'It is designed to significantly increase opportunities for building education-related connections around the globe while supporting cultural awareness and recognition of diversity.' It seeks to present ideas, examples and projects related to connecting educators and classrooms with a strong emphasis on promoting global awareness, fostering global competency, and inspiring action towards solving real-world problems.[6]

The Canadian Global Education network is rather different in that it is primarily based on the use of an online resource. It consists of teachers, students, and members of an educational community who

> believe that teaching and learning must integrate the interdependency of the social, economic, environmental, and political aspects of our world. As citizens of the world we have responsibilities towards our global community; a global education approach to teaching focuses on the students' place in the world community. To that end, we are creating an on-line directory of resources to be used in any curriculum area at any level.[7]

This third, more educational and delivery-focused type of network is most likely to be the dominant form of coordination within development education in the years to come, as internet-based and social networking become even more dominant. These forms of networking reflect wider trends within society and are particularly noticeable within education.

Each of these three network types, whilst different, demonstrates a number of common and apparently successful traits. They directly address the needs of the individual teacher or educator and exist to help them with their own practice. They also have relatively flat and democratic mechanisms for engagement and participation.

This range of types of network suggests that having some form of coordinating body within which individuals and organisations can share their experiences and provide a common voice to policy-makers, has been relatively successful. Periodic evaluations of Think Global, RORG and IDEA in Ireland clearly show this (O'Shea, 2010). What is noticeable and distinctive however about those networks with a formal structure is that their continued success and strength has been heavily influenced by their relationship to and funding support from appropriate national aid or development ministries.

A community of practice

The creation and sustaining of networks pose questions as to their purpose, function and distinctiveness. The value of the concept of 'a community of practice' is therefore worth exploring in relation to development education practice.

The concept of 'communities of practice' is most closely associated with the work of Wenger and his associates. They define the concept as 'groups of people who share a concern, a set of problems, or a passion about a topic and who deepen their knowledge, and expertise in this area by acting on an ongoing basis' (Wenger et al., 2002: 4). What defines a community of practice for them, as distinct from say a network or an ongoing set of activities within an organisation, is that 'communities of practice do not reduce knowledge to an object. They make it an integral part of their activities and interactions.'

They define the concept in relation to three elements: a domain, a community and practice. The domain refers to the area of knowledge, the issues and the basis for the engagement of members. The community is a community of people who care about this domain and are willing to interact and share ideas and trust fellow members; it is also a matter of belonging, of feeling part of some form of intellectual process. The practice is the set of frameworks, the activities, and the style that defines the way of doing things (Wenger et al., 2002: 26–28; Lave and Wenger, 1991).

A community of practice is seen as distinct from a network, a database or a website. It is a group of people who interact, learn together, build relationships and in the process develop a sense of belonging and mutual commitment.

Whilst Lave and Wenger take forward this framework into approaches to learning, this concept of a community of practice has some validity and value in itself, and is now used as a basis to review features of development education practice in some countries. Key to the conceptual framework developed by

Wenger and his associates is that a community of practice helps individuals and organisations not only to construct and manage the knowledge they have gained, but also to apply it and be effective agents for change.

How therefore do these concepts relate to development education?

The development education community

It is evident from the material referred to in the previous chapter, most notably the European Consensus document on development education, that stakeholders and organisations who practise under the banner of development education do so on the basis of some common principles, based on bodies of knowledge on development and global issues, values of social justice and equity, and an approach that promotes participatory forms of learning and voices of the dispossessed.

Where development education has become a feature of educational practice, the driver has often tended to be a voluntary organisation with a specific or major interest in development or a related area. Reviews of the landscape of development education in countries such as Japan (Ishii, 2003), Austria (Hartmeyer, 2008), Norway (O'Loughlin, 2010) and the Netherlands (North-South Centre, 2005) reflect this. In countries that have not had a strong development tradition, such as those of Central and Eastern Europe, the role of voluntary organisations has been less important in terms of creating a specific culture of practice. In countries where development education has become subsumed within broader global education traditions, as for example in Canada and Australia, there is a broader array of organisations who have come together covering areas such as human rights, the environment and intercultural education (Goldstein and Selby, 2000).

In countries where there is, or has been, a definable development education community that recognises and values this identity, then a number of common themes emerge. In her research on development education in the UK in 2001, Kanji suggested that there had been a development education community for the last fifteen to twenty years (Kanji, 2001). This community in the UK, she suggests, was focused around a network of local Development Education Centres in which the staff would clearly see themselves as part of a wider network (McCollum, 1996). This is in part due to the continuation under various bodies of a structure through which perspectives and experiences could be shared, collaboration could be identified, and common aspirations and identity promoted to external bodies.

Kanji summarises this as a 'symbolically constructed, imagined, transnational community'. She sees the defining features as being 'boundaries within which its members have a shared sense of meaning, a social and linguistic discourse and a body of symbols and rituals'. Influenced by the work of Anderson and Cohen and a shared 'aspiration to common interest and shared consciousness', Kanji notes 'that practice is shared and informed by perspectives (such as global – local and participant empowerment)', and that the development education community participates in certain rituals. This includes holding annual conferences and producing funding reports that serve to showcase the good practice of those involved in development education and that provide opportunities for networking among other things.

This view of a distinctly constructed body with common perspectives and practices has at certain periods in time been a feature of development education in the UK for example. One of the reasons for this was that within the UK the most dominant feature of development education practice from the 1980s until 2010 was a strong network of local Development Education Centres who shared common aspirations about their role, ways of working and nature of activities. This initially was through the National Association of Development Education Centres (NADEC), set up in the 1980s, which became subsumed within the Development Education Association, launched in 1993, re-named as Think Global in 2010. There is today a new structure, formed in 2009, the Consortium of Development Education Centres, which is in many respects a return to the days of NADEC.

This Consortium defines the Centres as 'independent local-based not-for-profit organisations whose core work is the support and delivery of global learning to schools and communities'.[8] They do this by providing training and workshops for teachers and community groups, running resource libraries, and running projects.

What is however noticeable about this identity and focus today is that it is far less based on a distinctive conceptual approach and much more on an area of activity in support of schools and communities. For example, if one looks at the research undertaken by McCollum in the mid-1990s, the emphasis of the Centres' practice was then much more on offering a distinct alternative to international NGOs and mainstream educational provision.

This change of emphasis was in part due to the extent to which in the UK during the first decade of the twenty-first century, development education themes became part of mainstream education. This mainstreaming, and the decline of funding for local Centres, also led to a lower profile for what were seen as distinctly development education organisations. Linked to this was the decision by the Development Education Association to change its name to Think Global and to promote the concept of global learning.

Elsewhere in Europe there has been less evidence of a distinctive 'development education community'. In part this is due to the size and scope of the organisations involved, but also to the fact that in many countries the sense of a distinctive development education identity is less clear. Even in countries with a long and strong tradition in this area, such as the Netherlands, development education is seen as just one element of the work of development NGOs.

The Peer Reviews of Global Education in a range of European countries reinforce the lack of distinctive and coherent communities of practice (see North-South Centre, 2005, 2006a, 2006b; O'Loughlin, 2010).

The only other countries in Europe, apart from the UK, that could be argued to have retained a distinctive and strong development education focus are Ireland and Norway. As in England, the influence and role of the national coordinating bodies, IDEA in Ireland and RORG in Norway, have played an important role in creating a sense of distinctive development education community.

In Ireland the evidence, particularly through an analysis of training needs of its members, shows a relatively high degree of engagement in the Association, interest in sharing ideas and developing joint activities (O'Shea, 2010). O'Shea's study identified that there was expertise within the membership of IDEA that could be harnessed in meeting current training and development needs and that these needs could be broadly categorised as relating to development education theory and practice, general training needs, and organisational/project management needs (ibid.: 31).

This suggests that IDEA does to a large extent act as a community of practice, in that there is a clearly identifiable domain within which the network works, it has a clear focus and it operates as a learning network.

Whilst RORG in Norway is not such a strong network as IDEA in Ireland, its agreement via dialogue with members and endorsement at its Annual Conference in 2006 suggests a sense of common values, set of principles and way of working. The principles agreed in 2006 included the following:

> Non Governmental Development Organisations (NGDOs) have both the right and the duty to conduct unbiased, independent and critical North/ South information based on their own ideological, political or religious basis, independent of pressure of economic or political nature from the state or others contributing financially to their activities and independent of their own economic interests.

> NGDOs have both the right and the duty to promote their own views and perspectives on important and current themes linked to North/South information, including critical views and perspectives related to the activities of Norwegian authorities and other development actors, but do also have the responsibility to ensure that different views and perspectives are expressed in an unbiased and respectful way.

> NGDOs have a responsibility to ensure that perspectives from the South are part of its development education.
>
> *(RORG, 2006)*

These examples suggest that there have been elements of communities of practice in development education in England, Ireland and Norway over the past twenty years. The nature of these practices has varied and evolved depending on the strength of the organisation, funding opportunities and above all the extent to which development education has become accepted within mainstream education. For example, in England in 1999 the then DEA produced a document on *Principles and Practices of Development Education* based primarily around how to produce good quality resources and training materials (DEA, 1999). A decade later the focus in its publication on quality development education and global learning was much more on case studies from within schools and mainstream education (DEA, 2008).

This reflects Wenger's comments about a community of practice going through a series of phases of growth and development and eventual transformation.

A comment often made about communities of practice is that they can become inward-looking, elitist and removed from the realities of everyday life. As Wenger et al. state, they 'can hoard knowledge, limit innovation, and hold others hostage to their expertise' (2002: 139). Whilst elements of this could be seen at various times in the history of development education, as McCollum notes, the evidence is of continuing creativity and willingness to learn and share ideas and above all be valued within the wider educational community.

Issue-based educational movements for social change

The third lens through which one could look at development education practice is as an educational movement for social change. McCollum in her review of development education practice in the 1990s refers to the 'development education movement' without necessarily stating what this means (McCollum, 1996).

Whilst development education could be regarded as an educational movement if one takes the criteria outlined above, a feature that makes it potentially distinctive from other issue-based approaches is its relationship to civil society and the desire of many of its proponents to see education as a vehicle for global social change. McCloskey (2011) refers to social change being the *raison d'être* of development education.

Whilst organisations involved with environment and human rights education included many with a strong civil society presence, the relationship between development education and civil society organisations has always been much stronger. This is somewhat strange, in the sense that in many Northern countries the concept of 'development' would have been about 'somewhere else'; yet there is a noticeable engagement of a broad range of organisations in the desire for societal change. In part this is due to the prominence given to concepts such as social justice, and the grassroots nature of much of the practice; but it is also for rather pragmatic reasons – there has always been, at least in many European countries, much more funding available for development education than say for human rights or environmental education. This has given development education in some countries a slightly more detached relationship with mainstream education; and has enabled a breadth of civil society involvement that could be argued to be one of its ongoing strengths.

What is less clear however is the extent to which you can define development education, either internationally or even in specific countries, as a social movement. Goodwin and Jasper, for example, see a social movement as 'a collective, organised, sustained, and non-institutional challenge to authorities, powerholders, and/or cultural beliefs and practices' (Goodwin and Jasper, 2003); while for Della Porta and Diani, it must be an informal interaction network which shares beliefs and solidarity, features collective action and makes use of protest (Della Porta and Diani, 1999: 14–15). These definitions share the contention that a movement should be collective, informal/non-institutional and challenging/protesting against something.

Development education in many countries evolved as a response and challenge to dominant beliefs and orthodoxies. Indeed McCollum in her review of development education in the UK called on practitioners to remind themselves of the radical heritage of much of the practice whilst not losing sight of current educational priorities. However this sense of a clearly organised collective of people is in the main not how development education is practised or perceived.

Other viewpoints suggest that a social movement is more than simply 'a reflex response to globalisation' (Thompson, 2006: 118), noting the importance of the second face: that of shared beliefs and collective voice in favour of something. In this understanding, the movement is both defensive and creative (McDonald, 2006: 25). Freire makes a similar observation, suggesting that people need to be armed with words and concepts (McLaren and da Silva, 1993: 61) which allow them to name the world, 'denounce' the negative and then 'announce the dream for which one fights' (Freire, 1972: 18).

A third approach in terms of development education as a social movement could be in seeing it as a form of practice – 'form of doing' (McDonald, 2006: 95). Tilly suggests that different forms of engagement largely fall within limited contextually defined sets (Tilly, 1987: 227). Here there is clearly some resonance with individuals and organisations involved with development education. For example in the UK there have been attempts over the years to develop models of good practice, so as to identify what is good development education. Development Education Centres were, and to some extent still are, seen as exemplar models of practice.

As indicated in the earlier chapters, development education has had close linkages with what have been called other adjectival educations, such as peace, human rights or environmental education. What these approaches to education share is a values-based approach to learning, often with a close allegiance to broader social movements for change. These educational movements have often related to challenging dominant orthodoxies within education, particularly the emphasis on economic needs, performance measurability, and basic skills (Goldstein and Selby, 2000).

The over-arching theme of Global Education has in some quarters (Richardson, Hicks, Selby and Pike) been seen as bringing these adjectival or issue-based educations together, with the following common principles as summarised by Lister:

- knowledge should have a social purpose – to ameliorate the human condition;
- the curriculum should include the study of major global issues;
- learning should include the learning of skills and not just content;
- in order to develop such skills, learning requires an action dimension;
- education should be affective as well as cognitive;

- the new movements require pluralism and diversity;
- the curriculum should have a global dimension;
- education should have a futures perspective.

(quoted in Hicks, 2008: 12)

For progressive educationalists these new movements in education were welcomed for their 'human-centred education' and 'global perspectives', giving a new process and outlook on the world (Lister, 1986: 54).

These separate identities reflect not only different issues but also different origins, cultures and support structures. Whilst most of these issue-based approaches have origins within international, often UNESCO, policies and statements, they have been linked to NGOs that reflect their interest and in some cases relate to broader educational support. For example, the growth in support for environmental education has been closely linked to a range of international conferences (Stockholm in 1972, Belgrade in 1975, Tbilisi in 1977), and its successor, sustainable development (Rio in 1992).

Peace education also emerged in the 1970s and drew heavily on the peace movement for its leadership and inspiration; but the political nature of this issue (Hicks, 2008) resulted in lack of broader political support or its transformation into conflict resolution or human rights education.

All of these issue-based educations had internal tensions, reflecting conservative, liberal and radical strands. For most of them however their broader educational support relied very often on short-term funding opportunities or the commitment of well-known international NGOs, such as the World Wide Fund for Nature (WWF) in the case of environmental education, and Amnesty International in the case of peace and later human rights education.

Development education was clearly seen as one of these educational movements, with a desire amongst its proponents for change in both the content and delivery of education; and also for transformation in society.

The extent to which these issue-based educations should be considered as educational movements could be assessed against the extent to which they:

- organise regular, national and international conferences on their issue;
- have a distinctive academic and intellectual focus, around some form of academic journal;
- provide a networking focus engaging both NGOs and educational practitioners as well as academics;
- promote initiatives that encourage policy support for their specific educational issue.

Of the various issue-based movements, probably the most successful over the past twenty years in terms of the features identified above has been environmental education, through national networking bodies in countries such as the UK and other European nations, Canada, the USA and Australia, regular national and international conferences, and an increasing academic focus through journals. Whilst in a number of countries these movements have been re-branded and in some cases re-focused around sustainable development education, their status remains comparatively high.

Human rights education has in a number of countries had a similarly high profile, helped considerably by international policy agreements, most notably in the Council of Europe. This area has however had a lower academic profile, despite considerable influence within a number of school curricula, linked to areas such as citizenship and civics.

Intercultural education has tended to be more of a theme within conferences, with an international association linked to an academic journal, but it has had considerable influence at a policy level, particularly within Europe.

Development education on the other hand has differed from these other movements in the following ways. It has been much more practitioner- and NGO-led and as a consequence in most countries been more on the margins of mainstream education provision. Yet at the same time it has probably, of all the issue-based educations, been the most heavily funded, particularly in Europe. There has been for example within the European Commission consistently for over thirty years a specific budget line for civil society-led projects on development education. The same cannot be said for environmental, human rights or intercultural education.

The potential for many of these issue-based educations to have continued influence may be found in areas of commonality under the banner of social justice and anti-oppression. This is starting to happen in North America where linkages are being made through connections to race equality, gender and critical education more widely.

Moving beyond networks, communities and social movements

The evidence identified in this chapter suggests that having some form of network having clear and common principles with common aspirations and goals is an important feature of the practice of voluntary organisations. Their role and functions however are likely to be heavily influenced by external factors such as funding, organisational capacity and relevance to wider society. There is some evidence to suggest that within the UK for example the effectiveness and value of these networks, communities and movements is closely related to how the sector perceives itself in relation to outside influences, whether positively or negatively.

But if development education is seen as more than a grouping of organisations then there is a need to look at the concept in a different way. This volume suggests that development education should be seen as much more than a grouping of organisations with common themes and values, but rather as an approach to learning, a pedagogy that engages a wide range of educationalists and is open to debate, dialogue and constant reflection and change.

Conclusion

This chapter has outlined the extent to which development education could be seen as a network of organisations, a community of practice and a social movement.

The extent to which these concepts are relevant to understanding development education needs to be situated within the specific social and historical context of a particular country. For example, where development education has a long and evolving tradition, there is evidence of a community of practice; but as development education organisations become closer to mainstream education, and their activities become more determined by policy-makers, this community of practice seems to be less evident.

The value of the concept of a social movement seems in most countries to be rhetorical and desirable, and only evident if there is a close relationship with wider movements or specific campaigns.

Finally in terms of a network, there is considerable evidence of this concept operating in a number of European countries and in Europe as a whole; but it is less evident beyond Europe, apart from to some extent in Japan.

There is evidence therefore of organisations who have been promoting themselves as part of a development education movement, as being part of a distinctive body of practice. This clearly has had value in a number of countries but it has also in some cases led to forms of exclusivity, and a potential marginalisation from mainstream practice.

Development education has been rightly criticised in the past for being too inward-looking and focused too much on being a movement for change; but the evidence suggests that during the first decade of the twenty-first century, in many European countries at least, it became more mainstream and more closely aligned to broader educational goals and agendas. This has been suggested by some (Selby and Kagawa, 2011; Cameron and Fairbrass, 2004; McCloskey, 2011) as leading to compromise and diminution of its 'soul' and '*raison d'être*'.

As will be suggested in the next chapter, the challenge is now more of an intellectual and theoretical one, ensuring that whilst development education continues to have a range of interpretations and perspectives, the discourse engages much more with theories around critical pedagogy, globalisation, human development and, above all, some of its intellectual roots in the work of Paulo Freire.

Notes

1   www.ideas-forum.org.uk
2   www.dear.or.jp/eng/eng01.html
3   www.deeep.org
4   www.gene.eu
5   www.lgtn.org.uk
6   www.globaleducationconference.com
7   www.global-ed.org/english/
8   http://globalclassrooms.org.uk/where-are-we/

References

Arnold, S. (1987) 'Constrained crusaders – NGOs and development education in the UK', *Occasional Paper*, Institute of Education, University of London.

Cameron, J. and Fairbrass, S. (2004) 'From development awareness to enabling effective support: the changing profile of development education in England', *Journal of International Development*, 16: 729–740.

DEA (1999) *Principles and Practice of Development Education Practitioners Working in Schools*. London: DEA.

DEA (2008) *Global Matters Learning – Case Studies*. London: DEA.

Della Porta, D. and Diani, M. (1999) *Social Movements: An Introduction*. Oxford: Blackwell.

Freire, P. (1972) *Pedagogy of the Oppressed*. Harmondsworth: Penguin.

Goldstein, T. and Selby, D. (ed.) (2000) *Weaving Connections*. Toronto: Sumach Press.

Goodwin, J. and Jasper, J.M. (2003) 'Editors' Introduction', in J. Goodwin and J.M. Jasper (eds) *The Social Movements Reader: Cases and Concepts*. Malden, MA and Oxford: Blackwell, pp. 3–7.

Hartmeyer, H. (2008) *Experiencing the World Global Learning in Austria: Developing, Reaching Out, Crossing Borders*. Munster: Waxmann.

Hicks, D. (2008) 'Ways of seeing: the origins of global education in the UK', unpublished paper.

Ishii, Y. (2003) *Development Education in Japan: A Comparative Analysis of the Contexts for Its Emergence, and Its Introduction into the Japanese School System*. London: Routledge/Falmer.

Kanji, S. (2001) 'Transformations in development education', unpublished MSc dissertation, University of Oxford.

Kirby, B. (ed.) (1994) *Education for Change: Grassroots Development Education in Europe*. London: Development Education Association.

Krause, J. (2010) *European Development Education Monitoring Report – 'DE Watch'*. Brussels: DEEEP.

Lave, J. and Wenger, E. (1991) *Situated Learning: Legitimate Peripheral Participation*. New York: Cambridge University Press.

Lister, I. (1986) 'Contemporary developments in political education: global and international approaches to political education', in C. Harber (ed.) *Political Education in Britain*. Lewes: Falmer Press, pp. 47–62.

McCloskey, S. (2011) 'Rising to the challenge: development education, NGOs and the need for urgent social change', *Policy and Practice, Development Education Review*, 12: 32–46.

McCollum, A. (1996) 'On the margins? An analysis of theory and practice of development education in the 1990s', unpublished PhD thesis, Open University.

McDonald, K. (2006) *Global Movements: Action and Culture*. Oxford: Blackwell.

McLaren, P. and da Silva, T.T. (1993) 'Decentering pedagogy: critical literacy, resistance and the politics of memory', in P. McLaren and P. Leonard (eds) *Paulo Freire: A Critical Encounter*. London: Routledge, pp. 47–89.

North-South Centre (2005) *Global Education in Netherlands: The European Global Education Peer Review Process*. Lisbon: North-South Centre.

North-South Centre (2006a) *Global Education in Austria: The European Global Education Peer Review Process*. Lisbon: North-South Centre.

North-South Centre (2006b) *Global Education in Finland: The European Global Education Peer Review Process*. Lisbon: North-South Centre.

O'Loughlin, E. (2010) *Global Education in Norway: Peer Review Process*. Amsterdam: Global Education Network Europe.

O'Shea, K. (2010) *A Study of the Current Training and Professional Development Needs of Members*. Dublin: IDEA.

RORG (2006) 'Be careful' poster – ethical guidelines for North/South-information in Norway, available at www.rorg.no.

Selby. D. and Kagawa, F. (2011) 'Development education and education for sustainable development: are they striking a Faustian bargain?' *Policy and Practice, Development Education Review*, 12: 15–31.

Thompson, S. (2006) 'Mapping transnational activism', *Democratiya*, 6: 115–119.

Tilly, C. (1987) 'The analysis of popular collective action', *European Journal of Operational Research*, 30: 223–229.

Wenger, E., McDermott, R. and Snyder, W.M. (2002) *Cultivating Communities of Practice*. Boston, MA: Harvard Business School Press.

Wilson-Grau, R. and Nunez, M. (2006) 'Evaluating international social change networks: a conceptual framework for a participatory approach', available at www.ngorisk.org/pdf/ Evaluating%20International%20Social%20Change%20Networks,%20Ricardo%20W.pdf

PART II

Theory of development education

5

TOWARDS A THEORY OF DEVELOPMENT EDUCATION

The previous chapters have outlined the history, main components and features of development education practice and suggested that whilst there is evidence of some coherent and common principles, they have tended to evolve rather than being based on, or heavily influenced by, theory.

If you asked development education practitioners who they thought were the main theoretical influences, most would probably make some reference to Paulo Freire and liberation education, but at the same time probably admitting they had not read much or any of his work (see McCollum, 1996; Brown, 2013). Within the UK, North America and Australia, practitioners might also state the influence of early American academics such as Tye or Hanvey, or UK figures such as Dave Hicks, Graham Pike or Robin Richardson. In Germany and Austria the work of Karl Seitz might well be mentioned.

This chapter summarises the work of two academics who are today probably the most influential theoreticians on development education. They are Annette Scheunpflug and Vanessa Andreotti d'Oliveria. The chapter then however suggests that in looking at the potential theories that could influence a pedagogy of development education, theories and ideas from development, globalisation, global citizenship, cosmopolitanism, postcolonialism and transformative learning need to be considered. As will be shown, development education touches on a myriad of social, philosophical and cultural theories. Developing a pedagogical approach does not mean adopting one or two theories but recognising their role and contribution to a process of learning. The chapter therefore concludes with a recognition of the importance of pluralism in order to develop a critical pedagogy for global social justice.

Scheunpflug and Andreotti

Annette Scheunpflug and Vanessa Andreotti are, as suggested above and reflected throughout this volume through numerous references and examples, the two most influential academics in the world today on development education, global education, global learning and global citizenship education.

Scheunpflug is a German education professor who, in developing a framework for Global Learning, has been very influential within both academic and practitioner-based debates, particularly in German-speaking areas of Europe. Andreotti is a Brazilian educationalist who has worked and been involved in research related to development education in the UK, New Zealand, Finland and Canada. Their importance is not only because they have developed concepts and thinking that have influenced practice, but they have themselves been engaged in working with practitioners and policy-makers and therefore have an influence way beyond that of many academics in the past. For example, both have been major speakers at conferences on global learning, global and development education and global citizenship in North America, Europe and New Zealand. They have also engaged in academic discourses relevant to the global learning theme in areas such as globalisation, postcolonialism and social justice education. Whilst their ideas and influence will be explored in various chapters in this book, a summary of their ideas is set out here.

Scheunpflug has been a key figure in Europe in promoting the concept of 'global learning' as a progression from development education or what was called in Germany 'third world pedagogy'. For her, the concept of Global Learning is understood as a 'pedagogical reaction to the development towards a world and global society' (quoted in Hartmeyer, 2008: 55). Global learning, she suggests, should not be a new subject in schools but a guiding principle defined by thematic issues such as development, environment, peace and interculturalism; by spatial dimensions; and by competences that need to be acquired to live in a global society. Her importance can be seen at three levels:

- recognition of the context of globalisation and what living in a global society means;
- competencies needed to live in a global society related to the dimensions of fact, temporal, space and social;
- evidence-based approach to ensure effective delivery.

Influenced by ethical and moral considerations regarding social justice, Scheunpflug sees globalisation as a key driver for education. For her, 'global learning should enable young people to learn to deal with the challenges of worldwide justice'. She goes on:

> Therefore they need some knowledge about globalisation, the root causes of poverty and the strategies of the Millennium Development Goals. They

should learn to acknowledge others, to deal with different cultural settings, to develop the ability to judge and to learn to see the world through other eyes.

(Scheunpflug, 2011: 38)

Her influences go back to the ideas of Kant and his concepts of ethical reasoning and freedom, and more recently the German sociologist Nicolas Luhman and his concept of the world society. Her importance to both the theory and practice of development education is not only in recognising the importance of a vision of a world for greater social justice but also the need to locate these debates within the context of learning, with recognition of different perspectives and voices and the legitimacy of dissent. This relates to her engagement in the need to distinguish between education, lobbying and campaigning (Scheunpflug, 2008: 24).

Andreotti, on the other hand, locates much of her thinking and writing within a postcolonial lens, based on critiques of western liberal and humanist traditions. Her work also builds on the thinking of Paulo Freire and epistemologies regarding construction of knowledge and the recognition of indigenous perspectives.

Central to her thinking is that learning in the twenty-first century required 'practitioners to perceive knowledge, learning and education in ways that were different to those of the previous century' (Andreotti, 2010). But she goes on to suggest that this shift is more than in the way learners think, but also in what they know and the ways in which they see things. This leads on to her third point: that this requires a shift in knowledge construction and the conceptual underpinnings of knowledge and future possibilities.

Andreotti sees the twenty-first century as the 'post-modern period', a time of change, fluidity and multiple sites of knowledge construction. This epistemological pluralism, she maintains, cannot be divorced from understanding social relations of capitalism, the impact of exploitation of peoples and exploitation of natural resources. In summary:

the local and global problems societies currently face are complex, interdependent and reflect the effects and failure of the Enlightenment ideals which have violently imposed and universalised, through colonialism and market globalisation, rendering other ways of knowing invisible.

(Andreotti, 2010: 9)

Taking this thinking forward, Andreotti suggests that global learning or global citizenship education needs to pluralise knowledge to enable dialogue, 'relationships of solidarity and, ideally the collective creation of non-hegemonic systems' (ibid.: 9).

Behind her thinking is the call for educationalists to resist instrumentalist thinking, to act as cultural brokers and encourage learners to see the world from different standpoints; and finally to critically engage in debates, to listen, negotiate and take responsibility for choices that are made.

The importance of Andreotti to the debates in development education and global learning is not just in questioning processes of learning and the need to recognise different perspectives and voices, but in locating her theories in the context of postcolonialism. This provides an important theoretical lens with which to understand and debate development education. As Andreotti states, 'post-colonialism champions a form of solidarity enacted as an ethical imperative toward the Other, where the Other is recognised as having a right to fundamentally disagree' (Andreotti, 2012: 3).

Both these academics provide important perspectives with which to build a theoretical framework of development education. They raise themes that resonate with development education practice, but also pose challenges regarding the location and role of learning and knowledge construction. Whilst they could be seen as at opposite ends of a theoretical spectrum, Scheunpflug taking a more cosmopolitan view whilst Andreotti takes a more postcolonial view, it is suggested here that both provide important building blocks for a theoretical framework. Both have developed bodies of research around their thinking, Andreotti through the journal, *Critical Literacy*, and Scheunpflug through the German language journal, *Zeitschrift fur Internationale Bildungsforschung und Entwicklungspädagogik (ZEP)*.

Whilst their ideas and importance should not be underestimated, and indeed their ideas are referred to in many places in this volume, it is suggested that in considering a theory of development education a range of other theories and influences need also to be considered, in order to provide a broader framework but also to situate their thinking within current discourses on globalisation, education and social change. It is suggested that debates around human development, social and educational transformation, critical pedagogy and global citizenship need also to be considered.

The reasons for this are as follows:

- Understanding development education requires an engagement with the debates around theories of international development.
- The twenty-first century is one in which globalisation is all-pervading, and any form of learning that includes consideration of the wider world has to take account of theories and influences in globalisation.
- In many countries around the world, the term global citizenship is increasingly being used as a way of summarising the aspirations of many development education practitioners. The various interpretations of this concept therefore need to be explored in relation to development education.
- The importance of understanding processes of learning and the construction of knowledge has been neglected in the history of development education.
- The continuing influence of Paulo Freire can be seen through the discourses within critical pedagogy, and needs to be applied in the context of development education.
- Central to much of development education practice is the notion of seeking social change, and therefore the discourse around critical pedagogy and transformative learning is particularly appropriate.

Reference to these broader theories, by their very nature, poses questions about linkages with practice. In bringing all of these different theories together through a more pluralistic approach, it is suggested that development education practitioners need to consider how these ideas relate and how they could help to conceptualise and clarify the aims of their own activities. What in essence is being said here is that as a discourse, development education needs to be aware of, and have the tools to respond to, the debates in development, globalisation, theories of knowledge and social change.

This means recognising that development education needs to see itself as a pedagogical approach that responds to both theoretical and practice-based debates within education. Scheunpflug and Andreotti provide an important basis for much of this thinking, although their ideas, as suggested above, could be perceived as inherently contradictory.

A theoretical framework for development education needs above all to respond to and address theories and practices related to debates on development and globalisation. Also underpinning development education is an implicit range of values that in part relate to universalist values such as social justice, but at the same time recognise power relations and inequalities. The debates around cosmopolitanism and global citizenship reflect some of these themes. Finally a theoretical framework for development needs to incorporate and make reference to broader educational questions concerning theories of learning, construction of knowledge and pedagogy.

Critiquing development

The evolution of development education cannot be divorced from an understanding of views about development. Indeed it could be argued that one of development education's greatest difficulties has been its failure to address and critique the assumption of development as just being about economic and social progress.

Lambert and Morgan (2012) in their study on learning about development within geography in the English school curriculum noted the ways in which the concept of 'development' was interpreted within that school subject. They note:

> In terms of teaching about development school geography still tends to define terms such as 'development' and then proceed to 'map' the patterns rather than delve into the question of how 'development' has been constructed. This leads to a failure to recognise the complex social formations that exist in space. For example, talking about whole countries as 'less developed' when there are important divisions within societies based around class, gender or locality.
>
> *(ibid.: 26)*

Any review of theories and practices of development education needs to take account of critiques of, and methodologies for assessing, concepts of development.

Bryan and Bracken (2011) in their review of development education and global citizenship education in Ireland suggest that there are a number of development discourses that can be seen within education in schools. Whilst the educational challenges behind these concepts of development are discussed in a later chapter, it is necessary to summarise here these theoretical traditions and their importance to development educationalists, in being aware of their roots and the implications for practice.

The roots of 'development' go back to the immediate post-1945 period and American President Truman's speech on development as modernisation (see Blum, 2000). This seeing of development as essentially modernisation gained particular prominence in the 1960s through the writings of Rostow, who saw development as essentially a path of progress from 'tradition to modernity', with the role of the west being to help in the process, through aid and technical assistance. Whilst aspects of this tradition have been discredited, its continuing influence can be seen in what Bryan and Bracken describe as 'development as luck'. They suggest this tradition assumes a sense of cultural superiority, with an approach based on compassion and pity, resulting in aid to the rescue, through, for example, celebrity humanitarianism (Bryan and Bracken, 2011: 61–73).

Baillie Smith (2004) refers to the need, in understanding development education practice, to critique NGO engagement, particularly within the context of development narratives. He notes that in the last decades of the twentieth century, the dominant discourse and practice around development was that the west possessed the skills and expertise that were somehow lacking elsewhere, with the emphasis on economic progress.

This approach has been critiqued from two perspectives, one that emphasises a human development and cosmopolitan viewpoint, as exemplified by Amartya Sen and Martha Nussbaum; and a post-development, structuralist perspective that sees the discourse as primarily about power, inequality and identity (Escobar, 1995).

Sen describes development as a 'process of expanding the real freedoms that people enjoy' (1999: 36), this being the primary end *and* primary means of development. He refers to the primary means of development as the instrumental role of freedom and describes five components – 'political freedom, economic facilities, social opportunities, transparency guarantees and protective security' – that contribute to the expansion of freedom in general (Sen, 1999: 38). Therefore, the aim of development is to expand the freedoms of everyone through enhancing their capabilities and supporting them to be actively involved in the process of development. This definition encompasses many aspects of development that have become part of the United National Development Programme's Human Development Index.

A postmodern critic of development, based on Michel Foucault's discourse analysis, argues that it is not progress, but power that is at the core of the development system, including its policy and practice: 'The real purpose of the development exercise [. . .] is to discipline and dominate' (Storey, 2003: 36). Particularly, it is argued that:

the principal effect generated by development discourse is to legitimise and reinforce Western dominance over the 'Third World' in part through its very definition or categorisation of the 'Third World' as being in need of Western-style development, and constituting an object of/for development.

(Storey, 2003: 35)

Escobar argues that development is being portrayed as necessary (Blum, 2000) and this measurement of underdevelopment justifies the intervention of NGOs and organisations like the World Bank (Storey, 2003).

Baillie Smith notes that poststructuralist-informed interventions into development theory and practice enable the analysis to go further, highlighting the ways dominant discourses of development convey particular conceptions of identity, agency and authority. He suggests that this discourse is particularly helpful in trying to understand the public and educative formulations of development, and their connections with citizenship.

Whilst the post-structuralist critiques do not offer an alternative development paradigm, they do provide insights helpful for engaging with the representation and communication of development in the UK. This maintains the connections to an emancipatory project in terms of the links between the representation of development and the responses that might engender, such as involvement in campaigns, changed consumer habits or donation to a charity. Put more broadly, the communication of development can be connected to issues around the emergence and formulation of a progressive global civil society and the development of global citizenship.

(Baillie Smith, 2004: 71)

It is suggested here therefore that theories of development need to be understood both for what they stand for and their influence, and also as a mechanism for understanding how educators respond to themes such as global poverty and social progress. Also, as Blum suggests in quoting Grillo, there is a tendency to see development as a monolithic enterprise, controlled from the top and almost conspiratorial and impervious to local knowledge or experience. She states that numerous studies confirm that people in the 'developing world' are not merely passive receptors of development interventions, but rather they engage with social change and economic opportunities according to their own understandings, needs and interests (Blum, 2000: 15). This poses a potential role for development education in the discourses in and around development, in making connections with debates about power, movements for change and terms such as global citizenship.

Understanding development and the debates around it today however also means engaging with the second theme which needs to be recognised in contributing to a theoretical basis for development education, and that is globalisation.

Critiquing globalisation

The second theme that needs to be included in debates about development education is theories around the concept of globalisation.

There is an extensive literature on globalisation (see for example Held and McGrew, 2000), and how it is interpreted around the world. A feature of many of the different perspectives on globalisation is that it should be seen as a complex process of transformation of economic, political and cultural social relations (Held and McGrew, 2000). Key to understanding these social relations is, as Giddens (1991) suggests, the way in which 'local happenings are shaped by events occurring many miles away and vice versa'.

Lewin (2009) suggests there are three main themes to the discourses on globalisation. The first is economic, in terms of the borderless nature of the production and marketing of goods. The second is the declining role of the nation state as the principal site of identity construction. The third is the nature of global communications and, resources permitting, instant access to knowledge, information and dialogue around the world. In many countries across the world, people have instant global access to information and knowledge (Kenway and Bullen, 2008).

A key theme therefore of much of the literature is the impact of globalisation on people's lives, which are now more interdependent with those of people elsewhere in the world. This leads, as Ray (2007) suggests, to a myriad of cultural influences that challenges one's own sense of identity and belonging within a community.

The debates around globalisation and education have been well covered by people such as Burbules and Torres (2000), Apple, Kenway and Singh (2005), Stromquist and Monkman (2000) and Edwards and Usher (2008). Whilst much of the discourse has been around the economic impact of globalisation on education, there has been a recognition that globalisation raises some major new challenges for education. These include instant global access to information and knowledge, increased social mobility, contact and dialogue with people from a wide range of cultural backgrounds, and the impact of events elsewhere in the world on what and how people learn in a specific locality (Jarvis, 2007).

Whilst it can be noted within some of these debates that learning needs to be more global in outlook, there has been less debate on the impact of globalisation in terms of approaches to learning and education. Such impact includes the impact of instant global access to information and knowledge, the opportunities to learn and engage with people from all over the world, and the implications this has for the form and content of learning, and above all the consequent influences on the development of an individual's identity.

A key theorist on globalisation and its relevance to education and the knowledge society is Ulrick Beck. He suggests that globalisation has led to making training longer rather than shorter, and to loosening or doing away with links to a particular job or occupation, gearing training instead to key qualifications that can be widely used in practice. Beck goes on to suggest that this should be seen not only in terms of 'flexibility' but also in terms of areas such as 'social competence, ability to work in a team, conflict resolution, understanding of other cultures, integrated thinking and a capacity to handle uncertainties and paradoxes of secondary modernity' (Beck, 2000: 137–138).

Beck also notes that learning within the framework of globalisation also poses questions about where, what and how people learn. Part of the exciting dialectic of globalisation, he suggests, is that it replaces 'traditional lecturing societies with dialogic attentiveness and courage to disagree – people beginning to realise transnationalisation of uneventful education and curricula' (ibid.: 138).

These observations, whilst coming from a critical viewpoint on globalisation, pose also the opportunities globalisation can create. Globalisation has, as several theorists have commented, led nation states to be more outward-looking, recognising the importance of learning about cultures and different viewpoints. Ray (2007) suggests that this involves increased hybridity in a more complex and fluid world. Living in a globalised world, he suggests, does not create homogeneity and polarisation but can create an eclectic mix of identities and perspectives. Globalisation can also, as France (2007) suggests, lead to the increased individualisation of societies, the dis-embedding of traditions and the emergence of uncertainty and fluidity.

Thus understanding concepts of and approaches towards globalisation leads to debates on approaches to learning, the purpose of education and how people themselves engage in a global society.

Cosmopolitanism and global justice

In response to the challenges that globalisation raises in terms of the impact of living in a more 'interconnected world', the concept of cosmopolitanism has gained renewed interest and become influential for both theorists and practitioners engaged in development education.

Central to the discourses around cosmopolitanism is that there are 'moral obligations owed to all human beings based solely on our humanity alone' (Wallace Brown and Held, 2010: 1). This, as Lu suggests, 'translates ethically into an idea of shared or common moral duties towards others by virtue of this humanity' (quoted in Wallace Brown and Held, 2010: 1). This moral cosmopolitanism often 'translates into corresponding duties of global justice, the protection of human rights, and reforming unjust international systems' (ibid.: 2).

Development education traditions, as mentioned in earlier chapters, have a strong values base to their practice around themes of global social justice, sense of world outlook and global responsibility. These themes have much in common with the writings of people such as Martha Nussbaum and have been influential in some sectors with her collaboration with Amartya Sen in promoting concepts of global social concern and awareness.

The influences of these views go back to the enlightenment and Kant, and have been promoted again in some of the writings of Scheunpflug.

Behind much of development education practice and thinking is an implicit assumption of a cosmopolitan worldview and a desire for global social justice. This, as Baillie Smith (2004) has noted, can be seen in the underlying goals and principles behind the practices of many development NGOs.

Sen talks about capability as the most pertinent space of comparison for purposes of quality of life assessment. Nussbaum (2011) in her volume on capabilities refers to quality of life and basic social justice being at the heart of the capabilities approach. She notes (ibid.: 62), for example, that the capabilities approach is closely allied with the international human rights movement, with the common ground being that all people have some core entitlements just by virtue of their humanity; and that it is a basic duty of society to respect and support these entitlements. There are some linkages here with debates around human rights in the context of education that have been promoted by Osler and Starkey (2005).

Nussbaum (2002) describes cosmopolitanism as representing a 'community of mankind' where all are of equal worth. This includes the ethics of compassion, of sharing the world with others from around the world, of respecting the dignity of reason and moral choice, and the value of shared values.

Nussbaum, in response to the dangers of a narrow national patriotism associated with certain practices and views in the United States, suggests that while we should not give up our special identities, 'we should also work to make all human beings part of our community of dialogue and concern'. She goes on to suggest that we need to learn 'enough about the different to recognise common aims, aspirations, and values, and enough about these common ends to see how variously they are instantiated in the many cultures and their histories' (Nussbaum, in Wallace Brown and Held, 2010: 158).

Tomlinson states that at its simplest: 'a cosmopolitan orientation is associated with an intellectual and aesthetic sense of openness towards people, places and experiences from different cultures, especially those from different nations' (cited in Szersynski and Urry, 2002). This relates to the concept of cultural cosmopolitanism which has been argued by Wallace Brown and Held as 'relating to how we might be able to cultivate a sense of global justice in a culturally pluralistic world' (2010: 10). They suggest further that: 'In its most basic form, cultural cosmopolitanism argues for moral duties and obligations that supersede or transgress localised obligations based solely on aspects of ethnicity, culture and nationality' (ibid.: 10).

But as Matthews and Sidhu have stated, cosmopolitanism has been criticised for producing little in the way of commitment to globally orientated citizenship, and for co-articulation with elitist and dominant governments and movements (2005: 53). They further suggest that a cosmopolitanism that 'extends the capacity to mediate between and within national cultures is positive if it creates possibilities for dialogue with the traditions and discourses of others and if it widens the horizons of one's own framework of meaning' (ibid.: 55).

These viewpoints and discourses are clearly relevant and important to the debates in development education and have been influential, if indirectly, in a lot of development education practice, particularly the activities of non-governmental organisations.

However, as Harvey (2009) comments, cosmopolitanism has tended to confuse rather than clarify agendas, because of the wide range of standpoints and views now associated with the concept. There are those like Nussbaum who take a moral cosmopolitan view; literary and cultural theorists who are concerned with cultural hybridities and multiculturalism; and social scientists who focus on rules of law and global governance. Harvey questions a perspective of universalism that is based on a moral discourse. He questions how cosmopolitanism can account for, let alone be sympathetic to, a world characterised by class and cultural divisions (Harvey, 2009: 80).

Cosmopolitanism may have many guises but central to the discourses is a form of liberal humanism. However, it is perhaps questionable as to how key this is in the context of a complex globalised world. Rizvi (2009) suggests a potential way through the labyrinth. Following Said, he sees cosmopolitanism as a model of 'critical learning that seeks to develop a set of epistemic virtues necessary for integrating discourses, practices and structures of global interconnectedness' in ways that are socially networked and have greater chance of developing 'some form of global solidarity' (Rizvi, 2009: 102).

As Sharon Todd has stated, the idea of 'humanity underpinning cosmopolitan efforts in education currently diminishes the potential to deal with human pluralism meaningfully' (2009: 152). She recognises the common bonds and values, but suggests that such commonalities 'grow out of the very differences that structure the plurality of human life' (ibid.). Todd goes on to suggest that in understanding this pluralism there is a need to look at conflict and violence, which are all too often ignored through the cosmopolitan lens. She contends that the disavowal of the humanness of violence lends itself to an 'idealised account of humanity'. Key to her argument is the recognition of an 'imperfect education', an education of humility not hubris (ibid.: 154).

> No universal principles can secure justice, since its promise lies in keeping open the question of justice itself. No fixed idea of humanity can substitute for the humanity that is always yet to come and never unified. No consensus can bring about equality or democracy, which requires dissensus and disagreement. No right can secure the well-being of a human life without acknowledging its never-ending place in processes of negotiation and translation. No principles or virtues can guarantee the moral betterment of society if individuals apply them unthinkingly as principles.
>
> *(ibid.: 154)*

She concludes that if one takes the example of young people learning about rights and democracy and citizenship, then central to that process is the understanding of the fractured nature of the ideas themselves.

These debates around cosmopolitanism and rights and their relationship to postmodernist approaches lie at the heart of many of the tensions within development education. This is why the work of Todd is perhaps important because she provides a valuable linkage between the various debates in development education and global learning, particularly in terms of dealing with the challenging and conflicting tensions regarding universalism versus pluralistic perspectives and voices.

Harvey (2009: 95) refers to the work of De Sousa Santos as perhaps an important bridge between postcolonialism and universalism. De Sousa Santos refers to the excluded populations of the world as needing 'a subaltern cosmopolitanism'. This 'cosmopolitan solidarity' needs an 'alternative concept of national and global friendship'.

One of the areas where the discourses within cosmopolitanism are relevant to the debates in development education can be seen in relation to discussions on social justice. Whilst the concept of social justice may equally have many interpretations and be subject to such questions as justice for whom, who defines it and when is it applied, it can be a useful concept in terms of the relationships to inequality in the world.

Brock (2009: 119) for example sees global justice as relating to every person having the right to be 'adequately positioned to enjoy prospects for a decent life'. She defines this in terms of meeting basic needs, enjoying basic freedoms, and fair terms of co-operation in collective endeavours, with the social and political structures in place to enable these to take place. This definition can however be interpreted in many different ways. It is suggested here that alongside the influence of Rawls who sees justice in terms of equity, or Sen who relates justice to capabilities and freedom, the concept of social justice needs to make reference to power relations and global divisions in the world, particularly when one comes to look at relevance to development education.

It is suggested here that the comments of the South African academic, Catherine Odora Hoppers, are particularly relevant. She notes that whilst one could find some consensus about the concept of social justice, its usage and interpretation often favoured the strong and the powerful. She states that social justice should be seen as the ideal condition in which all members of society have the same basic rights, security, opportunities, obligations and social benefits. She goes on: 'social justice is based on the idea of a society which gives individuals and groups fair treatment and a just share of the benefits of society' (Odora Hoppers, 2008: 608). However, she goes on to state that when it comes to deciding on 'fair treatment' and a 'just share', this is defined by whatever the strong decide. To her, key to incorporating concepts of justice is 'cultural justice', which 'takes us from tolerance to respect in cultural politics, arguing that what is needed is functional respectful co-existence'. This means not only listening to and recognising views of others, but directly engaging in forms of interaction that 'invokes the cultural worlds of the players' (ibid.).

As Ayers, Quinn and Stovall (2009) note, for social justice to have any meaning, it must have a political and active dimension. They talk about social justice education resting on three pillars: equity including the principle of fairness, equal access, activism related to full participation, and social literacy related to relevance – nourishing awareness of own identities and connection with others. Social justice education, they suggest, embraces the three Rs: 'relevant, rigorous and revolutionary' (ibid.: xiv).

As Rizvi suggests (in Ayers et al., 2009: 91), 'while, as an ideal, social justice may be universally applicable and aspired to, its expressions vary across different cultural and national traditions'. But whilst it may be difficult, as he suggests, to refer to a single set of goods, injustice does have a material reality that is recognised by those who experience it. This brings us back to the realities of the world and how as an individual you respond. It is an understanding and engagement with these challenges and how as a learner you respond to these questions that demonstrates the potential value of development education. The most popular manifestation of these debates is in how the concept of global citizenship is being perceived and in the role it can play in developing a theoretical framework for development education.

Concepts of global citizenship

The discourse on global citizenship has grown considerably over the past decade as agendas have converged on globalisation, citizenship, global social responsibility and development education. There are many different interpretations of global citizenship, reflecting many of the themes referred to earlier in this chapter, such as universalism, social justice, different perspectives, globalisation and development.

To some, global citizenship conveys the economic dimensions of globalisation; to others it conveys the idea of socially responsible behaviour; and to others it relates to global political institutions. It can be seen as part of a commitment to a broad global moral purpose or as a directly political form of social action that has global consequences.

Within the literature on global citizenship there are a number of direct connections to concepts referred to earlier in this chapter. For example, the term 'cosmopolitan' is used as distinctive from traditional notions of citizenship, but also because of linkages to global humanism. Examples of this can be seen in Dower (2003) and Osler and Starkey (2005).

A second tradition with the discourses on global citizenship is to see the concept as more radical, challenging dominant orthodoxies and essentially related to movements for change and social justice. Examples of approaches include Cogan and Derricott (2000), Noddings (2005) and Andreotti (2012).

A useful summary of the range of traditions and approaches to the concept of global citizenship can be seen in Table 5.1, devised by Oxley and Morris (2013).

This ever increasing body of literature around global citizenship is important and increasingly influential on debates within development education, for a number of reasons. First, the typology as outlined by Oxley and Morris in Table 5.1 can be a valuable lens by which to understand how individuals respond from their own

TABLE 5.1 Concepts of global citizenship identified from prevailing literature (Oxley and Morris, 2013: 6)

Conception	Examples of proponents/opponents	Focus and key concepts	More radical position(s)	Associated with the work of:
Political global citizenship	Held; McGrew; Linklater; Carter; Archibugi; Wendt; Dower; Cabrera; Tinnevelt; Patomaki	A focus on the relationships of the individual to the state and other polities, particularly in the form of *cosmopolitan democracy*	World state; anarchy	Kant; Rawls
Moral global citizenship	Singer; Appiah; Osler and Starkey; Kymlicka and Walker; Cabrera	A focus on the ethical positioning of individuals and groups to each other, most often featuring ideas of *human rights*	Strong cosmopolitanism; 'new' cosmopolitanism	Stoics; Kant; Sen; Nussbaum
Economic global citizenship	Garriga and Mele; Fombrun; Waddock and Smith; Logsdon and Wood	A focus on the interplay between power, forms of capital, labour, resources and the human condition, often presented as *international development*	CSR/fair trade; free markets, competition, free trade	Hayek; Friedman; Smith; Quesnay; Bowen
Cultural global citizenship	De Ruyter and Spiecker; Brimm	A focus on the symbols that unite and divide members of societies, with particular emphasis on *globalisation of arts, media, languages, sciences and technologies*	Multicultural awareness; cultural elitism	Nietzsche (*übermensch*)
Social global citizenship	Cogan and Derricott; Selcer	A focus on the interconnections between individuals and groups and their advocacy of the 'people's' voice, often referred to as *global civil society*	Multiple perspectives; relationships and communications	Habermas (communicative rationality)

Critical global citizenship	Andreotti; Tully; Walker	A focus on the challenges arising from inequalities and oppression, using critique of social norms to advocate action to improve the lives of dispossessed/subaltern populations, particularly through a *postcolonial agenda*	Post-Marxism; critical race theory; feminist	Escobar; Said; Gramsci; Marx; Frankfurt School; critical pedagogy (e.g. Freire)
Environmental global citizenship	Dobson; Lovelock; Richardson; Weiss	A focus on advocating changes in the actions of humans in relation to the natural environment, generally called the *sustainable development agenda*	Ecocentric; anthropocentric	Enviro-scientific research
Spiritual global citizenship	Noddings; Golmohamad; Lindner	A focus on the non-scientific and immeasurable aspects of human relations, advocating commitment to axioms relating to *caring, loving, spiritual and emotional connections*	Religious; humanist	Danesh; religious texts

personal standpoint to global themes. Secondly, in debates around global citizenship the mere use of the term poses questions about what is meant by 'global' and 'being a citizen' and consequently your role as an individual in a world of inequality and injustice. Finally, the discourses pose questions about the purpose and role of education.

Andreotti, in her review of the discourses and practices of global citizenship, refers to 'soft' and 'hard' approaches. To her, the goal of 'soft global citizenship' influenced by cosmopolitan notions is to 'empower individuals to act (or become active citizens), according to what has been defined for them as a good life or ideal world' (Andreotti, 2006: 48). On the other hand, she sees a harder and more critical global citizenship, influenced by postcolonialist and cultural literacy theory, as about empowering 'individuals to reflect critically on the legacies and processes of their cultures, to imagine different futures and to take responsibility for decisions and actions' (ibid.).

These discourses suggest that to engage and assess the value of the concept 'global citizenship', there is a need to assess one's own relationship to the broader themes and debates referred to elsewhere in this chapter. All too often, the term 'being a global citizen' is used without any debate or understanding of these different interpretations. For example the term is increasingly used in many countries as a goal of education systems: 'equipping our graduates to be good global citizens' is a common mantra in many universities. But to what extent is this an instrumentalist approach to learning, or a way of making connections between education and society?

The concept of global citizenship and its many interpretations therefore provides an important bridge between the debates on development, globalisation, cosmopolitanism and social justice, and processes of learning and pedagogy. Merely posing the question 'what do you mean by the term global citizen?' can result in a process of dialogue and debate that incorporates discussion about the role of the individual within the context of a globalised and unequal world, and what the individual needs to understand, know and be able to do, to engage in that world. Above all it poses the relationship between learning and social change.

Processes of learning

A feature of development education practice as indicated in earlier chapters has been a common assumption that learning about global and development issues in itself will lead to action for change. Many NGOs who have become involved in development education have done so on the basis that people, particularly young people, by learning about themes such as global poverty, unequal trade and human rights, will want to take action. This assumes that if the subject matter has a strong values base, this will lead to behavioural change. A central theme of this volume is to highlight the dangers and weaknesses of this approach, and to suggest that learning is important for its own sake: education can and should provide the tools to enable the learner to make sense of the world around them, but this should be done from a position of being well-informed.

Marshall outlines the dangers of an instrumentalist view of global citizenship education when she suggests that the practice requires 'an emotional and often active orientated commitment to, and understanding of, particular interpretations of economic, political, legal and cultural injustice' (2011: 418–419).

Therefore it is suggested that discourses on development education need to include engagement with debates on processes of learning, how people learn and the relationship between learning, personal experience, behavioural change and individual action.

In the 1930s Dewey wrote about reflective and experiential learning and how encountering a problem issue or dilemma in the real world sparked a process of reflective thinking and therefore learning (Dewey, 1938). A lot of development education practice, whether volunteering, school linking or exploring real world examples, is based on an assumption of the powerful impact of personal experience. This is discussed further in Chapter 7. But as Rogers and Horrocks (2010: 128) state, this leads on to consideration of the context and forms of social learning theory, learning as a process of constructing meaning and how people make sense of their experience. Learning, they suggest, is not discovering knowledge existing outside of themselves; rather, it is the construction of new perceptions. This relates to what Bourdieu (1990) has referred to in terms of personal construction of knowledge through feelings and ideas, the influence of places and people and their cultural backgrounds.

Others such as Kolb (1984) have written about experiential learning as a process of adapting to the world. Jarvis (2006, 2007), who sees learning in a lifetime context, suggests that education is the maturing of the development of the mind through the use of memory and experiential learning. For him, learning is 'the process of transforming the whole of our experience through thought, action and emotion and thereby transforming ourselves as we continue to build perceptions of external reality to our biography' (Jarvis, 2007: 5). This lifelong approach to learning, he suggests, combines the 'whole person–body (genetic, physical and biological) and mind (knowledge, skills, attitudes, values, emotions, beliefs and senses) experiences' and within a perceived context can lead to transformations 'cognitively, emotionally or practically (or through any combination) and integrated into an individual person's biography resulting in a continually changing (or more experienced) person' (Jarvis, 2007: 1).

In the course of his work, Jarvis acknowledges the insight gained from Freirean thought, which promoted a social active model of learning that rejected a passive acceptance of knowledge, values and beliefs in favour of a collaborative interchange that could revolutionise cognition and practice.

Illeris, another key figure on theories of learning, suggests that a convenient assumption is that we equate what is taught with what is learnt. This, he suggests, greatly oversimplifies the learning process, which should be understood as a holistic process comprised of cognitive, emotional and social dimensions. This means recognising that the process of learning brings in diverse experiences and prior knowledge, and the more the individual can actively participate in and take responsibility for their own learning, the more they will learn and retain (Illeris, 2003, 2009).

These theories on learning are very important for developing a pedagogy of development education because they directly address how people learn, which is complex, multifaceted and cannot be reduced to the mere accumulation of facts, data and bodies of knowledge.

Within the debates on processes of learning, it is suggested that an important contribution to these questions from a development education perspective is the work of Ajay Kumar (2008), whose work was referred to in Chapter 2. Building on the thinking of Gandhi, Kumar emphasises the importance of dialogue as a way of mediating learning. This dialogic or shared learning he suggests is a key element of development education:

> a dialogical approach to education is based on systematic and coherently organised representation by two or more interacting subjects of a phenomenon or a process about which they endeavour to know more about, increasing the possibilities of active interest in interpretation, meaning making, and knowledge creation, challenging all 'given' conceptions in ways that stimulate 'praxis', i.e. a synthesis of theory and action, theory and experimentation, knowledge and experience, work and science, and also actions based on rational deliberations (in the Aristotelian sense).
>
> *(Kumar, 2008: 45)*

For Kumar, learning is effective if it recognises the importance of dialogue and co-operation and a shared understanding of processes of learning. He sees 'intrapersonal and interpersonal relationships, dialogue and communication' as 'enhancing skills in the sphere of learning' (ibid.: 46). In posing development education as a form of 'critical humanist pedagogy', Kumar suggests that this implies the need to distinguish between 'merely useful knowledge' and 'really useful knowledge' with the latter 'enabling people to understand the root cause of the circumstances in which they find themselves in order to transform it' (ibid.: 41–42).

The themes addressed so far, from development and globalisation to cosmopolitanism and global citizenship, have posed questions about approaches towards learning. What they also pose is what is meant by knowledge within the context of these themes. It is to this area of knowledge that we now turn, and how concepts of knowledge relate to pedagogy, particularly the concept of critical pedagogy which is seen here as an integral component of development education.

Concepts of knowledge and the knowledge society

A perceived neglected area within the discourses on development education is the lack of attention to concepts of knowledge. One of the main critics of development education and global learning, Alex Standish (2012), has specifically raised this issue in relation to the school curriculum. Yet if one looks at the work of Scheunpflug and Andreotti and the influences on their thinking, one will see that there has been some debate on this, and they pose major questions that relate debates on knowledge to debates on pedagogy.

Scheunpflug suggests that 'because the more there is to know, the more an individual does not know, people must be aware that they can be wrong, even if they are generally knowledgeable' (2011: 33). Education, she suggests, has to assist the process of decision making under conditions of a relative lack of knowledge. One-dimensional solutions and linear processes do not address the complexities that often need to be addressed.

Andreotti, influenced by postcolonial and poststructuralist ideas, refers to the importance of 'pluralistic knowledge'. She suggests, for example, that teachers need to 'reclaim their role as cultural brokers' and increase 'their awareness and capacity to analyse and see the world from different perspectives'. Moreover, Andreotti states that we should not be posing what to think or offering universal pedagogies; and that educationalists should equip themselves to deal with all possibilities, equipping learners to be open and critical and able to deal with these possibilities. This, she suggests, requires an understanding of knowledges and identities within transient learning communities (Andreotti, 2010: 9–10).

Andreotti's perspective also relates to the debates regarding western hegemonic knowledges and indigenous knowledges. Whilst aspects of these debates are discussed elsewhere in this volume, with particular reference to the ideas of Odora Hoppers, it needs to be noted here that perhaps a role for development education is through some form of 'third space' (see Bhabha, 1994) to create opportunities for dialogue and negotiation. Breidlid (2013) suggests that the cultural-historical activity theory (CHAT) could be relevant here. He notes that in CHAT, contradictions are viewed as sources for change and development. In some ways these approaches are similar to points raised earlier by Kumar.

Behind these comments, however, is the need to address what is meant by knowledge. Jane Gilbert (2005) suggests we need to move away from thinking about knowledge as an object to be mastered, a static end-in-itself, to a view of knowledge as a resource, something that people think with, in order to solve real problems. If people need to make sense of and act on global influences, they first need to know a lot about themselves (ibid.: 197). They need to move away from an approach based on reproduction of knowledge to one of generating new knowledge. Gilbert further suggests that a systems-level understanding of a body of knowledge involves understanding how the body of knowledge works, both internally and in relation to other bodies of knowledge (2005: 209). This theme is discussed further in Chapter 6 with regard to learning about development.

Debates on knowledge and their relation to development education also lead to discussions about the influence of Paulo Freire, who suggests that the learner should be viewed as an independent thinker who must be actively engaged in the process of creating new knowledge and applying critical consciousness to their learning (Freire, 1972).

Freire and Giroux: critical pedagogy

Freire, as was mentioned at the beginning of this chapter, has been an influential figure for many development educationalists, perhaps more for what he has stood for, rather than in incorporating and using his thinking. To many development education practitioners, his importance is because of his challenge to dominant orthodoxies and his championing of the voices of the dispossessed.

Here it is suggested that Freire has much to offer a pedagogy of development education, rather than being a symbol against injustices in the world. To Freire, education is not a neutral process; it either functions as an instrument to facilitate conformity and support for the current social system, or it becomes the means by which learners make sense of and critically reflect on the world in which they live and the role they can play in transforming it. Freire believed that education is a political act and that it cannot be divorced from pedagogy. Freire defined this as the main tenet of critical pedagogy. This means that the way students are taught and what they are taught cannot be divorced from a political agenda.

One of the most influential aspects of Freire's thinking is his critique of what he called the 'banking' concept of education, in which the student was viewed as an empty account to be filled by the teacher. He notes that 'it transforms students into receiving objects. It attempts to control thinking and action, leads men and women to adjust to the world, and inhibits their creative power' (Freire, 1972: 77). To Freire, knowledge is constructed through dialogue – and only emerges through constant reflection and debate, invention and re-invention.

The influence of this dominant ideology within education, Freire suggests, requires the learner being prepared to question and develop a critique of the educational system. He wrote that 'men educate each other through the mediation of the world' and argued:

> Every human being, no matter how 'ignorant' or submerged in the 'culture of silence' he may be, is capable of looking critically at his world in a dialogical encounter with others. Provided with the proper tools for such an encounter, he can gradually perceive his personal and social reality as well as the contradictions in it, become conscious of his own perception of that reality, and deal critically with it. In this process, the old, paternalistic teacher–student relationship is overcome.
>
> *(Freire, 1972: 12)*

An important disciple of Freire's thinking has been Henry Giroux, an American academic, who has taken forward the debates to include the need to develop a critical awareness, so that individuals can take action against the oppressive elements of reality.

Giroux starts from a view that education is important not only for gainful employment but also for creating the 'formative culture of beliefs, practices, and social relations that enable individuals to wield power, learn how to govern and nurture a democratic society that takes equality, justice, shared values and freedom seriously' (2011: 4).

He goes beyond simply critiquing globalisation and power within education, and suggests a notion of critical pedagogy that addresses the democratic potential of engaging in how experience, knowledge and power are shaped in the classroom in different and often unequal contexts; and how teacher authority might be mobilised against dominant pedagogical practices as part of the practice of freedom – for example by enabling students to read texts differently as objects of inter-rogation rather than slavishly through a culture of pedagogical conformity (ibid.: 5). He goes on to argue for

> developing a language for thinking critically about how culture deploys power and how pedagogy as a moral and political practice enables students to focus on the suffering of others.
>
> *(ibid.)*

> – to educate students to lead a meaningful life, learn how to hold power and authority accountable, and develop the skills, knowledge and courage to challenge commonsense assumptions while being willing to struggle for a more socially just world.
>
> *(ibid.: 7)*

For Giroux, a recognition and understanding of the oppressive nature of education practice is crucial, but equally important are the processes for change and transformation: critical pedagogy is about transforming knowledge. To Giroux, educating young people in the spirit of a critical democracy means providing them with the 'knowledge, passion, civic capacities, and social responsibility necessary to address the problems facing the nation and the globe; this means challenging those modes of schooling and pedagogy designed largely to promote economic gain' etc. and substitute training for critical thinking and analysis (ibid.: 12).

Giroux also suggests that critical pedagogy is an 'ethical project with its roots in critical theory, so that it incorporates both a vision of how society should be constructed and a theory of how currently society exploits, dehumanises and denigrates certain groups of people' (Scott, 2007: 103). This sense of the other and recognising difference has, he suggests, political implications. First, as Scott summarises, Giroux suggests that

> student identities and subjectivities need to be understood as multiple and embedded constructs which may be contradictory, and furthermore need to be surfaced for and by students in the act of creating new, more satisfying and more socially just forms of identity.
>
> *(Scott, 2007: 104)*

Furthermore Giroux suggests curriculum knowledge should not be treated as a set of sacred texts but as part of 'ongoing engagement with a variety of narratives and traditions'. He further suggests there is a need to challenge the 'culture of positivism' within education about knowledge being seen as about objectifiable data – the separation of values from knowledge. Giroux suggests that the

> logic of positivistic thought suppresses the critical function of historical consciousness, for underlying all of the major assumptions of the culture of positivism is a common theme: the denial of human action grounded in historical insight and committed to emancipation in all spheres of human activity.
>
> *(ibid.)*

Moreover he suggests this culture presents a passive model of humanity.

Mclaren (2009) goes further. Building on the work of Giroux, he sees knowledge not only as a social construction but rooted in a nexus of power relations. He further suggests that critical pedagogy asks how our everyday common-sense understandings – our social constructions – get produced and lived out (ibid.: 63). The crucial factor here, he suggests, is that some forms of knowledge have more power and legitimacy than others.

Giroux and the discourse around critical pedagogy need also to be considered in relation to the debates around postmodernism. Whilst Giroux has some sympathy with postmodern ideas in relation to the continuing forming and re-forming of identities in relation to changing structures in society, he states:

> To reject all notions of totality is to run the risk of being trapped in particularistic theories that cannot explain how the various diverse relations that constitute large social, political and global systems interrelate or mutually determine and constrain one another.
>
> *(Giroux, 1992: 67)*

He makes clear that different forms of pedagogy produce different types of knowledge and identity in learners.

For Giroux, as Scott notes (2007: 108), there is an implicit assumption that certain pedagogical practices are foundational to his view. These are a respect for the views of others, the possibility of communicating an orderly exchange of views, an acceptance that one might be wrong and the need to be tolerant of other people's viewpoints.

Giroux is also important, as will be explored later, in terms of seeing teachers as 'transgressive intellectuals' who shape curriculum content and pedagogy so that dominant ways of thinking and acting are challenged. Giroux also notes the challenges of such transgressive activity in terms of daily practice.

These themes of critical pedagogy resonate closely with examples of practice and what is perceived as good development education practice, as outlined in Chapter 2. Above all, it is recognition of the political and ideological agenda within which learning and the production of knowledge take place that shows the value of critical pedagogy to development education. Learning and understanding about development, for example, is constructed within a context of power relations, inequalities and injustices in the world. Theories related to development, globalisation, cosmopolitanism and global citizenship clearly have some relevance to development education. But as suggested, to take the theories and practices forward, there is a need to recognise and relate these ideas to concepts related to power and inequality in the world and particularly the legacy of colonialism.

Postcolonialism

Development education practices have by their very nature raised questions and issues regarding the relationship between those who have power and those who do not, those whose historical and cultural influences come from imperialism and colonialism, and those who have been the subject of these influences. This is the origin of terms such as Global North and Global South.

A concept that has been increasingly influential in development education, most notably through the work of Andreotti, is postcolonialism. In general terms the concept could be summarised as dealing with effects of colonisation on cultures and societies (Ashcroft et al., 2000: 186). Central to much of the thinking around postcolonialism is recognising different histories that move beyond the dominant western and European notions of modernity.

Although a key founding influence for postcolonialism was the African revolutionary, Franz Fanon, probably the key academic influencers relevant to debates in development education are Edward Said, Homi Bhabha and Gayatri Spivak.

Edward Said has been a key figure in the development of thinking around power, empire and colonialism, most notably through his work on Orientalism (Said, 1978). This is a work that shows how knowledge about the Orient in the west was directly related to power and ideology. He argues that knowledge produced by the west about the Orient was not based on objectivity or scientific data but on negative images and stereotypes. Orientals were seen not as citizens but as problems to be solved or confined (ibid.: 207). Said went on to state that it was the west's cultural bias that was filtering the knowledge of the Orient. This leads to the west seeing the oriental as the 'other', as distinct from the superior and rational westerner.

Whilst Said's work has been clearly influential, criticisms have come from many quarters. However, central to many comments from those who have some sympathy with his overall perspective is his overemphasis on west–east binary traditions, not recognising the complex historical and cultural relations that have evolved around the world and the potential openings for change and transformation.

Homi Bhabha is the second key theorist, who, whilst recognising the contribution of Said, puts more emphasis on identity and the role of the coloniser. A key part of his thinking on development education is his conceptualisation of identities and stereotypes within the context of a notion of cultural supremacy.

Within Bhabha's thinking is an element of ambivalence. Whilst he notes that the coloniser and colonised might have similar assumptions and values, there is always a degree of superiority amongst the coloniser. This leads to what could be called a form of mimicry, which can be seen in a number of former British colonies in terms of cultural norms and values.

Bhabha's work is also important in terms of its linkages to other discourses mentioned in this section, most notably globalisation, regarding the ever-changing and therefore hybrid nature of these debates. Key to his thinking is his perception of culture, which he defines as 'an uneven, incomplete production of meaning, produced in the act of social survival' (Bhahba, 1994: 172). This perspective of cultural difference helps to avoid the traditional notion of seeing culture in terms of exoticism, with elements of an essentialist and static form as articulated in much of the discourse on and around multiculturalism.

The third key theoretician in the discourses on postcolonialism is Gayatri Spivak who argues that the economic differentiations in the world are linked to past and present colonial and imperial processes. She speaks much more about imperialism than colonialism. One of the main reasons she is so important in the discourses in development education is, as Andreotti suggests (2006: 72), that she problematises discourses on the Global South.

One of Spivak's distinctive contributions is associated with the usage of the concept 'subaltern'. She sees this term as related to everyone and everything that is denied or has limited access to 'cultural imperialism'. To Spivak, imperialism has been transformed into notions of western superiority with a division into First and Third Worlds. Poverty is for example constructed in terms of lack of resources and not in terms of power. This leads to a sense of triumphalism in the west as being at the centre of things, with a responsibility to others who are not global and part of this new world order (Spivak, 2003).

But unlike some theorists who are supportive of postcolonialism, Spivak argues for continual engagement and critiquing of dominant and hegemonic discourses. This also leads on to her proposition that engagement necessitates 'unlearning our privilege' and learning from below, from the subaltern. This process of unlearning and learning anew is developed further by Andreotti (2012).

Postcolonialism is an important element of the theory of development education for the following three reasons. First, it provides a critique of the relationships between the North and the South, the coloniser and the colonised, and provides the tools with which to assess notions of supremacy and relations between peoples. Secondly, it provides a framework for making a distinction between difference and diversity, for moving beyond notions of cultural diversity to recognising the complex and varied natures of peoples' identities. It moreover enables one to move from talking about Southern Voices as an essentialist notion. Finally, postcolonialism provides a political and ideological dimension that reminds us of the inequalities and injustices that exist in the world.

As this chapter suggests, there also dangers in seeing this as the only lens through which to look at development education. That is why this chapter has suggested the need to include reference to the ethical and justice-based influences that bring in discourses around development, globalisation and global citizenship. Postcolonialism can also engender a sense of pessimism, that change is impossible because of structural inequalities and power relations. That is why any theoretical framework for development education needs to take account of notions of change and transformation. It is to the concept of transformative learning that we now turn to complete the range of theoretical influences.

Transformative learning

Recent research (Ellis, 2013; Brown, 2013) that has looked at processes of change in development education and related themes has made reference to the importance of considering theories related to notions of transformation. One theorist who has become particularly influential in this research has been Jack Mezirow, who is one of the main proponents of transformative learning theory. Mezirow began developing his ideas in the 1970s and has been clearly influenced by the work of Freire and to some extent Habermas. His work, although mainly located within debates in adult education, has over time had wider impact and is seen as particularly relevant to educationalists interested in processes for social change starting from personal and individual transformations.

Mezirow defined transformative learning as:

> the process by which we transform our taken-for-granted frames of reference (meaning perspectives, habits of mind, mindsets) to make them more inclusive, discriminating, open, emotionally capable of change, and reflective so that they may generate beliefs and opinions that will prove more true or justified to guide action. Transformative learning involves participation in constructive discourse to use the experience of others to assess reasons justifying these assumptions, and making action decisions based on the resulting insight.
>
> *(2000: 8)*

Key to Mezirow's work is the concept of 'frames of reference', which has two dimensions: a habit of mind and a resulting point of view. This could be interpreted as a set of assumptions, whether social, cultural, political or scientific, which are expressed as points of view made up of values, beliefs, attitudes and value judgements. According to Mezirow it is through these 'frames of reference' that learning occurs. He sees this happening in four ways, from elaborating on existing frames of reference, learning new frames of reference, transforming points of view and finally through transforming a habit of mind (Mezirow, 2000: 19; Brown, 2013: 28).

It is this approach to transformational learning that is seen here as particularly relevant to debates in development education because it is based on questioning and challenging underlying assumptions and premises on which our beliefs are based. It requires being prepared not only for being open to other points of view but also re-framing our viewpoints and perspectives.

Criticisms of Mezirow (for example Brookfield, 2000) suggest that he puts too much emphasis on individual transformation and not enough on social action and change. Mezirow argues that social change can only come through personal change and one must first be aware of the need to change. But Brookfield suggests that for an act of learning to be transformative, it must include a re-thinking and re-ordering of how one thinks and acts. This he goes on to suggest must include examining power relations and hegemonic assumptions (Brookfield, 2000: 139–140; Brown, 2013: 32).

Whilst Brookfield may have some valid points, Mezirow's reference to personal transformations related to emotional feelings is particularly pertinent in an area where the issues for debate are concepts such as social justice, inequality and global poverty.

Another element of Mezirow's thinking that has particular relevance is his emphasis on critical reflection and critical thinking. At a general level, all forms of education could be argued as being transformative in that they involve 'a shift of consciousness that dramatically and permanently alters our way of being in the world' (Mezirow, 2000). If learning is seen as a socially-facilitated process which leads to new frames of thinking, then there is a need to recognise that there will be different levels of change in the learner.

One potential model that has relevance for the pedagogy of development education outlined in this volume is the different forms or frames in which changes take place. Sterling has argued the value of this approach in relation to sustainable development education:

> First order change and learning takes place within accepted boundaries. It is adaptive learning that leaves basic values unexamined and unchanged. By contrast second order change and learning involves critically reflective learning, which examines the assumptions that influence first order learning. At a deeper level still, when third order learning happens we are able to see things differently. It is creative and involves a deep awareness of alternative world views and ways of doing things.
>
> *(Sterling, 2001: 15)*

As the following chapter will outline, in developing a pedagogy for development education, development education needs to include an understanding of these levels of learning and their relationship to critical thinking and understanding global issues through different perspectives and viewpoints.

Plurality, power and positivity

Within many of the theoretical frameworks outlined above there is an underlying assumption that key to all the approaches is the importance and value of having a broader world or global outlook that moves beyond national or binary notions and that recognises the value of pluralism, particularly in the context of worldviews. Although Marshall (2011: 415) uses the term global citizenship education, she is in reality talking about the same discourse as outlined in this chapter. She notes that by recognising the plurality of global citizenship, you can expose a complex picture that can help to develop a set of conceptual tools to facilitate analysis.

Marshall, in referring to the work of Todd (2009), notes that pluralism is not simply about an aggregation of identities or communities to which one belongs but needs to take account of the specificity of contexts, relationships and languages to which one is attached.

Secondly, Marshall refers to the importance of concepts of power which enable the unearthing of relations and practices that reinforce traditional power structures. This theme is always present in debates within development education and related discourses, but it is not always mentioned overtly (Marshall, 2011: 415).

Thirdly, Marshall suggests a degree of positivity, the promotion of hope, with the future being recognised and promoted within the discourses. She notes that it is all too easy to be critical and demonstrate pitfalls. She notes that the role of hope and idealism in the classroom can be a positive force; and that taking a too strong anti-universalist position can have unhelpful pedagogical repercussions for teachers who have to work with notions of right, wrong and truth (ibid.)

It is suggested here that in bringing the various theories together, there is a need to refer back to some underlying principles that can help with analysing and identifying the most relevant theories to help inform practice.

Towards a critical pedagogy of global social justice

As has been suggested in this chapter, Andreotti and Scheunpflug are seen as key to developing a theoretical framework for development education. They provide two important building blocks, but as this chapter has suggested their work tends to focus on particular themes and areas, notably the more ethical and philosophical approaches. What has been suggested here is the importance of also recognising other factors such as the influence of economic and social factors, whether to do with development, or globalisation, or a sense of identity, as seen through the discussions on cosmopolitanism and global citizenship.

Development education practices have a tradition of making assumptions regarding the relationship between learning, transformation and change, at the individual or societal level. The perspectives of Mezirow and transformative learning theories are seen as important because they look at the relationship between the individual and society. However in understanding the practices within development education, it is also necessary to recognise the central role that ideology and construction of knowledge play. How people see their relationship to the wider world, and their understanding of concepts like poverty, depends both on their own personal experience and value base and on how their understanding is constructed in terms of access to knowledge and where that knowledge comes from. This reminds us of the continuing relevance and importance of Paulo Freire and his successors in critical pedagogy.

Wright, in reviewing the influence of Freire, Giroux, Spivak and others, notes that they all emphasise a mode of pedagogy that equips students to do three main things:

1. question dominant values;
2. achieve an increased level of critical consciousness regarding the ideologies that impact on their lives;
3. place the discourse of education itself in its formative geo-socio-political context.

(Wright, 2011: 61)

This means, he suggests, that within a school environment for example there would be a need for 'self-reflexive space' to consider what is behind Eurocentric universalism. Secondly, subjects should be taught that are global but in a form that includes 'non-dominant perspectives in other than tokenistic ways'. This also means a recognition of different forms of public and political engagement rather than just focusing on national and international institutions. Thirdly, in recognising difference, there needs to be the promotion of an understanding as to how difference is constructed. Wright calls all this 'divisive universalism' (ibid.: 64).

Whilst this framework is valuable, it is perhaps still too narrow in recognising the complexities and themes that underpin development education. It is suggested therefore that perhaps a more appropriate starting point, which may lead into the concepts and approaches outlined by Wright above, is the following underlying principles which can help to make connections between theories and practices:

- A sense of global outlook or mindset, or as Kenway and Fahey (2008) suggest, a 'global imagination'. This means looking beyond the immediate and recognising the global interconnectedness of the world in which we live.
- Understanding of power and inequality in the world, how this is caused and what are the social, cultural and ideological as well as economic ramifications. This brings in debates on globalisation, development, postcolonialism and tensions between western and indigenous knowledges.
- Concern with social justice and wanting the world to be a better place in terms of greater equity so that all peoples have the opportunity for their voices to be heard and understood, but on their terms. This brings in reference to discussions on cosmopolitanism, global citizenship and critical pedagogy.
- Recognition that engagement in these debates can lead to a process of critical reflection, dialogue and engagement in a period of transformation and change for both the individual and society more widely. This means ensuring that discussions on social change are based not on some form of activist model but on a depth of understanding through increased knowledge, engagement with debates on processes of learning, notably transformative learning, and notions of global citizenship.

These approaches should also, as alluded to in comments by Marshall, be located within the context of recognising the pluralistic nature of ideas and practices, promoting a sense of opportunity, positive thinking and the idea that change is possible. Moreover any theories need also to consider the power not only of economic and ideological forces, but social and cultural forces, and the consequential concerns with justice and equity.

It is in essence through the development of these concepts, their relationship, roots and connections to various theories, that a pedagogy of development education needs to evolve.

References

Andreotti, V. (2006) 'Soft versus critical global citizenship education', *Development Education, Policy and Practice*, 3(1): 40–51.

Andreotti, V. (2010) 'Global education in the 21st century: two different perspectives on the "post" of postmodernism', *International Journal of Development Education and Global Learning*, 2(2): 5–22.

Andreotti, V. (2012) *Actionable Postcolonial Theory in Education*. New York: Palgrave Macmillan.

Apple, M., Kenway, J. and Singh, M. (eds) (2005) *Globalizing Education: Policies, Pedagogies and Politics*. New York: Peter Lang.

Ashcroft, W., Griffiths, G. and Tiffin, H. (2000) *Post-Colonial Studies: Key Concepts*. New York: Routledge.

Ayers, W., Quinn, T. and Stovall, D. (eds) (2009) *Handbook of Social Justice in Education*. New York: Routledge.

Baillie Smith, M. (2004) 'Contradiction and change? NGOs, schools and the public faces of development', *Journal of International Development*, 16: 741–749.

Beck, U. (2000) *What Is Globalization?* Cambridge: Polity Press.

Bhabha, H. (1994) *The Location of Culture*. London: Routledge.

Blum, N. (2000) 'Doing development at home: education as a tool for social change', unpublished MA dissertation, University of Sussex.

Bourdieu, P. (1990) *In Other Words: Essays Towards a Reflective Sociology*. Oxford: Blackwell.

Breidlid, A. (2013) *Education, Indigenous Knowledges and Development*. New York: Routledge.

Brock, G. (2009) *Global Justice*. Oxford: Oxford University Press.

Brookfield, S. (2000) *The Power of Critical Theory in Adult Learning and Teaching*. Berkshire: Oxford University Press.

Brown, E. (2013) 'Transformative learning through development education NGOs: a comparative study of Britain and Spain', unpublished PhD thesis, University of Nottingham.

Bryan, A. and Bracken, M. (2011) *Learning to Read the World? Teaching and Learning about Global Citizenship and International Development in Post-Primary Schools*. Dublin: Irish Aid.

Burbules, N. and Torres, C. (eds) (2000) *Globalization and Education: Critical Perspectives*. New York and London: Routledge.

Cogan, J.J. and Derricott, R. (2000) *Citizenship for the 21st Century: An International Perspective on Education*. London: Kogan Page.

Dewey, J. (1938) *Experience and Education*. New York: Macmillan.

Dower, N. (2003) *An Introduction to Global Citizenship*. Edinburgh: Edinburgh University Press.

Edwards, R. and Usher, R. (2008) *Globalisation and Pedagogy*. London: Routledge.

Ellis, M. (2013) 'The critical global educator', unpublished PhD thesis, Institute of Education, University of London.

Escobar, A. (1995) *Encountering Development: The Making and Unmaking of the Third World*. Princeton: Princeton University Press.

France, A. (2007) *Understanding Youth in Late Modernity*. Berkshire: Oxford University Press.

Freire, P. (1972) *Pedagogy of the Oppressed*. New York: Continuum.

Giddens, A. (1991) *Modernity and Self-Identity: Self and Society in the Late Modern Age*. Cambridge: Polity Press.

Gilbert, J. (2005) *Catching the Knowledge Wave*. Wellington: NZCER Press.

Giroux, H. (1992) *Border Crossings, Cultural Workers and the Politics of Education*. New York: Routledge.

Giroux, H. (2011) *On Critical Pedagogy*. New York: Continuum.

Hartmeyer, H. (2008) *Experiencing the World Global Learning in Austria: Developing, Reaching Out, Crossing Borders*. Munster: Waxmann.

Harvey, D. (2009) *Cosmopolitanism and the Geographies of Freedom*. New York: Columbia University Press.

Held, D. and McGrew, A. (eds) (2000) *The Global Transformation Reader*. Cambridge: Polity Press.

Illeris, K. (2003) 'Towards a contemporary and comprehensive theory of learning', *International Journal of Lifelong Education*, 22(4): 396–406.

Illeris, K. (ed.) (2009) *Contemporary Theories of Learning*. Abingdon: Routledge.

Jarvis, P. (2006) *Towards a Comprehensive Theory of Human Learning*. Abingdon: Routledge.

Jarvis, P. (2007) *Globalisation, Lifelong Learning and the Learning Society*. London: Routledge.

Kenway, J. and Bullen, E. (2008) 'The global corporate curriculum and the young cyberflaneur as global citizen', in N. Dolby and F. Rizvi (eds) *Youth Moves: Identities and Education in Global Perspective*. New York: Routledge, pp. 17–32.

Kenway, J. and Fahey, J. (eds) (2008) *Globalizing the Research Imagination*. London: Routledge.

Kolb, D. (1984) *Experiential Learning: Experience as the Source of Learning and Development*. Englewood Cliffs, NJ: Prentice-Hall.

Kumar, A. (2008) 'Development education and dialogic learning in the 21st century', *International Journal of Development Education and Global Learning*, 1(1): 37–48.

Lambert, D. and Morgan, J. (2012) *Geography and Development: Development Education in Schools and the Part Played by Geography*, DERC Research Paper no. 3. London: IOE.

Lewin, R. (ed.) (2009) *The Handbook of Practice and Research in Study Abroad: Higher Education and the Quest for Global Citizenship*. New York: Routledge.

Marshall, H. (2011) 'Instrumentalism, ideals and imaginaries: theorising the contested space of global citizenship education in schools', *Globalisation, Societies and Education*, 9(3–5): 411–426.

Matthews, J. and Sidhu, R. (2005) 'Desperately seeking the global subject: international education, citizenship and cosmopolitanism', *Globalisation, Societies and Education*, 3(1): 49–66.

McCollum, A. (1996) 'On the margins? An analysis of theory and practice of development education in the 1990s', unpublished PhD thesis, Open University.

Mclaren, P. (2009) 'Critical pedagogy: a look at the major concepts', in A. Darder, M.P. Baltodano and R.D. Torres (eds) *The Critical Pedagogy Reader*. New York and London: Routledge, pp. 69–96.

Mezirow, J. (2000) 'Learning to think like an adult: core concepts of transformation theory', in J. Mezirow and Associates (eds) *Learning as Transformation: Critical Perspectives on a Theory in Progress*. San Francisco: Jossey-Bass, pp. 3–34.

Noddings, N. (2005) *Educating Citizens for Global Awareness*. New York: Teachers College Press.

Nussbaum, M. (2002) 'Capabilities and social justice', *International Studies Review*, 4(2): 123–135.

Nussbaum, M. (2010) 'Patriotism and cosmopolitanism', in G. Wallace Brown and D. Held (eds) *The Cosmopolitan Reader*. Cambridge: Polity Press, pp. 155–162.

Nussbaum, M. (2011) *Creating Capabilities*. Cambridge, MA: Belknap Press of Harvard University Press.

Odora Hoppers, C. (2008) *South African Research Chair in Development Education –Framework and Strategy*. Pretoria: University of South Africa.

Osler, A. and Starkey, H. (2005) *Changing Citizenship: Democracy and Inclusion in Education*. Maidenhead: Open University Press.

Oxley, L. and Morris, P. (2013) 'Global citizenship: a typology for distinguishing its multiple conceptions', *British Journal of Educational Studies*, 61(3): 1–25.

Ray, L. (2007) *Globalisation and Everyday Life*. Abingdon: Routledge.

Rizvi, F. (2009) 'International perspectives on social justice and education', in W. Ayers, T. Quinn and D. Stovall (eds) *Handbook of Social Justice in Education*. New York: Routledge, pp. 91–94.

Rogers, A. and Horrocks, N. (2010) *Teaching Adults*. Berkshire: Oxford University Press.

Said, E.W. (1978) *Orientalism*. London: Routledge & Kegan Paul.

Scheunpflug, A. (2008) 'Why global learning and global education? An educational approach influenced by the perspectives of Immanuel Kant', in D. Bourn (ed.) *Development Education: Debates and Dialogues*. London: Bedford Way Papers, pp. 18–27.

Scheunpflug, A. (2011) 'Global education and cross-cultural learning: a challenge for a research based approach to international teacher education', *International Journal of Development Education and Global Learning*, 3(3): 29–44.

Scott, D. (2007) *Critical Essays on Major Curriculum Theorists*. London: Routledge.

Sen, A. (1999) *Development as Freedom*. New York: Anchor Books.

Spivak, G. (2003) *Death of a Discipline*. New York: Columbia University Press.

Standish, A. (2012) *The False Promise of Global Learning*. New York: Continuum.

Sterling, S. (2001) *Sustainable Education: Re-Visioning Learning and Change*. Dartington: Green Books and the Schumacher Society.

Storey, A. (2003) 'Measuring development', in G. McCann and S. McCloskey (eds) *From Local to the Global: Key Issues in Development Studies*. London: Pluto, pp. 25–40.

Stromquist, N. and Monkman, K. (2000) *Globalisation and Education*. Oxford: Rowman & Littlefield.

Szersynski, B. and Urry, J. (2002) 'Cultures of cosmopolitanism', *The Sociological Review*, 50(4): 461–481.

Todd, S. (2009) *Toward an Imperfect Education: Facing Humanity, Rethinking Cosmopolitanism*. London: Paradigm.

Wallace Brown, G. and Held, D. (eds) (2010) *The Cosmopolitan Reader*. Cambridge: Polity Press.

Wright, C. (2011) 'Postcolonial cosmopolitanisms', in V. Andreotti and L.M. de Souza (eds) *Postcolonial Perspectives on Global Citizenship Education*. London: Routledge, pp. 47–67.

6

A PEDAGOGICAL FRAMEWORK

So far this volume has reviewed the history and common themes that underpin development education practice, and the potential roots of a theoretical framework.

The first three chapters focused on the history and current practices in development education and identified a number of definitions that help us to understand why and how the activities of NGOs in particular are constructed. These chapters also identified a number of distinctive themes such as understanding what living in an interdependent world means, valuing the voices and perspectives from the Global South, encouragement of a more values-based approach to learning and the connections between learning, sense of moral concern about global poverty and wanting to make the world a better place.

Chapter 5 showed through the work of Scheunpflug and Andreotti and debates on development, globalisation, cosmopolitanism, global citizenship, postcolonialism and transformative learning potential linkages and connections between the themes mentioned above and these theories. Incorporating elements from these theories into a new conceptual framework that builds on the existing practices can help to provide greater rigour and clarity to what is meant by development education and particularly a pedagogical approach.

Bringing these theoretical influences together provides the basis for a new pedagogical framework based around four underlying principles. They are as follows:

- Global outlook
- Recognition of power and inequality in the world
- Belief in social justice and equity
- Commitment to reflection, dialogue and transformation.

They should be seen as underlying principles that in the case of the first three could be interpreted also as learning outcomes whilst the fourth is focused more directly on pedagogy. But together they form a framework that emphasises the importance of processes of learning. This framework also aims to take account of the philosophical and ethical perspectives developed by Scheunpflug (2008, 2011, 2012), and recognises the ideological framework within which development education operates. This includes how knowledge is constructed, and the influence of western and hegemonic thinking on development and global themes. It also brings in the ideas of Andreotti (2008, 2012), particularly her work on Through Other Eyes, which is discussed in later chapters.

This chapter will now explore in more detail what these four underlying principles mean, their importance and relevance to debates in development education, and how they are being interpreted in practice. These principles are seen not as replacing the different interpretations of development education as outlined in Chapter 3, but as complementing them, providing a pedagogical framework that can make connections between theory and practice.

A global outlook

Three levels

Implicit in all of the theories and practices that have underpinned development education has been the importance of some sense of global outlook or global mindset, or as Kenway and Fahey (2008) suggest, a 'global imagination'. Learning and understanding about development and global issues could in itself be said to encourage a 'global outlook'. But this is not necessarily always the case, as people could and do respond to themes such as global poverty as not directly relevant to them, but as being 'about people elsewhere' in the world.

In proposing the concept of 'a global outlook', it is suggested that this should be seen as a process of learning and engagement. Through developing a global outlook, learners will get drawn into debates about their own sense of identity and place in the world, and how, as individuals, they relate to inequality and poverty.

A development education approach could therefore be one that encourages a journey towards a global outlook. This is where some of the literature and debates on cosmopolitanism are particularly relevant (cf. Scheunpflug, 2008; Wallace Brown and Held, 2010). This is an approach to learning that moves beyond a concern for the poor to one that recognises the value of social justice and international solidarity. This leads to the final element of the approach, a sense of global responsibility. Without a sense of concern and belief in the value of social change within which one, as an individual, has a responsibility, the learner could feel detached and alienated from forms of social engagement.

The three levels can therefore be summarised as:

- Towards a global outlook
- From concern for the poor and dispossessed to concern for social justice and solidarity
- Sense of global responsibility.

Towards a global outlook

To promote a global outlook within education, some understanding of the existing visions and perspectives of the learner needs to be in place. For example, the dominant identity in many countries may be related to national cultural perceptions. But in an increasingly complex society, the dominant identities and perspectives could equally be local, cultural, linguistic or some hybrid combination of these.

To the learner, the relevance of understanding global themes and issues poses the question of how they see their relationship to the wider world. Research by Kirkwood-Tucker et al. (2011) with student teachers in Florida in the USA notes a 'severely limited understanding of the world among American teacher candidates' (ibid.: 10) and also a lack of training and understanding as to how to integrate global perspectives into the classroom.

In response to this challenge, Kirkwood-Tucker et al. suggest the promotion of the concept of worldmindedness as a 'worldview in which one sees oneself as a member of the world community with a responsibility toward the other members of that community' (ibid.: 7).

They go on to suggest that a framework developed by Merryfield (2009) could help to clarify what this concept of 'worldmindedess' might mean. For example, they suggest that the belief systems of future teachers can be broadened by integrating into their education global concepts which develop this worldmindedness, including a sense of personal responsibility, awareness of cultural pluralism, a sense of efficacy and a sense of interconnectedness.

The evidence from their research with student teachers shows that those who were proficient in two or more languages were likely to have a broader, more liberal political identity, women rather than men; and those who had been involved in foreign exchange programmes, were born outside of the United States, or had taken specific courses on global themes were more 'worldminded'. Whilst these comments may at one level appear obvious, they are an important reminder of the challenges many educators have in promoting areas such as development education.

The challenges in promoting a sense of 'worldmindedness' or 'global outlook' were also highlighted in the research by Hicks and Holden (2007), also with student teachers. This showed that those student teachers who had travelled abroad were more 'worldly', and those who had a range of not only cultural experiences, but direct engagement with social and economic issues, through either employment or personal life, were likely to be more socially responsible.

But a global outlook could be neo-colonialist, even imperialist in outlook. It could at a more subtle level start from a position that our own viewpoint is the best.

Scheunpflug, in reviewing how teachers respond to challenges regarding developing a global outlook, notes that it is important to be sensitive to students' tendencies to 'take European superiority for granted', and that teachers have a 'sense of how to get students to look through other lenses and perspectives' and are able to activate their own students' 'reconceptualisation of these issues' (2011: 30).

This means that engaging in learning about global development themes may well have to start from demonstrating the value of looking beyond one's own environment. Therefore a necessary initial point for any engagement in learning must be the process of demonstrating that we live in an interconnected world, that events elsewhere in the world have an impact upon us, and that we now live in a 'global village'.

Whilst obviously cultural, economic and social situations will influence any sense of 'global outlook', there is evidence that encouraging an outlook amongst young people that goes beyond their immediate horizons can not only be beneficial for their personal and social development, but can also equip them with the skills to engage in the world into which they will be growing up (see Bourn and Brown, 2011).

There is also evidence from all sectors of education that learners need to be more globally conscious today. Examples of this include:

> A curriculum for the 21st century should encourage learners to be aware of global issues. Learners should evaluate information and events from a global perspective. By exploring the connections between the local and the global, they can also realise that it is possible to play a part in working towards solutions to challenges such as climate change and global poverty. Our aim is that all students will be more globally aware as a result of being at the College.
>
> *(Hilary Anson, Principal, King George V College,*
> *Southport, quoted in Bentall et al., 2010: 9)*

However this promotion of a global outlook, in line with some of the criticisms of the concept of global citizenship (see Bourn, 2009), could lead to a form of elitism, to some form of ideal lifestyle to work towards.

An example of this is the following quotation from Marquardt, which whilst having some rhetorical value could be interpreted as some form of ideal model.

> People with global mindsets seek to continually expand their knowledge, have a highly developed conceptual capacity to deal with the complexity of global organisations, are extremely flexible, strive to be sensitive to cultural diversity, are able to undertake decisions with adequate information and have a strong capacity for reflection. A person with a global mindset thinks and sees the world globally, is open to exchanging ideas and concepts across borders . . . The emphasis is placed on balancing global and local needs, and being able to operate cross functionally, cross divisionally, and cross culturally across the world.
>
> *(Marquardt, quoted in Jameson, 2006: 6)*

The dangers of promoting some form of ideal could be disempowering to many people. As research undertaken with undergraduate university students in London has shown, on being asked whether they saw themselves as being a global citizen, 'the majority who responded to this question were dubious about the term'. For some it was seen as an elitist concept. 'Only a very few people could be considered as global citizens', was one observation. For the majority who did respond, the term 'global citizen' was seen in terms of globalisation. Those who were sympathetic to the concept saw it as going beyond national boundaries and being able to communicate with and learn from others. Those who were most positive about the term were those who had spent time in different countries and had more of a hybrid cultural identity (Bourn, 2009).

This suggests that promoting a 'global outlook' by itself may well not challenge or question existing assumptions. It may well reinforce existing notions. Therefore it is suggested here that having a global outlook must not be the only key component in a conceptual framework for development education. It should also encourage ethical and social justice questions as well.

Moving beyond concern for the poor

A lot of the research into how young people and adults perceive international development issues is based on an approach that sees the poor of the world as either helpless victims or beneficiaries for aid, in other words in a negative context; and the role of the 'enlightened' person in the North as to provide help, either through fundraising, project work or campaigns to support the poor from a humanitarian perspective (VSO, 2002; Hunt, 2012).

This section outlines how to move on from this to a mindset of social justice and sense of solidarity. This can come through promoting stories about people and communities in the Global South that challenge the mindset, stories that are positive and show evidence of change. Development education practices often have to respond to notions that may exist in the learner about aid and helping the poor.

However there are dangers in taking too narrow a view and being over-critical of a humanitarian approach. It is suggested here that the educational approach should not be to condemn or directly criticise, but rather to show that a moral concern for the poor by itself will not necessarily lead to change, and could well result in a reinforcing of existing dependency relations.

This relates to Andreotti's comments about soft and hard global citizenship, with the former emphasising a moral concern and the latter a more critical social justice approach (Andreotti, 2006). Andreotti herself notes that in certain circumstances the soft and moral standpoint may well be appropriate and could be recognised as an important starting point. She states however that unless the learners become 'critically literate', which enables them to engage with assumptions about poverty and inequality, they may well, however unintentionally, reproduce the systems and ways of thinking they are trying to question (ibid.: 49).

Whilst Andreotti develops her thinking on this through her Through Other Eyes initiative, there are dangers of seeing this critique in terms of binary opposites and not as a process of learning, reflection and critical engagement.

Central to any pedagogy of development education should be the promotion of knowledge, skills and a values base that enables learners to develop on their own terms.

Sense of global responsibility

Finally, within the conceptual framework of developing a global outlook there is a recognition of the consequences of one's own actions and those of others. One cannot divorce having a global outlook from having a sense of global responsibility.

This theme builds on approaches promoted by Oxfam in its Framework for Global Citizenship. For example, this refers to being a Global Citizen as including someone who 'participates in the community at a range of levels, from the local to the global', 'is willing to act to make the world a more equitable and sustainable place' and 'takes responsibility for their actions' (Oxfam, 2006).

This approach directly relates to the relationship of development education to themes such as citizenship and civics, with an emphasis on an individual's responsibility to respond to what they have been learning about. This also includes where and how development education practices relate to areas such as changes in personal lifestyle, for example purchasing ethical goods, being conscious of one's own carbon footprint and supporting social justice-based organisations.

In the context of the conceptual framework outlined in this chapter, a sense of global responsibility would be seen more in terms of being aware of, and informed about, the consequences of one's own actions. It is not suggested here that development education practices should include lifestyle changes. This may be a consequence of an individual's learning, but should be seen as an outcome from development education practice and not as an integral component of it. As noted by Bourn and Brown, 'the over-emphasis on engagement as participation can mask the importance of the learning process and the complex relationships between learning and behaviours' (2011: 26).

Recognition of power and inequality in the world

Introduction

Development education practices, as indicated in Chapter 1, grew out of a concern for and solidarity with the poor. For many practitioners, this concern for the poor was linked to a broader social and political viewpoint that was inherently critical of dominant economic forces around the world and the consequences these had in reproducing inequalities. However many of these practices have tended to be subsumed within broader initiatives, sometimes for funding reasons or because the activities came from specific NGOs or organisations with a distinctive political or social perspective where there was no need to explain or explore the relationship of these perspectives to concepts of power and inequality in the world.

A constant but unwritten theme within the debates and practices in development education is the underlying assumption that we live in an unequal world where economic, political and social power rests in the Global North, to the detriment of the Global South.

There has been a tendency in many of the publications for practitioners in development education to locate this power in predominantly economic terms. Examples of this can be seen in such activities as the popular role-play game, the Trading Game (Christian Aid, 2010). The issues regarding economic power and development education are also explored in research by Egan (2011). Whilst these approaches have some validity, there are dangers of reducing learning about power and inequality to stereotypical 'bad capitalists', not looking at the complex and subtle influences of power, particularly at a social and cultural level.

McMichael raises this in a review of a role-play activity, where she suggests there are dangers of 'caricatured positions and binaries such as us/them and privilege/subordinate' (2012: 53).

Foucault, power and development

A valuable starting point that helps to look at these concepts in a more complex manner is the work of Michel Foucault, who is particularly relevant in seeing the close relationship between power and knowledge. To Foucault, power is dispersed and is not a thing but a relationship. Power is also more than the state; it is exercised through society. For Foucault, no body of knowledge can be formed without a system of communications, records, accumulation and displacement which in itself is a form of power (McNay, 1994).

This approach can be particularly important when looking at power in relation to development. For example, Rai (2007) suggests that there is a need to move beyond seeing power as something one has or does not have, as a matter of control over key institutions. She also suggests that debates about power should not be separated from empowerment. She further notes that critiques of notions of development have looked at how the 'power of development discourse' has defined development as a 'technical problem that requires intervention by Northern experts'. Rai notes that the 'supposedly powerless' have often managed to turn development discourse on its head, using it as a base for legitimising their demands (Rai, 2007: 8).

Power and understanding of what it means is suggested here as an important component of a pedagogy of development education. If understanding concepts of development is a key element of development education, as suggested in the previous chapter, then what this means for peoples around the world needs to be recognised within any educational programmes that address the relationship between the Global North and the Global South. But, as suggested above, this should include promoting narratives and stories challenging these power relations and showing that change is possible through the actions of people.

Understanding of historical forces – colonialism, imperialism and their implications

It is suggested here that in looking at power and inequality in relation to development, there also needs to be an understanding of the historical forces, social, cultural and economic, that have shaped and informed the power relations and inequalities that exist in the world.

Here, theorists such as Said, on Orientalism, and Spivak and Bhabha with regard to postcolonialism, are relevant: in the context of a conceptual framework for development education, learning needs to include an understanding of the changing dynamics and relationships between states around the world. For example, an activity within the school classroom that looks at, say, food production in India needs to include reference to the historical role India has played as a colony of the UK.

Postcolonialists will moreover state that merely knowing the historical context is not sufficient; the learning needs to look at the causes and implications of these relations at social, cultural and economic levels. Thus, in looking at inequalities within and between states, a historical, economic and cultural context needs to be included.

But it is suggested here that simply having a postcolonial lens is not sufficient because it can tend to reduce debates to binary opposites, and can ignore the changing influences related to globalisation.

Understanding of the forces of globalisation

As indicated in Chapter 4, globalisation has transformed many of the social, cultural and economic relationships that exist around the world. Globalisation is a process of social, cultural and economic change. For example, countries such as China, India and Brazil are becoming global economic players today whereas a decade ago the dominant lens though which they were seen economically and politically was as part of the Global South. Whilst both Brazil and India are still in many respects heavily influenced by social and economic forces from the Global North, there is a need to recognise that their relationship to the wider world today is much more complex and multi-layered.

An example of this complexity is that whilst China, India and Brazil will soon have the largest economies in the world, their living standards have a long way to go before they catch up with those in Europe, the USA and Japan. As Straw and Glennie (2012) note, 'only 31 per cent of people in Latin America and 13 per cent of people in Asia' are part of the 'global middle class'.

Globalisation is however not just about economics; it is as much to do with social and cultural forces. Appadurai states that it is not 'simply the name of a new epoch in the history of capital' but a 'new role for the imagination in social life' (2005: 14). Globalisation can not only lead to disjuncture and dislocation; it can lead to new forms of social interaction, forms of dissent and collective action (ibid.: 6).

As discussed in the previous chapter, there is a relationship between globalisation, citizenship and a sense of identity. Whilst it can lead to new forms of homogenisation, particularly in terms of cultural norms, globalisation can, as Stromquist and Monkman state, 'open spaces for new identities and contestation of established values and norms, many detrimental to the achievement of true social justice' (2000: 21).

This means that in the context of learning about development and global issues, there is a need to include a recognition of the changing nature of social, economic and cultural forces and that these factors are likely to have a direct impact upon the learner.

In much of the literature around globalisation and skills there has been a tendency to refer to skills that reflect the increasingly multicultural nature of societies, to be more flexible and adaptable, and to recognise the need for constant innovation (see Trilling and Fadel, 2009). But all too often these approaches pay little attention to the development of knowledge and values that address the impact of globalisation on a person's life: enabling them to make sense of the rapidly changing world around them and giving them the confidence, knowledge and value base to make a positive contribution to both the economy and society more widely (Bourn, 2008: 23).

These themes are developed further in Chapter 7.

Implications of power and inequality for the Global North and Global South

Bringing these different themes and elements together within a process of learning requires inclusion of a complex array of social, economic and cultural factors that pose political and ideological questions that may be challenging for many educators. It is therefore suggested that any forms of learning about power and inequality in the world need to make reference to themes such as globalisation and identity, and encourage a sense of a historical perspective, to enable an understanding of the changing nature of social relationships around the world. This means addressing one of the key aims of development education practice, which has been to understand the global economic, social, political and environmental forces which shape our lives.

This includes addressing what Bryan (2011) has noted: that development education practices have all too easily accepted the brief to prepare young people to compete and consume in the global economy, and to view development aid as a virtuous moral endeavour rather an integral element of neoliberal globalisation. Is development education, as Bryan argues, accepting rather than questioning 'the ideologies and institutions that have created excessive wealth and persistent poverty' (Bryan, 2011: 9)?

Postcolonial theory does address aspects of these themes, but as Lazarus (2011) observes, this discourse has tended to be framed in cultural and social rather than economic and political terms. Also postcolonialism, as the previous chapter indicated, by focusing on the North-South binary, does tend not to address in any significant way the characteristics and changing nature of global economic and social forces. Moreover, as suggested in this chapter, binary North-South perspectives can tend to ignore the increasingly complex nature of the growing economies of countries such as Brazil and India, let alone the impact of other global cultural forces such as Islam.

As Egan (2011) has suggested, development education practices have tended to: 'focus more on the negative impacts of unequal power and control in terms of the human and environmental damage caused in the global South'.

It is the relationship of this learning to questions of social justice and equity that is perhaps one of the most challenging aspects of development education. It is to this area that we now turn in terms of its inclusion within a conceptual framework for development education.

Belief in social justice and equity

Introduction

Underlying much of the practice and theories relevant to development education has been a value base of concern for a more just and equitable world. This phrase, or variations of it, can be seen in most definitions of development education. Yet concepts of social justice by their very nature can be ideologically and culturally laden: in whose interests of social justice, for example; and in terms of equity, on what basis?

Many of the academic debates around the term social justice, particularly in relation to education, tend to focus on academic attainment and the culture of the school (Smith, 2012).

The previous chapter made reference to different theories of social justice and equity. Building on that discussion, it is proposed that a potential lens for looking at social justice and equity in the context of development education is to recognise that it is, like the other concepts referred to in this chapter, a process of learning and engagement. A belief in social justice will come from a wide range of personal, social and cultural influences. This means recognising that for many people their concern about global poverty is likely to start from a moral position that might be influenced by factors such as personal experience, religion, peer group and family, and the media. It is in the process of learning more about social justice issues and the impact this has on the learner's own value systems that development education becomes relevant.

At the other end of the spectrum, you may also find an individual who has been campaigning against global poverty but has not seen the relationship of the values behind this, in terms of social justice and desire for greater equality, to other aspects of their own lives or those of other people. Their response has been based on moral or political standpoints.

Social justice implies a sense of wanting to change and move from the status quo. It also implies seeing connections between learning and wider societal concerns.

Sense of concern and care for a better world

Tallon (2012) makes reference to the use of altruistic emotions within education and their relevance to debates in development education. Referring to the work of Boler (1999), Tallon notes the influence of altruistic emotions in the classroom such as pity, compassion, empathy and even guilt. Boler further notes the danger of a 'passive empathy' that seeks an emotional reaction but absolves the learner from reflection or responsibility through the denial of power relations. Tallon goes on to link these questions to notions of the 'other'. Learners might be concerned, even wish to help and support people in poverty, but this is from a sense of cultural distance.

These practices, as Tallon notes, have often been the ways in which international development organisations (NGOs) have engaged in activities within schools. There might be an overt learning component, but the real motivation of the organisation is to secure some form of passive support, usually through raising money, for a particular campaign (Tallon, 2012: 9).

During the first decade of the twenty-first century there were conscious moves by some NGOs to move from this approach of 'guilt' to one of taking action, about what you can do. The most obvious example of this was the 2005 Make Poverty History campaign which, whilst raising awareness of global poverty, did little to deepen understanding or transform viewpoints. As Osler and Starkey (2010) have commented, whilst the dominant messages of Make Poverty History were framed in cosmopolitan terms, namely global solidarity, it never had a strong human rights agenda and the 'predominant sentiments' were those that were 'largely charitable'. In other words, please give on our behalf and we shall feel good about helping the poor (ibid.: 82).

Chouliaraki (2010) has raised similar questions in relation to NGO practices in general, reinforcing comments made by Bryan (2011) and Biccum (2010). These themes are explored further in Chapter 9.

Therefore, central to any development education programme has to be the task of identifying learners' starting points for concern about global poverty, and the basis for their viewpoint, and promoting a process of learning that encourages a more social justice perspective.

Belief in social justice

For many educators who are supportive of development education, there is a connection between their interest in the pedagogy and their own personal value system. Oxfam, for example, refer to a sense of 'moral outrage' (Oxfam, 2006), implying that you need to take action to challenge the injustices that exist. However evidence on teachers' reasons for supporting development education, whilst suggesting a personal enthusiasm, suggests less interest in taking action (Hunt, 2012; Hicks and Holden, 2007).

Jones (2009), in her research with teachers in England for example, identified a strong connection between teachers' support for global themes within schools and their own personal value base. She found a strong connection for many teachers who were supportive of learning about global themes within the school classroom, to their own Christian faith. She found that global themes matched the Christian social justice values of 'conservation justice and equality'. One person said: 'as a practising Christian I believe in fairness and think that every person in the world has a right to enough food and drinking water, and a comfortable way of life, free from war and intimidation'. This was a view expressed by many respondents, not just professed Christians; but the difference was that all of the Christians used their faith as a reason to be interested in the global dimension, to lead by example. One respondent said: 'As a Christian teacher I am concerned about the promotion and seeking of money, sex and power. I believe the western world needs to model sustainability and to reject materialism', and that he 'tries' to be a moral leader. Another commented that in her role as a deputy head at a Catholic school, 'I have a role as a spiritual leader too which encompasses the ethics/principles of the global dimension' (Jones, 2009: 62).

A key hypothesis in the research by Jones was that implicit in global dimension approaches was a moral vision. Her research found that the overwhelming majority of teachers who were interested in or supportive of the 'global dimension' in schools were interested because of some form of moral vision, with particular resonance to justice-based concepts such as 'equality', 'fairness', 'tolerance' and 'respect'. She identified an example of this in the comments of a male primary school teacher:

> a place where all people have equal access to resources, are tolerant and respectful of their and others' cultural and religious beliefs, are aware and actively engaged in implementing sustainable approaches to resource management, and look beyond material concerns in their values systems.
>
> *(ibid.)*

The research by Jones also identified that many of the teachers sympathetic to this approach held an ideological viewpoint of the world that questioned many of the dominant aspects of 'western society', with the vision of a society where 'the environment and other people are seen as having intrinsic value rather than a consumer society where people are judged on how much they consume, and where the environment is treated as a dustbin'.

The wish to see a more equal and sustainable world

These beliefs in social justice, and wanting the world to be a better place in terms of greater equity so that all peoples have the opportunity for their voice to be heard and understood, lead on to discussion about global citizenship and the relationship between education and social change.

This is where, within the context of debates in development education, the viewpoints, perspectives and skills around engagement in society come to the fore, and particularly the agendas of NGOs. As indicated, learning about global and development issues inevitably leads the learner to begin to question and re-think their own views about the world, the reasons for inequality and power differentials. Standish (2012) has criticised development education and global learning for being too driven by instrumental agendas, and whilst there may be evidence in some quarters of NGO practice to support this, the materials and practices of most organisations tend to leave the route and direction of the learning up to the teachers and educators. All the NGOs are doing is putting forward perspectives and viewpoints. This area is discussed further in Chapter 8.

This perspective of moving beyond informing learners about global injustices has been supported by research from Bryan and Bracken (2011: 202) with teachers in Ireland. Teachers noted that they felt they had a 'responsibility and a duty to make the world a better place'. Above all, they found, there was a view from those teachers sympathetic to development education that this area of learning and practice was about 'making a difference'.

However, Bryan and Bracken also go on to note that elements of this approach can lead to a form of development activism which can all too easily be reduced to individualised forms of action, 'such as fasting, fundraising or other forms of charitable giving' (ibid.: 203).

Commitment to reflection, dialogue and personal and social transformation

Development education by its very nature can be unsettling to the learner, leading learners to question their own assumptions about themselves and their relationship to the wider world. It suggests notions of critical thinking, reflection, dialogue and engagement that could lead to some form of personal transformation. This may, as posed in the previous section, lead to concerns for social change. This means ensuring that discussions on social change are based not on some form of activist model but on depth of understanding through increased knowledge, engagement with debates on processes of learning, notably transformative learning, and notions of global citizenship.

Critical thinking

A theme of much development education practice has been that of questioning existing views about the world; this approach to learning has much in common with the discourses around critical thinking. At one level, critical thinking could be reduced to simply looking at different sorts of information, weighing up evidence and building an argument in order to solve problems. But as Paul suggests, it is more than this. In essence, he says, 'critical thinking is thinking about your thinking while you're thinking in order to make your thinking better'. Related to this, he states, is the importance of self-improvement (Paul, 1995: 91). Paul also poses the need to make a distinction between the monological: views that can be discussed within an established logic; and the multilogical: questions that can be approached from different viewpoints (Paul, 1990: 36).

Brookfield refers to critical thinking as about 'hunting assumptions', 'without trying to assess their accuracy and validity, their fit with life' (Brookfield, 2012: 7). He suggests seeing things from different viewpoints and taking informed action, which means 'action that is based on thought and analysis' (ibid.: 13). It is this last area around the linkage to action that makes Brookfield so relevant to the discourses in development education, because as he suggests it means entering the realm of values, 'action for what'. Brookfield also suggests that questioning assumptions means engaging with ideological questions. He suggests three types:

- paradigmatic – how we view the world;
- prescriptive – how we think the world should work and how people should behave;
- causal – why things happen in the way they do.

(ibid.: 24–25)

Eleanor Brown (2012: 42) in her research on development education notes that learning about global issues necessitates recognition of different interpretations, but also recognition of bias and dealing with complexity.

Brown also found out from her research with development education practitioners that there was recognition, particularly in the UK, of learning to read different interpretations of an issue. One practitioner she interviewed stated:

I would define critical thinking as being able to think, when you're told information, being able to question it, question why am I being told this, who's come up with that information, what's their agenda, why have they told me this, is that actually the truth of the situation, or are there other perspectives.

(Brown, 2012: 187)

Think Global has focused on the importance of modelling as a way of encouraging teachers to reflect and be more critical:

Modelling is crucial in teaching, and to support students to be self-reflective, and to respond to complexity and change, teachers need to be doing so themselves. Anecdotal evidence from practitioners who support educators suggests that some teachers hold views that reinforce stereotypes on global issues. Hence fostering critical thinking means teachers, as well as students, questioning their own understanding and assumptions.

(Shah and Brown, 2010: 24)

Within the framework of development education, critical thinking might include the following:

- imagining a range of global perspectives – looking at topics and issues through different lenses;
- looking critically at the images of other countries that are presented in the media and by other organisations such as NGOs;
- challenging assumptions about 'how poor people live';
- looking at the causes of inequalities;
- exploring power relations – including questions such as who has power, who is voiceless, and who benefits?
- exploring our own prejudices about poorer countries.

This questioning of assumptions, looking at issues from different perspectives, and exploring and reflecting upon our own viewpoints, has been central to the two web-based educational initiatives led by Andreotti, Open Space for Dialogue and Enquiry and Through Other Eyes. She summarises this process as: learning to unlearn, learning to listen, learning to learn and learning to reach out (Andreotti, 2008: 29). These initiatives are discussed in more detail in Chapter 9.

Self-reflection and a dialogic approach to learning

Thinking critically and engaging with different viewpoints and assumptions often leads to the learner reflecting upon their own viewpoints and engaging in dialogue to listen, question and respect different views.

A criticism of some development education practice (Standish, 2012) suggests that there is a tendency to be doctrinaire in approach and not listen and engage in dialogue. This is a theme that Eleanor Brown (2012) explores by noting that it is easy, especially for NGOs, to lead learners towards one perspective and approach. But she also notes the danger of complete relativism and instead, following Golding, proposes a community of enquiry approach that can lead to the construction of a critical and rational dialogue. The community of enquiry approach 'seeks reasoned or reflected judgement, where ideas are judged better or worse depending on the quality of reasoning supporting them' (Golding, 2011: 481).

A useful approach within development education discourses on these areas has been the work of the Indian academic, Ajay Kumar, referred to in Chapters 2 and 4. His emphasis on dialogic rather than dialogue is an important distinction that is very relevant in this conceptualisation of development education. Whilst noting that dialogue can be defined as 'shared enquiry or talk amongst consenting adults', he suggests instead the term dialogic, which he characterises as 'the interactive, responsive, democratic, fair and impartial nature of dialogue' (Kumar, 2008: 44). A dialogic approach helps, he suggests, locate dialogue within the context of change and a process of learning and engagement (ibid.: 44). Kumar concludes that a

> dialogic approach to education is based on systematic and coherently organised representation, by two or more interacting subjects, of a phenomenon or a process about which they endeavour to know more about, increasing

the possibilities of active interest in interpretation, meaning making and knowledge creation, challenging all given conceptions in ways that stimulate praxis, theory and experimentation, knowledge and experience, work and science and also actions based on rational deliberation.

(ibid.: 45)

This sense of seeing learning as a process of 'dialogic encounters within a group or community of learners who together pose problems, enquire and seek solutions for change' (ibid.) can provide an excellent conceptual basis for development education because it locates the dialogue and engagement within wider processes of learning, and yet ensures space for reflection, questioning and exploring new ideas and thinking.

A popular educational tool that uses similar approaches is that of Philosophy for Children (P4C), a technique used in a number of schools to help children and young people develop questioning and enquiry skills. This method presents students with a stimulus and encourages them to ask imaginative questions, listen to the ideas of others and collectively decide on which questions to explore. The approach is based around a professional development approach to teachers that you can use in a classroom environment.

- It is seen as a way to open up children's learning through enquiry and the exploration of ideas.
- It gives children the possibility of seeing that their ideas have value, and that others have different ideas that have value too.
- They realise that they don't always have to be right.
- They have the confidence to ask questions and learn through discussion.
- All learners (including teachers) have opportunities to genuinely enquire.
- It is seen as a chance to speak and be heard without fear of getting an answer wrong.
- Intelligence grows.
- It gives children who are not considered 'academic' a voice and a chance to flourish.
- It gives the 'academic' children a chance to think outside the box and to see that the non-academic have inspiring ideas.
- It gives all children value.[1]

P4C is well known within development education and global learning in the UK and other industrialised countries as a particularly valuable methodology. With its emphasis on encouraging an environment that values listening, respect and valuing different viewpoints, P4C can provide a valuable pedagogical approach to learning about global issues.

Transformation

Dialogue, reflection and questioning one's own assumptions, outlined in this section, are themes common to many discussions on learning (see Illeris, 2007). However, in relation to development education, the term 'transformation' has become commonly used. For example, Scheunpflug notes that she sees global learning as contributing to a sort of 'transformational identity' (2012: 38). Andreotti's Open Space for Dialogue and Enquiry (OSDE) methodology approach refers to 'transforming relationships' (2012: 193). There is however an important distinction that needs to be made and that is between personal and social transformation. Whilst it could be argued that you cannot have one without the other, there has been a tendency in aspects of development education practice to emphasise the social side without looking at changes within the individual. Whilst at a general level, all forms of education may be seen as transformative if they involve 'a shift of consciousness that dramatically and permanently alters our way of being in the world', it is the nature of this transformation that is particularly pertinent in the debates on development education.

It is here perhaps that the work of Mezirow, as noted in the previous chapter, becomes valuable and important. Illeris, in reflecting upon Mezirow's work, summarises 'transformative learning' as 'about being conscious of, considering and reviewing one's meaning, perspectives, and the habits of mind that follow from them'. This, Illeris goes on to suggest:

> typically occurs when one discovers in one or other connection that the meaning perspectives do not fit with what one experiences or does. Then dissonance or a dilemma arises which one feels one must solve, and this takes place first and foremost through reflection, leading to revision or transformation of the meaning perspectives, i.e. through transformative learning.
>
> *(Illeris, 2007: 63)*

Ellis (2013: 11) notes that Mezirow suggests: 'learners challenged by a disorienting dilemma solve problems by self-examination, critical assessment of assumptions and exploration of options for new relationships, roles and action'. She notes that he demonstrates how 'critically reflective rational discourse can enable adults to gradually reconcile and take responsibility for even painful experiences, transforming frames to more inclusive, differentiated, permeable and integrated perspectives'.

These processes of learning have some similarity with debates regarding systems and frame theory. For example learning could be understood as a socially-facilitated process by which an epistemological frame is either constructed and consolidated or, more importantly, transcended, leading to a new, more adequate, frame (Bourn and Morgan, 2010).

There are however dangers of seeing transformation as some form of linear process. Mezirow (2000) had noted that transformation could be slow and gradual or it could be sudden.

Eleanor Brown (2012) in her research with NGO workers noted that very often this process of transformation and change was directly linked to learning taking place within courses or in aspects of personal experience.

What is evident from development education practice in many countries is that transformation and change in the learner is seen as the goal of the practice. Funding and projects led by NGOs particularly focus on this area, albeit because impact is usually measured in terms of behaviour change. This theme is discussed further in Chapter 10.

This chapter has had as one of its underlying messages the need to challenge and question this simplistic approach. Whilst development education practice may well lead to change in views, perspectives, and lifestyle in the learner, this should come as a result of deepening learning, reflecting, dialogue and critical thinking. Transformative learning may well be the fourth stage in a process but this process is not linear or straightforward, and may not be an outcome of some development education activity.

The next two chapters take forward this framework, and apply it in the context of reflecting upon practice that addresses learning, first within international development, and secondly within a global society.

Note

1   www.philosophy4children.co.uk/home/p4c/

References

Andreotti, V. (2006) 'Soft versus critical global citizenship', *Policy and Practice*, 3: 40–51.

Andreotti, V. (2008) 'Poverty and development', in D. Bourn (ed.) *Development Education: Debates and Dialogues*. London: Bedford Way Papers, pp. 45–63.

Andreotti, V. (2012) *Actionable Postcolonial Theory in Education*. New York: Palgrave Macmillan.

Appadurai, A. (ed.) (2005) *Globalisation*. Durham, NC: Duke University Press.

Bentall, C., Bourn, D. and Blum, N. (2010) *Learning and Skills in a Global Economy*. London: Learning Skills Improvement Service (LSIS).

Biccum, A. (2010) *Global Citizenship and the Legacy of Empire*. Abingdon: Routledge.

Boler, M. (1999) *Feeling Power: Emotion and Education*. New York: Routledge.

Bourn, D. (2008) *Global Skills*. London: Centre for Excellence in Leadership.

Bourn, D. (2009) 'Students as global citizens', in E. Jones (ed.) *Internationalisation: The Student Voice*. Abingdon: Routledge, pp. 18–29.

Bourn, D. and Brown, K. (2011) *Young People and International Development, DERC Research Paper no. 2*. London: IOE.

Bourn, D. and Morgan, A. (2010) 'Development education, sustainable development, global citizenship and higher education: towards a transformatory approach to learning', in E. Unterhalter and V. Carpentier (eds) *Global Inequalities and Higher Education: Whose Interests Are We Serving?* Basingstoke: Palgrave Macmillan, pp. 268–286.

Brookfield, S. (2012) *Teaching for Critical Thinking*. San Francisco, Jossey-Bass.

Brown, E. (2012) 'Transformative learning through development education NGOs', unpublished PhD thesis, University of Nottingham.

Bryan, A. (2011) 'Another cog in the anti-politics machine? The de-clawing of development education', *Policy and Practice: A Development Education Review*, 12: 1–14.

Bryan, A. and Bracken, M. (2011) *Learning to Read the World*. Dublin: Irish Aid.

Chouliaraki, L. (2010) *The Ironic Spectator*. Cambridge: Polity Press.

Christian Aid (2010) *The Trading Game*. London: Christian Aid.

Egan, A. (2011) 'Development education and corporate power', unpublished MA dissertation, Institute of Education, University of London.

Ellis, M. (2013) 'A critical global educator', unpublished PhD thesis, Institute of Education, University of London.

Golding, C. (2011) 'The many faces of constructivist discussion', *Educational Philosophy and Theory*, 43(5): 467–483.

Hicks, D. and Holden, C. (2007) *Teaching the Global Dimension*. London: Routledge.

Hunt, F. (2012) *Global Learning in Primary Schools, DERC Research Paper no. 9*. London: IOE.

Illeris, K. (2007) *How We Learn*. London: Routledge.

Jameson, J. (2006) (ed.) *Leadership Practices in Lifelong Learning in a Global Society*. London: DEA/Centre for Excellence in Leadership.

Jones, C. (2009) 'Moral leadership: an investigation of global dimension leadership in UK schools', unpublished MA dissertation, Middlesex University.

Kenway, J. and Fahey, J. (eds) (2008) *Globalizing the Research Imagination*. London: Routledge.

Kirkwood-Tucker, T.F., Morris, J.D. and Lieberman, M. (2011) 'What kind of teachers will teach our children? The worldmindedness of undergraduate elementary and secondary social studies teacher candidates at five Florida public universities', *International Journal of Development Education and Global Learning*, 3(3): 5–28.

Kumar, A. (2008) 'Development education and dialogical learning in the 21st century', *International Journal of Development Education and Global Learning*, 1(1): 37–48.

Lazarus, N. (2011) 'What postcolonial theory doesn't say', *Race and Class*, 53(3): 3–27.

McMichael, C. (2012) 'Understanding theories of International Development through role-play: a critical discussion on a post graduate seminar activity exploring two contrasting theories', *International Journal of Development Education and Global Learning*, 4(3): 41–54.

McNay, L. (1994) *Foucault: A Critical Introduction*. Cambridge: Polity Press.

Merryfield, M. (2009) 'Moving the center of global education: from imperial worldviews that divide the world to double consciousness, contrapuntal pedagogy, hybridity, and cross-cultural competence', in T.F. Kirkwood-Tucker (ed.) *Visions in Global Education*. New York: Peter Lang, pp. 215–239.

Mezirow, J. (2000) 'Learning to think like an adult: core concepts of transformation theory', in J. Mezirow and Associates (eds) *Learning as Transformation: Critical Perspectives on a Theory in Progress*. San Francisco: Jossey-Bass, pp. 3–34.

Newell-Jones, K. (2007) *Global Skills and Lifelong Learning*. London: DEA.

Osler, A. and Starkey, H. (2010) *Teachers and Human Rights Education*. Stoke-on-Trent: Trentham Books.

Oxfam (2006) *Education for Global Citizenship*. Oxford: Oxfam.

Paul, R.W. (1990) *Critical Thinking: What Every Person Needs to Survive in a Rapidly Changing World*. Rohnert Park, CA: Centre for Critical Thinking and Moral Critique.

Paul, R.W. (1995) *Critical Thinking: How to Prepare Students for a Rapidly Changing World*. Santa Rosa, CA: Foundation for Critical Thinking.

Rai, S. (2007) 'Re-defining empowerment, measuring survival', paper presented at workshop in Canada, available at: www.ethicsofempowerment.org/papers/RaiEmpowerment.pdf

Scheunpflug, A. (2008) 'Why global learning and global education? An educational approach influenced by the perspectives of Immanuel Kant', in D. Bourn (ed.) *Development Education: Debates and Dialogues*. London: Bedford Way Papers, pp. 18–27.

Scheunpflug, A. (2011) 'Global education and cross-cultural learning: a challenge for a research-based approach to international teacher education', *International Journal of Development Education and Global Learning*, 3(3): 29–44.

Scheunpflug, A. (2012) 'Identity and ethics in global education, becoming a global citizen', in L. Jasskelained, T. Kaivola, E. O'Loughlin and L. Wegimont (eds) *Proceedings of the International Symposium on Competencies of Global Citizens*. Amsterdam: GENE, pp. 31–39.

Shah, H. and Brown, K. (2010) 'Critical thinking in the context of global learning', in T.L.K. Wiseley, I.M. Barr, A. Britton and B. King (eds) *Education in a Global Space*. Edinburgh: IDEAS, pp. 37–42.

Smith. E. (2012) 'Social justice and inequalities in education', in J. Arthur and A. Peterson (eds) *Routledge Companion to Education*. London: Routledge, pp. 350–361.

Standish, A. (2012) *False Promise of Global Learning*. New York: Continuum.

Straw, W. and Glennie, A. (2012) *The Third Wave of Globalisation*. London: IPPR.

Stromquist, N.P. and Monkman, K. (eds) (2000) *Globalisation and Education*. Oxford: Rowman & Littlefield.

Tallon, R. (2012) 'Emotion and agency within NGO development education: what is at work and what is at stake in the classroom?', *International Journal of Development Education and Global Learning*, 4(2): 5–22.

Trilling, B. and Fadel, C. (2009) *21st Century Skills*. San Francisco: Jossey-Bass.

VSO (2002) *The Live Aid Legacy*. London: VSO.

Wallace Brown, G. and Held, D. (eds) (2010) *The Cosmopolitan Reader*. Cambridge: Polity Press.

PART III

The practice of
development education

7

BUILDING A KNOWLEDGE BASE –
LEARNING ABOUT DEVELOPMENT

To assess the relevance and value of this conceptual framework in terms of improving the quality and focus of development education practice, three areas are now addressed in this and the next two chapters. This chapter looks at the contribution of the conceptual framework in relationship to learning about development. The following chapters look at the framework in relation to globalisation and global justice, the latter particularly with regard to the practice of NGOs.

Any educational programme that aims to be located within the traditions of development education has to include a knowledge base around understanding different interpretations of international development, and basic data about global poverty. If it does not, then it cannot be called development education. This does not mean an acceptance of the concept 'development'; rather that it has to be located within and promote learning about different interpretations and under-standings as to what is meant by development.

A theme in this volume is that practice under the label of development education has tended to give insufficient attention to this knowledge base. Projects and initiatives funded by aid and development bodies may have made reference to development themes, but all too often specific themes have been referred to, whether fair trade, Millennium Development Goals or climate change. These themes are then promoted and supported through resources and training but usually in a form that does not look at the topics in a critical manner, or from different viewpoints and perspectives. The knowledge component of development education needs, it is suggested here, to be much more visible and central to any learning, for without this, on what basis can learners make informed decisions as to their viewpoints? All too often knowledge has been seen in terms of providing data to support a campaign, an initiative or a specific viewpoint.

Knowledge about development

Earlier chapters discussed this knowledge element. If we accept that knowledge is much more than data and facts, and includes, as Scheunpflug (2011) suggests, several levels, and as Andreotti (2012) suggests, different perspectives and approaches, then understanding about development needs to be seen as posing problems and raising debate rather than as resolving issues.

Development knowledge needs to include some understanding about different interpretations of data, to critically assess the evidence and then to review this knowledge in terms of its applicability and impact within societies.

All too often, however, development knowledge is presented as a series of facts and data, with an acceptance of the dominant paradigms about development and aid. This practice has been critiqued by a range of academics around the world (Andreotti, 2012; Cameron and Fairbrass, 2004) and has been noted in a number of research studies (Egan, 2011; Tallon, 2013).

Perhaps the most valuable comment on these debates has been that of Baillie Smith (2004) who has referred to the 'mediating role NGOs have played'. He has suggested that because of the role they have played in presenting examples of practice to schools, it has led to them, however unintentionally, closing debates on the need to see different viewpoints.

Tallon (2013) in her research in New Zealand noted similar points when, as an educationalist working with teachers, she found that a dominant view was to accept the role of NGOs and their practices, and to support what they were doing as the norm. Similarly, Hartmeyer (2008) has noted that for an educationalist to just accept and work within the Millennium Development Goals framework, for example, presumes an acceptance of the approach of target setting and a dominant learning framework. If development raises important issues regarding power, inequality, justice and change, then surely it should be assessed within such a pedagogical framework.

The approach taken in this chapter therefore is to look at some examples of educational practice that are located within the discourse on development, through the framework outlined in the previous chapter. This means asking the following questions:

- To what extent in the process of learning about development are connections made to its implications for developing a global outlook, having a concern for the poor, and being disposed to be supportive to a sense of social justice and solidarity?
- Within the debates on development, to what extent is there a recognition of its historical antecedents of colonialism, consequential divisions between North and South in the world, and their implications for how countries, societies, economies and cultures 'develop'?
- A charitable mentality is often a natural starting point and response to learning about development, but to what extent does the learning progress to bring in an understanding of social justice and equity?

- Learning about themes such as poverty and inequality poses challenges to the learner about their own viewpoints, sense of place in the world and how they should respond. To what extent does the learning about development encourage critical thinking, reflection and dialogue, and pose challenges in terms of personal and social transformation?

This chapter now looks at examples of research that has looked at learning about development. Examples are taken from school textbooks, a specific examination course on world development, projects based on personal experiences of developing countries, and a review of research into school linking. Each of these examples is then assessed in terms of the extent to which the evidence demonstrates engagement with the questions posed above.

Learning about development through school textbooks

Within formal education, development themes are most prominent in geography or related subjects. To assess how development is taught and promoted within school education, it is appropriate to look at examples of textbooks because they give perhaps the best sense of how the theme is constructed and taught.

Material for this section is taken primarily from research undertaken in Ireland by Bryan and Bracken (2011) and observations from a research paper by Lambert and Morgan (2012) with regard to geography education in the UK.

Bryan and Bracken specifically look at textbooks related to the Geography Leaving Certificate because it is there that one can see approaches to some detailed learning about development. Within the certificate, development themes are referred to with regard to Population, Settlement Patterns and Urbanisation, and Patterns of Economic Activity. Themes covered include global distribution of wealth, trade, aid and causes of inequality around the world. In 2005 the curriculum body for Ireland, along with Irish Aid, suggested that 'having completed the study of this unit (Patterns of Economic Activity), students should have a critical understanding of different views and approaches towards development' (NCCA & Irish Aid, 2005: 8, quoted in Bryan and Bracken, 2011: 103).

Bryan and Bracken observed that in comparison with other subjects they looked at, geography showed a more 'substantative critical engagement with a broad range of global themes and issues which enable students to critically reflect on the development enterprise itself and how the developing world is portrayed in the media' (2011: 104).

However in looking at specific textbooks promoted within the curriculum, there is clear evidence that questions the extent to which the processes of learning about development include 'making connections to a more global outlook, a concern for the poor, and to be disposed to be supportive to a sense of social justice', as posed in this volume.

For example Bryan and Bracken note that blanket statements are made in textbooks that refer to themes such as child mortality as attributable to 'uneducated and ignorant mothers' (ibid.: 104). This reflects a tendency in many books in Ireland and elsewhere (see Lambert and Morgan, 2012) to make over-generalised comments that suggest crude divisions between 'developed' and 'developing'.

Lambert and Morgan, in reviewing a textbook, *Horizons*, first published in 2006, state that it tends to locate 'development' within 'some sort of socio-biological realm'. Whilst they note that various definitions are discussed, the effect of this mapping is to represent development as rather static. The causes of poverty, they report, are listed as 'a series of factors with little in the way of explanatory theories that might help the student to put the figures in perspective' (ibid.: 23). Moreover they suggest there is an unproblematic acceptance of the dominant narratives of development, with the role of geography to map and observe what is 'out there' in an objective sense.

Bryan and Bracken found that some of the most problematic references to development were in relation to the material on urbanisation, where there were examples of observations on communities through the lenses of Irish development workers. The 'poor but happy' representation is a common theme in many textbooks and publications on development. This approach is most evident when poverty is simply described with no analysis of the causes.

It is easy to focus in on texts that are uncritical in their approach, but as Bryan and Bracken acknowledge there were several publications that did look at differences and inequalities within countries as well as between them, and that critiqued different theories of development. They also found examples that did question assumptions about the historical antecedents of colonialism, consequential divisions between North and South in the world, and their implications for how countries, societies, economies and cultures 'develop'.

For example, Bryan and Bracken found references to the need for 'critically examining Eurocentric thinking and images relating to the South' and that the idea that 'one model of development fits all countries is questionable' (ibid.: 108–109).

In many publications with a development focus, visual images are often used as a tool to bring to life the stories or the issues being portrayed in the text. However the use of visual images is often problematic, and can all too often reinforce traditional notions of pity which in turn reinforce a charitable mentality. Bryan and Bracken found several examples of this 'development pornography', but at the same time found examples that showed more positive images, including examples of fair trade initiatives, health clinics and local co-operatives (ibid.: 115). But as they state, replacing one image with a counter one can all too easily fail to address the causes of poverty and the impact of inequality.

This relates to the extent to which there is encouragement of progression within the learning to move from a charitable mentality to one of social justice, and to encourage questioning, reflection and critical thinking to help the learner in their understanding of development.

Bryan and Bracken note that it is in geography that the contradictory faces of development are most evident; there were examples that challenged the 'moral supremacy and universality of Western ways of interpreting and knowing the world' (ibid.: 123). One theme they refer to, that is referred to elsewhere by Smith (2004), Standish (2012), Tallon (2013) and Hartmeyer (2008), is the role and usage of NGO materials, which can often reproduce a one-sided perspective.

What is most noticeable from the textbooks is the absence of any discussion of the relationship of the learning to individuals' own worldviews and their own sense of place in the world. This may be partly explained by how a subject like geography is often taught, which is to separate out 'home' from 'far away'' and not to look at interconnections or personal and social engagement. Bryan and Bracken are particularly critical of what they term 'development activism'. All too often this form of activism is located in a school or educational institution as quite separate from any process of learning or discussion about development.

Publications giving data and evidence are important to building an under-standing of development, but they are not neutral or value free. Therefore for the teacher and educator more broadly, learning about themes such as global poverty through one particular publication would be insufficient. Different viewpoints and interpretations have to be part of the narrative of understanding development.

Learning about development through a specific course and examination

A good example to take from the UK is the post-16 examination on World Development which is a specialist course over two years, as a pre-higher education qualification. The evidence from this example is based primarily on two research studies: Miller, Bowes, Bourn and Castro (2012); and Bowes (2011).

Although the course has to date only been taken by a relatively small number of students, it has proved popular with those who have undertaken it. It is a unique course that emphasises the multi-disciplinary nature of development issues. It combines the spatial characteristics of geographical study alongside international relations, institutions and systems of governance within political studies, with historical perspectives vital for an understanding of current situations. The course also includes aspects of sociology in exploring human interrelationships; and economics through discussion on production and exchange.

The course includes an in-depth study of the relationship between development, people, poverty and their environment, plus the nature of poverty and inequality. It encourages students to develop an understanding of real world complexities from a range of perspectives, political, social, economic and environmental.

It provides space for students and teachers to learn in different ways, often more in partnership than through traditional didactic knowledge transfer. An important and distinctive feature of the course is that it offers different opportunities for learning, including collaborative approaches, space for students to follow their own interests, and learning through research. The course does not encourage activism, but does enable young people to respond intellectually to what they see as injustice and inequality. One of the most important opportunities within the course is for students to develop *informed* personal opinions and judgements. This is reflected strongly in the evaluative nature of many examination questions, as well as in the individual report the students have to complete.

Bowes (2011), in her research into this examination, explored the views of students and teachers regarding the relevance of the World Development qualification to their own lives and future careers. Students commented that it helped their understanding of global issues, of the world and 'how it is inter-connected', how it changed their outlook, and encouraged an interest in current affairs. Many students in Bowes's study stated explicitly how much more informed they felt about world issues and concerns. Knowledge enabled the students to discuss with confidence (ibid.: 96–112).

There is some evidence in the research on this examination of changes in perceptions of development. Whilst there was evidence of increased understanding of the complexity of issues surrounding global poverty, viewpoints remained predominantly at a moral level (Miller et al., 2012: 39).

There is less evidence within the course of engagement with the relationship between colonialism and the consequential divisions between the Global North and the Global South in the world, and the implications for how countries, societies, economies and cultures 'develop'.

A more complex theme within the research on this examination is the extent to which the course promotes and encourages a sense of critical engagement with charitable perspectives and themes around social justice. A feature of development education practice, as this volume has indicated, is to challenge perceptions people may have about poorer places in the world, particularly sub-Saharan Africa. Therefore a key indicator of the extent to which the course reflects development education approaches is whether it has changed the students' perceptions and images of lower-income countries. There were examples that the examination did have an impact such as: 'need to recognise had pre-conceived ideas', 'Africa is not as bad as I thought', or recognition that the media tended to manipulate the images of Africa. One student commented that there is 'much more to Africa than just extreme poverty', whilst five students highlighted how 'development' can be interpreted in different ways, 'taking many forms and working on varying levels'. Other issues such as aid and debt were raised, with one student expressing how 'I now understand the reasons for poverty and how it is often linked to exploitation by foreign interests'. Another student explained that before the course they had not appreciated how 'issues with Aid were so complicated, and how much conflict there is'. There was also recognition that the media have a role to play in how images of the developing world are presented, especially amongst charities and their strategies to fundraise. However, these views need to be balanced against the majority, who did not see the course as changing their perceptions (Miller et al., 2012: 30–32).

Finally, learning about themes such as poverty and inequality poses challenges to the learner about their own viewpoints, sense of place in the world and how they should respond. To what extent does the learning about development within this course encourage critical thinking, reflection and dialogue, and pose challenges in terms of personal and social transformation? In other words, to what extent did the course change students' perceptions about global and development issues?

The evidence revealed that the majority of students felt that their perception of inequality had increased. The poverty and inequality theme had most impact, while political development and the people/resources themes had least. It should however be noted that a relatively small number of students studied the political theme, and much of the people/resources theme was broadly familiar for most students (ibid.).

There is clear evidence of the strong social and moral influence of the course. The relatively low number of responses regarding political views and perceptions may also in part be due to students' and teachers' confidence about which issues to study.

The research shows the complex nature of learning about development: its many aspects and the wide range of themes and topics that are challenging in terms of knowledge and skills gained, and that also raise questions about values of justice and fairness in the world. What is less clear however is the extent to which the course resulted in further engagement by young people in international development.

It is clear that although the development community places more emphasis on values and attitudes, the students themselves responded more positively to the factual content of the course. What is also important from the evidence is that increased knowledge did not automatically lead to a desire to further their knowledge and to engage in follow-up actions. But this should not be surprising for 17- and 18-year-olds whose main concerns are about securing a good university place and having some sense of personal security for their future career (ibid.: 34–36).

Finally, in terms of the evidence gained from this study in relation to pedagogical concepts underpinning development education, what is noticeable from the comments by students is the extent to which this examination has resulted in some questioning of aid and development, and particularly the role of NGOs. The participatory approach of the course undoubtedly helped, alongside the use throughout the course of 'real world' examples. The themes addressed therefore seem relevant, topical, but also open to different interpretations.

Analysis of this examination course suggests that learning about development can pose questions, raise issues and encourage critical reflection; but to be effective the subject matter needs to be covered in some depth, from a range of viewpoints, and taught in a manner that is seen as relevant to everyday lives. However, as the next section will identify, the role of wider and more personal experience needs to be reviewed regarding the contributions it makes to processes of learning.

Learning about development through personal experience

There have been very few empirical studies that have explored young people's experience of opportunities to engage with development issues, and fewer still that have compared this experience across different contexts, exploring the relationship between context and forms of learning and engagement. One significant study is that by Asbrand, a German academic who compared two groups of young people learning about globalisation and development, one group through critical and intellectual discussion at school, the other through volunteering in organisations outside of school. She found that compared with the learning which took place in a school environment the construction of knowledge of the young volunteers was much more certain and secure. The latter group felt 'certain about their knowledge and there is no consideration of non-knowledge or different perspectives' (Asbrand, 2008: 36). They took their knowledge as true and objective, allowing clarity regarding the options of acting in a complex world society, and 'a self-image of being active' (ibid.: 37).

However, there is evidence that knowledge gained from experience, particularly if it is part of some form of overseas travel, visit or volunteering project, can often result in a partial level of understanding, affected by personal perceptions and motivations (see Jorgenson, 2010). For example, for many young people in Europe, North America, Japan and Australia, the whole area of 'overseas experience' is often part of some form of rite of passage between school and university, or prompted by a desire to 'do good' or 'broaden horizons'.

Evidence from research with young adults (18–20-year-olds) involved in these types of activities identifies perceptions of communities they visit as being 'poor-but-happy', with little evidence of increased understanding of the reasons for poverty (Simpson, 2004).

It is where this form of experience is part of a broader learning process that includes training and discussion on development education themes before, during and after the experience, that understanding of development issues has resulted in some questioning of perceived assumptions and approaches.

For example, Davies and Lam's (2010) research on a study visit to Zambia by a group of students from a British university reflects the positive and negative challenges that a 'personal experience' approach can bring to learning about development. The aim of this study visit was to support students in their undergraduate module on Education in Africa. It aimed through firsthand experience, to 'provide participants with insight into lives outside of their own and to help them make links between their own experiences of education, their potential future professional lives as teachers and the very different context of education in the "South"' (ibid.: 35). The research identified evidence of gains in awareness, appreciation and understanding of Zambian culture, but also the continuation and in some cases reinforcement of ethnocentric stereotypes. Typical comments were: 'it made me realise how lucky I am'; 'you respect what you've got more'; 'we take so much for granted' (ibid.: 46).

The authors of this research, who organised the trip and taught on the course, stated that they had learned that they needed to bring in a stronger 'critical literacy dimension to the preparation for the visit' and 'provide students with a framework informed by post-colonial theory'. The other change they were going to consider was to include more emphasis on reflection and self-examination before, during and after the visit (ibid.: 50–51).

Another study, by an employee of a small UK-based enterprise, Partner Ghana, showed similar evidence, including the importance of training and support for the young people (Love, 2013). Partner Ghana sends groupings of young people to Ghana for a three-week volunteering experience. Their experience includes engaging in a series of educational, cultural and construction projects. Love interviewed the young people before, during and after their visit, and found that the experience did not significantly develop 'participants' understanding of causes and solutions to global inequality' (ibid.: 34–39). This would seem to support claims that short-term volunteering experiences do not necessarily result in more critical reflection on development issues (Trewby, 2007).

The students' perceptions of poverty prior to their visit were heavily influenced by negative views about the role of the west through unfair and unequal trade relations. The volunteering experience had a mixed impact on participants' thoughts about the causes of inequality. Four participants reported having their initial understanding confirmed by their experiences in the country. Three participants also recorded some deeper reflections on the importance of education (Love, 2013: 30–34).

A specific theme that emerged from Love's research was that the volunteering experience tended to confirm participants' initial thoughts on solutions to inequality. Interestingly also, the research did not confirm that such volunteering experiences reproduced paternalistic relationships. Love noted:

> Prior to volunteering, these participants unanimously stated that they felt they could learn 'equally' from their peers. This may be a case of social desirability bias but responses during the (volunteering) experience further demonstrated that the volunteers felt they learnt a lot from their student partners. Furthermore, the majority of participants stated that they wished to volunteer both to help those less fortunate but also to learn from the host community. This indicates a fairly equitable approach to their relationship with their peers.
> *(ibid.: 37)*

Whilst the cohort for this study may have been a particular grouping of young people who had already shown some level of awareness and understanding of development and global themes, Love's research does show the dangers of coming to simplistic conclusions regarding such volunteering experiences.

Similar evidence can be found in research for VSO, a UK volunteering NGO, which looked at the impact of a one- or two-year international volunteering placement on a range of adults (Bentall et al., 2010).

The evidence showed a desire to develop a greater understanding of development as a factor in deciding to do a VSO placement. This thirst for more knowledge about development continued for many of them after their return to the UK, although this was frequently accompanied by a change of viewpoint. Several volunteers stated that they had become much more cynical or questioning about aid and the role of NGOs in development after having the chance to see what was happening on the ground. Another frequent comment was that the placement had led them to see that development is much more complex than they had thought beforehand. This recognition of the need to better understand the complexities of people's lives and the everyday issues they face was a common message to emerge.

Another theme that emerged from the research with these volunteers was a concern about not reproducing stereotypes, or reducing the complexities of their experiences to slogans and simple stories. Others emphasised 'the need to encourage learning about different viewpoints and perspectives'.

> In most cases, the volunteers were keen to share both the negative and positive aspects of their experiences, including not only the problems they encountered but also funny stories, in order to both communicate the complexities of development and encourage people to engage with important issues.
>
> (Bentall et al., 2010: 18)

What this study and Love's research show is that in terms of learning about development, personal experiences can reinforce views and perceptions, but can also change them. What personal experiences such as those outlined above can also do is challenge assumptions that an individual may have, and lead them to be more critically reflective.

It also appears from the two organisations referred to in this study that training, learning and support for the volunteers is very important. Where development education-related training sessions are included pre- and post-experience, then the volunteers seem better able to reflect more positively and relate to a broader worldview.

We can perceive a similar pattern when considering the question: to what extent did the visits encourage critical reflection about the causes of, and solutions to, global inequality? Although most of the participants already displayed a fairly nuanced, complex understanding of global inequality, the experience seemed to have little impact on further developing their critical thinking on this subject. A possible reason for this is that the volunteer experience included very little supported reflection. Spending time in a local community may give one a more complex understanding of that particular community's experience of poverty, but it is arguably unlikely to build any insight into the structural causes of poverty such as debt, unfair trade and exploitation.

All of these studies on the contribution of personal experience demonstrate the value that such initiatives can provide as a contribution to learning about development and global themes. But they can all too often reinforce existing notions and views of the learner, unless the 'experience' is part of a broader learning process that includes space and time for critical reflection, dialogue, and engagement with looking at the causes of inequality and global poverty.

Learning about development through a school link

Another feature of the proposed value of 'personal experience' and 'direct contact' between peoples and communities has been international partnerships, particularly through linking schools around the world. This has been a particularly popular feature of development education practice in the UK over the past decade (Leonard, 2008) and has also become a feature of the landscape of development education practice in Ireland (Toland, 2011). The rationale for funding these initiatives was that real world examples and direct contact with people were seen as ways of bringing development to life and showing at first hand what poverty and development mean.

The evidence from a range of research-based studies on such links suggests a rather mixed and complex picture. Whilst there is evidence that direct contact can motivate students' learning, the extent to which there is increased depth of understanding is more questionable (Leonard, 2008; Bourn and Cara, 2012, 2013; Edge, Frayman and Lawrie, 2009).

Where the link included curriculum-based activities with external support from NGOs, and resources for the professional development of the teachers, there was evidence of learning about development (Edge, Creese, Frew and Descours, 2011; Bourn and Cara, 2012, 2013).

Research for Link Community Development, an international NGO which supported a number of linking programmes between 2000 and 2012, showed evidence that pupils in the UK and Ireland had increased their knowledge and understanding about development and global issues as a result of having a partnership with a school in Africa. But this was more effective and long-lasting if and when the learning was directly related to curriculum themes and resources such as environment, health and social justice. There was also evidence that despite the aims of the NGO and the project having a clear development education focus, many pupils from schools in the UK and Ireland still saw their relationship to their partner school in Africa in terms of helping them, providing resources and support, and not as a mutual learning process. Indeed the final evaluation report for this project showed that it was as much, if not more, to do with the curriculum materials and support to the schools, rather than the direct contact with the partner school, that were the main factors in securing increased learning about development amongst pupils (Bourn and Cara, 2012, 2013).

Leonard (2008), in reviewing research in this area, notes there is evidence that linking does tend to result in a rather thin understanding of development issues. But as she identified from her in-depth study of one link, where the partnership is long-standing and there is healthy dialogue and debate between the schools, learning can be significant and sustainable (Leonard, 2012). She also shows that a link can provide an opportunity to promote pedagogical approaches within the partner school in the Global South that resonate with development education approaches. A link can result in both partners questioning their own assumptions about the country of their link, its people and cultures. It can also encourage styles of teaching and learning that may well be different from the norm within the school.

What links appear to do quite well is promote greater intercultural understanding. Behind the motivation of many school links is a cosmopolitan viewpoint, promoting a 'common sense of humanity and belief in being part of a global community' (Bourn and Cara, 2013: 17). Links can also be an important motivator for teachers. Direct experience and contact can help to increase confidence, broaden perspectives and perhaps challenge assumptions. But unless there is curriculum development work alongside it, the evidence suggests that there is a danger that such links and partnerships can reinforce dependency relationships, a sense of paternalism, and stereotypes that both teachers and pupils may already have.

Conclusion

So what do these examples tell us about processes of learning about development, in the context of the pedagogical framework outlined in this chapter?

To what extent, in the process of learning about development, are connections made to the implications for developing a global outlook, having a concern for the poor, and being disposed to be supportive to a sense of social justice and solidarity?

All of the examples referred to demonstrate evidence that learning about development can lead to promoting a more global outlook; but there is also evidence from all the examples that it can equally reproduce patronising and paternalistic perspectives. It is where learning is based on looking at different viewpoints and encouraging self-reflection that a sense of change and transformation takes place in the learner.

The evidence reinforces themes raised in the previous chapter about the importance of the process of learning, 'opening up the minds' of the learner and providing an appropriate support and professional development programme for the educators.

Understanding development also means being exposed to different interpretations and viewpoints. Development education practice in many countries has not been particularly strong in promoting and encouraging understanding and critical reflection on different views on themes such as poverty, aid and development. This, as will be explored in Chapter 8, is in part due to the influence and agenda setting of international development NGOs.

But there is also another reason for this, and this relates to the lack of inclusion within many programmes of the historical antecedents of colonialism in relation to development. A probable reason for this is that within the practices of many NGOs and the priorities of funders, there is a constant requirement to promote the value of aid.

Where moving beyond a charitable mentality to one of social justice is most evident is where there have been opportunities for critical reflection, questioning and considering the implications of one's own personal engagement.

Finally, and perhaps most challenging of all, is this: that learning about development does pose challenges to the learner about their own viewpoints, sense of place in the world, and how they should respond. Once again, it is in initiatives that have encouraged and provided space for the learner to address these areas that some of the most long-lasting impact and depth of understanding about development can be seen.

References

Andreotti, V. (2010) 'Global education in the 21st century: two different perspectives on the "post" of postmodernism', *International Journal of Development Education and Global Learning*, 2(2): 5–22.

Andreotti, V. (2012) *Actionable Postcolonial Theory in Education*. New York: Palgrave Macmillan.

Asbrand, B. (2008) 'How adolescents learn about globalisation and development', in D. Bourn (ed.) *Development Education: Debates and Dialogue*. London: Institute of Education, pp. 28–44.

Baillie Smith, M. (2004) 'Contradiction and change? NGOs, schools and the public faces of development', *Journal of International Development*, 16: 741–749.

Bentall, C., Blum, N. and Bourn, D. (2010) 'Returned volunteers and engagement with development', unpublished report for VSO. London: Development Education Research Centre.

Bourn, D. and Cara. O. (2012) *Partners in Development: Link Community Development Mid-Term Evaluation Report*. DERC Research Report no. 6. London: IOE/DERC.

Bourn, D. and Cara. O (2013) *School Linking – Where Next – Partnership Models between Schools in Europe and Africa*. DERC Research Report no. 10. London: IOE/DERC.

Bowes, E. (2011) 'World Development A Level: its perception and status amongst students, teachers and universities', unpublished Masters of Arts dissertation, University of East Anglia.

Bryan, A. and Bracken, M. (2011) *Learning to Read the World*. Dublin: Irish Aid.

Cameron, J. and Fairbrass, S. (2004) 'From development awareness to enabling effective support: the changing profile of development education in England', *Journal of International Development*, 16: 729–740.

Davies, D. and Lam, E. (2010) 'Role of first hand experience in the development education of university students', *International Journal of Development Education and Global Learning*, 2(2): 35–52.

Edge, K., Creese, B., Frew, E. and Descours, K. (2011) *Plan School Linking – Research and Development Findings, Third Year*. London: IOE/Plan UK.

Edge, K., Frayman, K. and Lawrie, J. (2009) *The Influence of North-South School Partnerships: Final Report*. London: IOE.

Edge, K., Khamsi, K. and Bourn, D. (2009) *Exploring the Global Dimension in Secondary Schools: Final Research Report*. London: Institute of Education.

Egan, A. (2011) 'Development education and corporate power', unpublished MA dissertation, Institute of Education, University of London.

Hartmeyer, H. (2008) *Experiencing the World – Global Learning in Austria: Developing, Reaching Out, Crossing Borders*. Munster: Waxmann.

Jorgenson, S. (2010) 'De-centering and re-visioning Global Citizenship Education Abroad Programme', *International Journal of Development Education and Global Learning*, 3(1): 23–38.

Lambert, D. and Morgan, J. (2012) *Geography and Development: The Role of Development Education in Geography Curriculum.* DERC Research Report no. 3. London: IOE.

Leonard, A. (2008) 'Global school relationships: school linking and modern challenges', in D. Bourn (ed.) *Development Education: Debates and Dialogues.* London: Bedford Way Papers, pp. 64–98.

Leonard, A. (2012) *The Aston-Makunduchi Partnership: South-North School Link: In Depth Case Study.* DERC Research Report no. 8. London: IOE, DERC.

Love, J. (2013) 'International voluntary service within a school partnership: "voluntourism" or effective development education?' unpublished MA dissertation, Institute of Education.

Miller, G., Bowes, E., Bourn, D. and Castro, J.M. (2012) *Learning about World Development at A Level.* DERC Research Report no. 7. London: IOE.

Scheunpflug, A. (2011) 'Global education and cross-cultural learning: a challenge for a research based approach to international teacher education', *International Journal of Development Education and Global Learning*, 3(3): 29–44.

Simpson, K. (2004) 'Broad horizons? Geographies and pedagogies of the gap year', unpublished PhD thesis, University of Newcastle.

Smith, M. (2004) 'Contradiction and change, NGOs, schools and the public faces of development', *Journal of International Development*, 16(5): 741–749.

Standish, A. (2009) *Global Perspectives in the Geography Curriculum.* London: Routledge.

Standish, A. (2012) *The False Promise of Global Learning.* New York: Continuum.

Tallon, R. (2013) 'What do young people think of development?' unpublished PhD thesis, Victoria University of Wellington, New Zealand.

Toland, P. (2011) 'A development education evaluation of a teacher study visit to Africa', unpublished MA dissertation, Institute of Education.

Trewby J. (2007) 'A pedagogy of the gap year', unpublished Masters thesis, University of Reading.

8
LEARNING AND SKILLS
IN A GLOBAL SOCIETY

This chapter reviews the conceptual framework outlined in Chapter 6 in relation to practices and approaches to learning in the context of a global society. It looks particularly at how young people perceive their relationship to the wider world, the concept of a global dimension in schools, the value of the concept of global skills, and initiatives in higher education. The material for this chapter is based primarily on research in the UK.

These approaches and practices have tended to be influenced by broader themes and concepts than those most commonly associated with development education. Terms like global learning, global youth work, global education, global dimension, global perspectives and global skills have tended to be used as a way of broadening beyond the discourses and practices located in development. These terms also aim to make linkages with broader global challenges, including sustainable development; or to recognise the interdependent nature of the world we now live in.

At one level, some of these terms have been used consciously, rather than the term development education, as these terms have a broader resonance with education and learning, or they represent recognition that the dominant lens should today be globalisation rather than development.

The rationale for addressing these themes is that the dominant social, economic and cultural context influencing development education practice today is that of globalisation, and its impact in terms of why and how people learn and make sense of their place and role in the wider world.

The themes outlined in Chapter 7, and building on the conceptual framework, are applied also in this chapter. Thus, the following themes and questions are posed here:

- To what extent in the process of learning about globalisation and learning in a global society are connections made to its implications for developing a global outlook, concern for the poor, and being disposed to be supportive to a sense of social justice and solidarity?

- Within the debates on globalisation and related areas, to what extent is there recognition of the historical antecedents, the consequential divisions between North and South in the world, and the implications for how countries, societies, economies and cultures have responded to the rapidly changing world?
- To what extent does the learning progress to bring in an understanding of social justice and equity?
- Learning about themes such as globalisation and global inequality poses challenges to learners about their own viewpoints, sense of place in the world, and how they should respond. To what extent does the learning about globalisation and global forces encourage critical thinking, reflection and dialogue, and pose challenges in terms of personal and social transformation?

Young people and a global society

For young people in many industrialised countries, the first decade of the twenty-first century has been a period dominated by the increasing influence of global-isation and the wide range of economic, cultural and political activities across the world landscape which 'cut across national boundaries, integrating and connecting communities and organisations in new space-time combinations' (Hall, 1992: 299).

Global social, political and economic change often appears to affect young people disproportionately. Many sociologists specialising in youth affairs have portrayed young people as being at the forefront of such change (Furlong and Cartmel, 2007; Miles, 2000), with globalisation having profound and far-reaching effects on their lives. In particular, a large body of evidence explores the ways in which the flows of globalisation impact on young people's identification, whether that be through internet communities (France, 2007: 157), consumption in a global marketplace (Miles, 2000) or mass communication systems (Nayak, 2003).

Research by IBT in the UK indicates that young people become interested in issues affecting the developing world through a wide range of opportunities for engagement, including: programmes on TV; the news; reading articles about these issues; discussions with family; teachers; activities at school; going on holiday/ travelling; charity advertisements; getting involved with a charity; religious institu-tions; cinema films; friends' experiences; having family/friends from another country; talking to people from charities (Cross et al., 2010: 23).

Recognition of this changing relationship between young people and society became evident during the 1990s, and there was an emerging body of both research and practice that showed different forms of engagement in global issues (Bourn and McCollum, 1995). This research found that while young people are primarily interested in issues involving their own lives, they are also concerned about the wider world. This recognition of the connections between the personal and local, and the wider world became the focus of this new term 'global youth work'.

The concept of global youth work was in part a recognition that for many young people, their understanding and engagement with wider world issues came not through school but through more informal areas, through youth work or their own personal engagement. The concept became defined as 'informal education with young people that encourages a critical understanding of the links between the personal, local and the global and seeks their active participation in actions that bring about change towards greater equity and justice'.

Central to this concept was that young people's concerns about the wider world needed to be seen 'in the context of their own images of themselves and their future in society' (DEA, 2002, 2007).

The hallmarks of good global youth work came to be seen as the following:

- starting from young people's everyday experiences;
- engaging young people in critical analysis of local and global influences on their lives and communities;
- raising awareness of globalisation, the world's history and rich diversity of peoples, particularly in relation to issues of justice and equity;
- encouraging young people to explore the relationships between their personal lives and local and global communities;
- seeking young people's active participation to build alliances and create change, locally and globally (DEA, 2007; Adams, 2010).

A 2009 report identified a range of initiatives and organisations bringing global issues into youth work; however, it stated that it is 'difficult to get a clear picture of the proportion of young people who experience youth work', let alone the proportion that have the opportunity to learn about poverty and development in informal education contexts (Cotton, 2009: 12).

In his review of the history of global youth work, Adams states that global learning can 'still be seen as a curriculum area or campaigning issue'. However he goes on to suggest that the ambition of global youth work is more subtle, based on the notion that there is a global dimension to every issue (Adams, 2010). This is particularly seen in relation to environmental issues, but is also evident in the activities of a number of organisations on themes such as migration and refugees, fashion, food and healthy lifestyles (White, 2002). This suggests a move within global youth work to avoid common assumptions about young people's engagement with development issues.

One of the challenges for global youth work has been the tension between education and campaigning, with NGOs particularly seeking to engage young people in taking action. The DEA's global youth work training manual aimed to address this through a series of model training activities that encouraged promotion of different voices and perspectives. An example of this was encouraging discussion through an 'agree/disagree' series of statements about globalisation. Another was to undertake a role-play exercise between the youth worker and young people that looked particularly at negotiating skills, supporting the young people in the development of their understanding of issues, and not prescribing outcomes (DEA, 2007).

So, in reviewing the progress and activities on the theme of young people in a global society in the UK, how do these relate to the conceptual framework of development education that has been outlined here in relation to globalisation? There is evidence that a number of activities under the banner of 'global youth work' did develop a global outlook, and promoted a sense of social justice and solidarity. There is also evidence of a strong values base, particularly where there were connections to the perspectives of specific organisations, especially religious-based organisations.

There was less evidence of recognition of the historical antecedents and the consequential divisions between North and South in the world. There was however one particular initiative on Black Perspectives on Global Youth Work (Joseph et al., 2002) which included this element. Where this example of global youth work was at its most innovative was in relation to personal and social transformation. Through engaging in youth projects, there was evidence of changes in viewpoints about the wider world and the individual's relationship to it. What was particularly distinctive about 'global youth work' from other forms of engagement with young people was the connections to personal identity.

An evaluation study undertaken by De Montfort University for Y Care International regarding a global youth work project with marginalised young people in England shows evidence of the value of a young-person-led approach. Key themes to emerge were the recognition of the links between their lives and those of young people in the Global South; and seeing the world differently as a result of reflecting on their own relationship to the wider world (Sallah, 2013).

Unfortunately due to funding constraints and organisational priorities, the organisations who led on this area of practice in the UK are no longer actively engaged in global youth work. It has been left to Y Care International, a local Development Education Centre, Global Education Derby, and De Montfort University in Leicester to be the main standard-bearers for this area of practice.

The global dimension in schools

In England, the term Global Dimension was promoted as a key concept within the school curriculum in 2000, and by 2005 had become recognised as a cross-curricular theme. Influenced by broader traditions within global education, the concept was perceived as bringing together a range of values-based approaches to learning and incorporating themes such as human rights, sustainability, conflict resolution, citizenship, and intercultural understanding.

The main publication that promoted this concept, the Education ministry's *Developing a Global Dimension to the School Curriculum* (revised in 2005) stated:

> Including the global dimension in teaching means that links can be made between local and global issues. It also means that young people are given

opportunities to: critically examine their own values and attitudes; appreciate the similarities between peoples everywhere, and value diversity; understand the global context of their local lives; and develop skills that will enable them to combat injustice, prejudice and discrimination. Such knowledge, skills and understanding enables young people to make informed decisions about playing an active role in the global community.

(DFES, 2005: 3)

This publication moved the dominant thinking forward from seeing learning about development and global issues as about faraway places, to recognising the interdependent nature of people's lives, and the importance of a values-based approach with the emphasis on social justice, equity and fairness.

Hicks (2007), a key influence on the development of the global dimension concept, stated that he saw the term as four linked dimensions: issues, spatial, temporal, and process. He stated that a minimum requirement is to draw together: 'i) relevant contemporary global issues; ii) ways in which they are spatially related; iii) ways in which they are connected over time; iv) the pedagogy that is most appropriate for investigating such matters' (Hicks, 2007: 25–26). He goes on to say that doing a project on, say, an Indian village or setting up an international link are 'not good examples of good global education' (ibid.) because they do not locate the learning in the context of living in an interconnected world, or because learning about global issues has to include different dimensions and interpretations, recognising the changing dynamics of particular issues. Hicks further suggests that the most appropriate pedagogy for the Global Dimension is one that is based on participatory and experiential teaching and learning:

It needs to involve both head and heart (the cognitive and the affective) and the personal and political (values clarification and political literacy). It needs to draw on the learner's direct or simulated experience and it requires the development of interpersonal, discussion and critical thinking skills, as well as skills of participation and action.

(Hicks, 2007: 27)

An example of how these concepts were interpreted in schools can be seen from the research with a range of secondary schools by Edge et al. (2009). This identified how teachers saw the Global Dimension as a valuable mechanism for equipping pupils to understand the wider world and their place within it. The term was interpreted in a variety of ways, including:

- awareness of and exposure to other and different cultures and the world context; and a sense of global social responsibility;
- bringing students to understand that they are citizens of the world and to demonstrate the interconnectedness of the world we are living in;
- teaching about global issues and understanding the impact of our actions;

- promoting and sustaining international links;
- understanding the bigger picture and their place in it;
- helping students to link their complex and different identities and their place in the world.

Research by Bourn and Hunt (2011) showed similar evidence, from interviews with teachers, of a strong theme of equipping young people to be global citizens and expanding horizons and ways of thinking beyond local contexts.

> It's a way of helping the learners within our school look at global issues, their complexity, and try and work out their place in the world, and figure out the links between their own lives and people elsewhere in the world, and issues that affect them, either directly or indirectly within the world.
>
> *(ibid.: 16)*

> It's having an idea of, thinking of, the big picture in terms of education and worldwide issues.
>
> *(ibid.)*

> A means to mitigate the effects of the distortions of the world presented to children and teachers everyday by the media, popular culture, politicians and the curriculum. It is essential that all teachers confront these distortions and present children with a more accurate picture of the world. Children should then be able to make decisions about how to become involved with issues that interest them.
>
> *(ibid.)*

This emphasis on cultural understanding and awareness was a key theme emerging from the interviews with teachers when relating the Global Dimension to schooling approaches:

> Because we want our pupils to understand that other people do have their different ways of looking at life, they have their own cultures, religions, lifestyles, etc. And we're helping them to be able to communicate with people from different cultures and backgrounds, and help them to respect others that is not something they would automatically do, but to understand, to respect and be able to communicate with those people.

> Enabling pupils to feel that they part of a global community of students and that they can understand something of the way in which they all learn and participate in a whole range of activities, both together, and you know, in their own home countries.

> The global dimension would be the extent to which, within all our lessons, we refer to ourselves in relationship to others in the world, and that our

whole curriculum is imbued with understanding the different cultures, customs, rituals.

(ibid.: 18–19)

Research with teachers suggests that whilst there was evidence of promoting approaches to learning that broadened pupils' worldview, there was less evidence of encouraging critical perspectives. This means that in relation to the pedagogical framework outlined in this chapter, there is less evidence of critical thinking or making connections with broader debates around inequality in the world. Andreotti (2008) in her criticism of the 2000 edition of the Global Dimension publication raises these issues and concerns. She states that the Global Dimension Framework emphasises change and progress in terms of a 'non-negotiable universalised epistemology that would work for everyone' (ibid.: 59). This results in much of the practice leading to a lack of engagement with different viewpoints about themes such as development, poverty and inequality.

Global skills

The concept of global or twenty-first-century skills has become increasingly popular in recent years amongst both policy-makers and practitioners. It has been most noticeably picked up in discussions regarding post-16 vocational education. This section looks at three interpretations of the concept and critiques each one of them against the pedagogical framework posed in this chapter.

It is suggested that global skills could be seen through one of three lenses, as linked to skills to compete in the global economy; or to be able to understand and engage with people from a range of cultures and backgrounds; or as a vehicle for presenting a more critical and transformatory pedagogy.

A necessary starting point however is to address the question as to whether we are talking about generic skills in the context of globalisation, or specific skills that require enhancement and support, for people to effectively engage in society and to equip them to work in the global economy.

Global skills are likely to be seen by business and employers as equipping the learner and therefore the worker to be an effective employee. However what is noticeable from a range of studies in the UK in recent years is the emphasis increasingly given to areas such as transferable skills, team working, good interpersonal skills and the capacity to deal with uncertainty and solve problems (LSC, 2006). Research by Newton et al. for the UK government's Department for Work and Pensions reinforces the value that employers are placing on softer skills, including positive self-esteem, reliability and initiative (Newton et al., 2005).

Such generic skills are acknowledged within large companies, for example through workforce requirements in terms of ability to work in a range of complex social and cultural environments, being culturally sensitive and able to communicate to a wide range of customers.

KPMG, the international audit company, state the following:

> So what exactly are we looking for when we recruit new people? Naturally, we want you to have good technical skills, problem-solving abilities and commercial focus. We're also looking for people with a lot of integrity − good team workers who can build effective relationships, learn from experience and bring out the best in others.
>
> *(quoted in Bourn, 2008: 19)*

Therefore whilst a global perspective may not emerge specifically within employer needs, there is evidence to suggest that some understanding, experience and ability to work within a range of social and cultural settings are being seen as increasingly important. The German Employers Association (BDA) has pointed out that it expects its workers to

> have the capacity for integrated thinking and knowledge about world economics and ecology, as well as an ability to work in teams, deal with complexity, take responsibility, have a strong personality, refer to a stable set of values, feel empathy and be interculturally competent.
>
> *(Toepher, 2003: 16)*

There is thus some evidence at least from large international companies that global skills are seen as being linked to having the skills to work in a range of cultural environments, and being adaptable; and to having a recognition of broader social needs and agendas. But this should not detract from the context within which employers and policy-makers see global skills, that is, related to economic competition and working within existing dominant social norms.

Another facet of 'global skills' that has perhaps less profile but is equally needed, is the skills to respond to the impact of globalisation on a person's life, to enable someone to make sense of the rapidly changing world around them, and to give them the confidence, knowledge and values base to make a positive contribution to both the economy and society more widely.

This could be summarised as covering the following areas:

- understanding what globalisation means, particularly in relation to planned or current areas of employment;
- ability to understand and engage with global challenges, such as climate change and poverty, in order to be a more informed and engaged citizen;
- development of skills to understand and respect a range of cultures and values and to be able to reflect critically upon one's own values base.

This broader perspective on global skills has been suggested by organisations in the UK with links to development education, notably the Development Education Association:

The essential skills for the 21st Century are to do with flexibility, ability to learn and transfer learning to new contexts, personal fulfilment, community development, intercultural understanding and above all, the ability to understand and engage with the environmental challenges facing us this century.

(DEA, 2003: 2)

Similar perspectives can be seen in the work of Catteeuw (2006), a Flemish government adviser on skills, in his framework for intercultural competences for business purposes. He identified the following key skills: critical awareness, openness, flexibility and empathy, communicative skills, solution-orientated attitude and cultural knowledge.

This broader perspective on global skills could be summarised as recognising the importance of generic skills of communication, team work, adaptability and respect for others, but in a context which recognises the nature of society, its cultural base, its rapidly changing economic forces and the challenges of dealing with the unknown. As I have mentioned elsewhere, building on the work of the Open Space for Dialogue and Enquiry initiative, key to the skills needs of the global society are skills that enable people to deal with complexity, uncertainty and insecurity (Bourn and Neal, 2008).

In the UK, strategies for promoting global skills have included recognition of the skills to live and work in a multicultural society, and this means 'completely repositioning institutional approaches to international education' (CEL, 2007). The main manifestation of these programmes within further and higher education has been in terms of partnerships between institutions, including study visits of staff and exchanges of students.

Behind the strategies for partnerships and links is the assumption that mere intercultural experience can help to gain greater understanding of the wider world. What is suggested here is that all too often these exchanges and experiences reproduce dominant notions of cultural superiority. Intercultural dialogue is not really dialogue but a form of reproduction of cultural domination.

Only when the exchange and the partnership are part of a broader process of learning and engagement with global issues and questions, and address questions of power and domination, can such experiences perhaps lead to a broader and more questioning global consciousness.

The third approach to global skills recognises complexity, and critical thinking is linked closely to a more values-based approach around social justice. Building on the work of Paulo Freire and Giroux, this approach is based on recognition of an approach to learning that is open, participatory but also deeply political, with a recognition of power. Giroux (2005) talks about critical pedagogy starting, not with test scores, but with questions. He states it is also about recognising competing views and vocabularies, and opening up new forms of knowledge and creative spaces.

These influences can be seen in the following approach to global skills that I developed for the Learning and Skills Improvement Service, a UK government-funded research and training body for further education (Bourn, 2008). Here global skills are based on the following concepts:

- an ability to communicate with people from a range of social and cultural backgrounds;
- an ability to work within teams of people from a range of backgrounds and other countries;
- openness to a range of voices and perspectives from around the world;
- willingness to resolve problems and seek solutions;
- recognition and understanding of the importance of global forces on people's lives;
- willingness to play an active role in society at local, national and international level (Bourn, 2008: 25).

These concepts include elements of the first and second themes expressed on how to interpret global skills. But they also incorporate an approach that has direct linkages to ideas expressed by Freire and Giroux. Bringing all of these elements together can provide opportunities for creative and more radical perspectives to emerge from practice.

Providing openings and opportunities for a more critical approach can result in global skills implying the following:

- recognising the value of learning about different perspectives and approaches;
- equipping the learner with the skills to question, and developing the ability to critically enquire and reflect upon a range of social, economic and cultural influences;
- emphasising the importance of positive social engagement and of seeking solutions;
- recognising the impact of globalisation on people's lives and the need to equip them with the ability to make sense of a rapidly changing world;
- making reference to the forces that shape societal and economic change (ibid.: 25–26).

One example of this approach has been a global skills project at Preston College in the north of England, which has used topics linked to the Millennium Development Goals in lessons on English as a second language and basic literacy (Bourn, 2008). Their approach has been developed in partnership with a local Development Education Centre that has expertise in participatory and social justice-based approaches.

There are examples in UK further education colleges that have implemented a more critical approach to global skills through projects and initiatives on themes such as Black History month and Refugee Week, organised in such a way as to encourage a sense of celebrating diversity: they promoted this diversity in a way that moved beyond a traditional multi- or intercultural approach to one that located the learning within the context of globalisation, social change, causes of inequality and injustice and what the learners could do themselves (Bourn, 2008).

These different lenses for interpreting global skills show that there is evidence of learning that makes connections to living in a globalised world and promoting a wider world outlook. They also show that critical pedagogical approaches in line with the framework outlined in this volume are possible to implement within further education.

Global perspectives in higher education

Over the past decade universities have begun to address their role and relationship to the wider world beyond merely recruitment of students and sharing academic debates. Influences have come in part from globalisation, the impact of new technology and increased economic mobility, recognition of the need to address issues around sustainable development, and the interest from students in wider world issues.

Within the UK, for example, there is evidence from universities as diverse as Bournemouth, University College London (UCL), Leeds Metropolitan, Gloucester and Plymouth of policy and curriculum reviews to address global and sustainability concerns (Caruana and Spurling, 2007; Jones and Brown, 2007; Bourn et al., 2006). There is also evidence from elsewhere in the world that universities are re-thinking their role in relation to the impact of globalisation, global citizenship and the environmental challenges of the twenty-first century (Corcoran and Wals, 2004; Gough and Scott, 2007; Schattle, 2008; Stearns, 2009).

These trends are in part influenced by the agendas of policy-makers, students and employers who are for different reasons calling on universities to recognise their role within a rapidly changing global society and economy. For a variety of reasons, terms like 'preparing students to be global citizens' are being promoted by universities (Shultz, Abdi and Richardson, 2011: Shiel, 2007). This has taken two main forms: a broader vision about the university as a global institution; and promotion of its students as potential global citizens. Examples of this can be seen in a range of different universities in the UK, from UCL to Bournemouth.

This trend can also be seen in teacher education, through a variety of initiatives and courses that encourage understanding of the global dimension as an element of the qualification to be an effective teacher (Hicks and Holden, 2007; Wade and Parker, 2008). Medicine and engineering are other areas where there has been an expansion of interest in global issues (Bourn and Neal, 2008). It is these last two areas that this section will specifically address.

Influenced by the work of the Development Education Association (DEA) on global perspectives in higher education, and making connections with emerging trends around internationalisation, a number of universities have begun to look at international development and globalisation not as areas of study but as drivers for re-thinking how the institution relates to global forces and influences. Through a range of publications and events between 1997 and 2006, the DEA evolved a development education approach towards higher education that came under the heading 'global perspectives': 'This means promoting ways of understanding society by making connections between local and wider world issues. It means looking at an issue or area of learning through the impact of globalisation and international development.'

The DEA gave as its rationale in promoting global perspectives that it enabled the learner to 'understand their own situation in a wider context', to 'develop skills and knowledge to interpret events affecting [their] lives' and to 'learn from experiences elsewhere in the world' (Bourn et al., 2006: 7).

In developing its thinking for its work in higher education, the DEA developed a framework for learning around knowledge, cognitive, social and practical skills, and values and attitudes. Central to this framework is the interrelationship of these concepts. One cannot learn about understanding the causes of poverty and inequality without the development of critical and analytical thinking, respecting views and having a commitment to social justice (ibid.).

Related to these developments has been the increased use of the concept 'global citizenship'. Whilst this term is to some extent an expansion of some of the debates in development education and education for sustainable development, its origins and discourses in Europe and North America have had a rather different focus.

In North America particularly, references to global citizenship emerged in a number of universities in the 1990s in response to globalisation and the need for graduates to be more globally aware, to travel and have the skills to work anywhere around the world. The events of 9/11 reinforced this notion, although giving it a particular slant in some institutions. The result is that you can see evidence from institutions such as George Mason University (Stearns, 2009), Chapman University and Tufts University (Schattle, 2008) of a desire to equip students to have greater knowledge, experience and positive outlook on wider world affairs.

The influences on this tradition have come from a variety of sources. At Soka University of America (Schattle, 2008), the influence came from a particular faith-based perspective, in this case Buddhist. In others it was due more directly to economic forces, through the impact of globalisation in terms of the need for the institution to be more globally competitive. Finally it was in some cases due to a response to the changing nature of the international student body and the promotion of international volunteering (Stearns, 2009).

The term global citizenship has also been linked to the drive for higher education institutions in the UK to have international strategies that not only encourage more international students, but also address the extent to which the university is 'internationalising' its ways of working. This has resulted in some institutions linking discourses on internationalisation to a set of pedagogical principles based around empowering students to develop as critical beings, to show the relevance of global issues to their own lives and demonstrate the relationship between local actions and global consequences (Caruana and Spurling, 2007; Killick, 2006; Shiel, 2007).

Critics of the term global citizenship suggest that it is elitist, not grounded in realities of political systems and makes assumptions, usually by people in the North on behalf of the rest of the world, about best forms of global social change (Dobson and Valencia, 2005). Carter (2001) suggests that if the term is seen more as a form of opening up dialogue and debate and as a spectrum of theories and interpretations, then it can become the basis for a constructive discourse. Andreotti (2006) for example makes a distinction, as noted in Chapter 5, between a 'soft' or passive form of global citizenship versus a 'hard' or more active form linked to notions of social justice and critical thinking.

Regardless of the discourses around global citizenship in higher education, what can be noted is that the mere promotion of the term has in a number of universities opened up a debate about the role of higher education in equipping its graduates to live and work in the global society of the twenty-first century.

Bournemouth University offers an example of developing a strategy on global perspectives that makes connections about wider world agendas: with critical thinking, valuing different methodologies and approaches, and questioning the dominance of Eurocentric and rich world viewpoints. The strategy also makes connections to a more values-based approach by 'challenging and discarding prejudice'; it acknowledges the 'global forces that affect us all' and promotes 'justice and equality' (Shiel, 2007).

Developing a global perspective is therefore seen as about broadening curricula and incorporating pedagogic approaches that empower students to develop as critical beings who are able to challenge orthodoxy and bring about change. It involves above all a shift in approach, rather than a radical change of content (Shiel, 2007).

Other examples can be seen at Leeds Metropolitan University (Jones and Brown, 2007) and University College London. At Leeds Metropolitan students are enabled to 'develop both an awareness of the global context of their subjects and themselves as global citizens' (Killick, 2006: 12). Their internationalisation strategy includes links to sustainable development (Jones and Brown, 2007), and reflects a strong values-based approach, with the aim of ensuring an international, multicultural ethos and the development of graduates with 'world-wide horizons'.

University College London is a very different type of institution from Bournemouth or Leeds Metropolitan. The latter two are post-1992 universities, formerly polytechnics and used to looking at courses and initiatives in an inter-disciplinary way. They are also less likely than say UCL, a much older institution, to be concerned about aiming to be one of the leading universities in the world.

UCL has however since 2005 begun a programme of promoting itself as a global university and the university for global citizenship. It states that as an institution with a strong liberal tradition, 'going global' should mean 'actively promoting a sense of global citizenship, social justice and environmental responsibility' (UCL, 2007).

The goal of UCL's strategy is to develop graduates who are:

- critical and creative thinkers;
- ambitious – but also idealistic and committed to ethical behaviour;

- aware of the intellectual and social value of culture difference;
- entrepreneurs with the ability to innovate;
- willing to assume leadership roles: in the family, the community and the workplace;
- highly employable and ready to embrace professional mobility (UCL, 2007).

It is evident from developments in the UK at Bournemouth University and to a lesser extent at UCL and Leeds Metropolitan, that there are potential spaces or openings for new approaches to learning that could rise to the challenges raised in this volume concerning transformative learning, for both students *and* teachers/lecturers. Sterling notes that whilst there is evidence of change within faculties and courses, there is much less in terms of institutional change. He gives an example of Hawkesbury College in Australia, an agricultural college where the mission became one of learning to think not only critically but in a way that necessitated a change in perception about engagement in the world (Sterling, 2004).

These initiatives in higher education demonstrate, as in further education, evidence of the promotion of a more global outlook, but tempered by the tensions regarding the influence of economic forces. There is evidence of critical reflection, but noticeably in higher education there is less focus on a more values-based approach related to concerns for social justice and a more equitable world.

Conclusion

In all of the areas mentioned, informal work with young people, in schools, further education and higher education, there is increasing evidence of educational bodies recognising the need to equip their learners to respond to the challenges of globalisation. What is less clear is the extent to which this learning moves beyond economic to social and cultural perspectives that bring in elements of social justice and global responsibility. There are elements of this, but only where some creative spaces have been possible at an institutional level, and where there is less pressure to demonstrate impact against external agendas such as examinations.

It is noticeable in nearly all of the sectors around the world that there is a lack of inclusion of any discussion of these themes in relation to historical antecedents, and recognition of power and inequality around the world. Competitive market forces, albeit under the guise of universal humanism, tend to dominate. There is more evidence of the promotion of critical thinking and multiple perspectives, but again this is heavily influenced by the pressures on the specific area of education.

The use of the term global can be an important lens through which to address a pedagogy of development education, but it can equally lead to distractions towards addressing global themes purely in terms of a competitive marketplace. Whilst it could be argued that that this could be a way into addressing issues of power, social justice and inequality, the evidence suggests that for this to happen, there needs to be strong leadership within an institution, that understands and recognises this more critical approach.

References

Adams, P. (2010) *History of Global Youth Work*. Think Global thinkpiece. London: Think Global.

Andreotti, V. (2006) 'Soft versus critical global citizenship education', *Development Education, Policy and Practice*, 3(1): 40–51.

Andreotti, V. (2008) 'Poverty and development', in D. Bourn (ed.) *Development Education: Debates and Dialogues*. London: Bedford Way Papers, pp. 45–63.

Bourn, D. (2008) *Global Skills*. London: Centre for Excellence.

Bourn, D. and Hunt, F. (2011) *Global Learning in Secondary Schools*. DERC Research Report no. 1. London: IOE/DERC.

Bourn, D. and McCollum, A. (1995) *A World of Difference*. London: DEA.

Bourn, D., McKenzie, A. and Shiel, C. (2006) *The Global University: The Role of the Curriculum*. London: DEA.

Bourn, D. and Neal, I. (2008) *The Global Engineer*. London: Engineers Against Poverty.

Carter, A. (2001) *Political Theory of Global Citizenship*. London: Routledge.

Caruana, V. and Spurling, N. (2007) *The Internationalisation of UK Higher Education: A Review of Selected Material*. www.heacademy.ac.uk/assets/York/documents/ourwork/tla/lit_review_internationalisation_of_uk_he.pdf

Catteeuw (2006) 'Framework for intercultural competence', quoted in D. Humphries (2007) *Inter Cultural Communication Competence: The State of Knowledge*. Report prepared for CILT. London: CILT.

Centre for Excellence in Leadership (CEL) (2007) *Leadership for Globalisation*. London: CEL.

Corcoran, P.B. and Wals, A.E.J. (2004) *Higher Education and the Challenge of Sustainability*. Dordrecht: Kluwer.

Cotton, N. (2009) *Global Youth Work in the UK: Research Report*. London: DEA.

Cross, S., Fenyoe, A., Wagstaff, M. and Gammon, A. (2010) *Global Generation: How Young People in the UK Connect with the Wider World*. London: IBT.

DEA (2002) *Young People in a Global Society*. London: DEA.

DEA (2003) *Global Success for All: A Skills Strategy in an Unequal World*. London: DEA.

DEA (2007) *Global Youth Work Practice Training and Resource Manual*. London: DEA.

DFES (2005) *Developing a Global Dimension to the School Curriculum*. London: DFES.

Dobson, A. and Valencia, A. (eds) (2005) *Citizenship, Environment and Economy*. London: Routledge.

Edge, K., Khamsi, K. and Bourn, D. (2009) *Exploring the Global Dimension in Secondary Schools: Final Research Report*. London: IOE.

France, A. (2007) *Understanding Youth in Late Modernity*. Berkshire: Open University Press.

Furlong, A. and Cartmel, F. (2007). *Young People and Social Change*. Berkshire: Open University Press.

Giroux, H. (2005) *Border Crossing*. New York: Routledge.

Gough, S. and Scott, W.A.H. (2007) *Higher Education and Sustainable Development*. London: Routledge.

Hall, S. (1992) 'The question of cultural identity', in S. Hall, D. Held and T. McGrew (eds) *Modernity and Its Futures*. Cambridge: Polity Press in association with the Open University, pp. 273–326.

Hicks, D. (2007) 'Principles and precedents', in D. Hicks and C. Holden (eds) *Teaching the Global Dimension*. London: Routledge, pp. 14–30.

Hicks, D. and Holden, C. (eds) (2007) *Teaching the Global Dimension*. London: Routledge.

Jones, E. and Brown, S. (eds) (2007) *Internationalising Higher Education*. London: Routledge.

Joseph, J., Akpokavi, K.B., Chauhan, V. and Cummins, V. (2002) *Towards Global Democracy: An Exploration of Black Perspectives in Global Youth Work*. London: DEA.

Killick, D. (2006) 'The internationalized curriculum: making UK HE fit for purpose', *Academy Exchange: Supporting the Student Learning Experience*, 5(Winter): 13–15.

Learning and Skills Council (LSC) (2006) *National Employer Skills Survey, 2005*. London: LSC.

Miles, S. (2000) *Youth Lifestyles in a Changing World*. Buckingham: Open University Press.

Nayak, A. (2003) *Race, Place and Globalisation*. Oxford: Berg.

Newton, B., Hurtsfield, J., Miller, L., Page, R. and Akroyd, K. (2005) *What Employers Look for When Recruiting the Unemployed and Inactive: Skills, Characteristics and Qualifications*. London: Department for Work and Pensions.

Sallah, M. (2013) *Evaluation of the Global Youth Work in Action Project (2010–13)*. London: De Montfort University/Y Care International.

Schattle, H. (2008) *The Practices of Global Citizenship*. Lanham, MD: Rowman & Littlefield.

Shiel, C. (2007) 'Developing and embedding global perspectives across the university', in S. Marshal (ed.) *Strategic Leadership of Change in Higher Education*. London and New York: Routledge, pp. 158–173.

Shultz, L., Abdi, A. and Richardson, G.H. (eds) (2011) *Global Citizenship Education in Post Secondary Institutions*. New York: Peter Lang.

Stearns, P. (2009) *Educating Global Citizens in Colleges and Universities*. New York: Routledge.

Sterling, S. (2004) 'Higher education, sustainability and the role of systematic learning', in P.B. Corcoran and A.E.J. Wals (eds) *Higher Education and the Challenge of Sustainability*. Dordrecht: Kluwer, pp. 47–70.

Toepher, B. (2003) 'Global education in adult and vocational education – why is it a must in the 21st century?' *The Development Education Journal*, 9(2): 15–17.

University College London (UCL) (2007) *What Is Meant by Global Citizenship?* www.ucl.ac.uk/global-citizenship.

Wade, R. and Parker, J. (eds) (2008) *Journeys Around Education for Sustainability*. London: London South Bank University.

White, P. (2002) *Global Youth Work: Improving Practice Series*. London: DEA.

9

NON-GOVERNMENTAL ORGANISATIONS AND EDUCATION FOR A MORE JUST WORLD

This chapter looks at the role that international non-governmental development organisations have played in relation to development education, and how their practice can be assessed in terms of the framework outlined in this volume for a pedagogy for global social justice. Evidence for this chapter is based on research looking at the practice of NGOs in Canada, Australia, New Zealand, the UK and Ireland.

NGOs in this chapter are seen as those international development and aid agencies whose primary function is to support and promote development themes, within which educational programmes may play a role. This chapter does not address the role of organisations whose sole focus is development education or global learning. The main organisations therefore referred to in this chapter are those that are part of international alliances of NGOs, such as Oxfam, Plan International, Save the Children and Christian-based development agencies.

As mentioned in Chapters 1 and 3, the agendas of NGOs with regard to development education are often blurred, running alongside activities that may have a campaigning, awareness-raising or even fundraising function. This blurring of roles clearly has implications as to how NGOs perceive the role of educational programmes; this lack of clarity is often given as a reason for the rather chequered history of development agencies' engagement with development education.

Although development NGOs, as Bond (2013) notes, have long been attempting to deepen the connections between their domestic constituents and the economic and social realities faced by citizens, communities and countries where they operate, there has been a lack of clarity amongst many of them as to what this has meant. If a trend can be identified it is that NGOs in the last decade or so have moved much more to a rights-based approach, which has enabled potential connections to themes such as global citizenship.

Underpinning this chapter are three themes that relate directly to the conceptual pedagogic framework outlined in this volume. They are:

- the nature of the global outlook promoted by the NGO and its relationship to notions of development and poverty;
- a distinctive values base particularly with regard to concepts of justice and equity;
- the perception of the role of education within the NGO, and how this perception relates to the broader goals of the organisation.

NGOs – global outlook, development and poverty

The primary function of most international development NGOs is to support communities in the Global South in reducing global poverty. The particular focus of this will vary, with some specialising in particular sectors, and some in specific countries or regions; for example with women, disability, or children; or with regions such as South Asia or sub-Saharan Africa. Some support their development work through advocacy and campaigning. A number in addition are involved in humanitarian relief in response to disasters and emergencies. To support their work, these NGOs rely on income from both the general public and governments and other donors, whether private sector or international agencies.

Common to these NGOs is a strong values base and a commitment to human rights and an end to global poverty. For example, British Overseas NGOs for Development (BOND), the umbrella body for development NGOs in the UK, states that its vision is a 'world of justice and equality, free from poverty, where human rights and the environment are respected'. To be members of BOND, NGOs have to sign a Charter that includes the following:

> We share a core belief that social and economic injustice drives global poverty and conflict, and that change must take place for peaceful sustainable development to happen. Women and men living in poverty have least voice, least power, least control over decisions affecting them, and least recourse to justice for the injustices, violence and discrimination they suffer.[1]

These themes are central to most NGOs. The relative importance of specific values will vary according to the focus and ethical basis of the organisation. For example those that have a strong faith base are more likely to promote themes related to social justice. Others who may have a more specialist development function are more likely to refer to access and contribution to development goals.

The changing role of development NGOs has also included a move within many of the larger agencies to 'engage their constituencies in "changing the world" through public action' (Rugendyke, 2007: 222). This sense of personal responsibility, often through social networking and new media, aims to provide information and encourage people to lobby for change by policy-makers.

NGOs and development education

Development NGOs have played a central role in the evolution and growth of development education in most industrialised countries. Their role has been the subject of numerous studies since the 1980s (Arnold, 1988; Osler, 1994; Harrison, 2008). As noted in Chapter 2, NGOs have dominated educational practice in Europe particularly (Rajacic et al., 2010). Criticisms of this practice have tended to focus on the emphasis on charitable approaches, fundraising, fasting and having fun (Bryan and Bracken, 2011), but as Tallon (2012) has noted, there are a range of approaches from a 'charitable or soft approach' to a more 'critical and hard edged' approach.

NGOs have also been criticised for being too concerned with promoting their own agenda within education, for promoting particular viewpoints, securing support for their actions and using young people as advocates for global change (Standish, 2012). These criticisms are not unique to development education. Gearon has made similar comments in relation to human rights and citizenship education and 'uncoordinated implanting of ideological bias by those who presume they know they are right' (Gearon, 2006: 17).

But NGOs could also be seen as part of promoting alternative views of changing the world to those of governments and policy-makers. For example, Marshall (2005) in her review of NGO practices noted the emphasis in their practice on being aligned to movements for global social justice.

Development NGOs have also been said to promote messages within school classrooms that are taken as the norm, as inherently true and correct, rather than as one perspective (Tallon, 2013). The use of the expert visiting speaker is one example of this. Another is the way in which NGOs have used educational systems to secure income and broader endorsement of their campaigns.

Before we review the nature of these NGO practices in development education, there are three areas that need to be considered that can help us reflect on their practice:

- how they perceive and promote development;
- the values base of the organisation and relevance to development education;
- their perceptions about individual engagement in development, particularly in relation to the links between awareness raising, learning, advocacy and change.

Concepts of development

Development NGOs have been the subject of considerable literature that questions the images they have presented to the public through their promotional, fundraising and advocacy material (Dogra, 2012). An example is the way in which an NGO informs and engages the public in the Global North about poverty in the Global South. Dogra has noted that despite attempts through fundraising and communication strategies, the dominant images presented and perceived by the public are ones of paternalism, doing good and helping others. She further notes that NGO messages overwhelmingly promote the Global South as rural communities, in a form that gives an image of timelessness and ahistoricity (Dogra, 2012: 69). Whilst NGOs have attempted to give greater consideration to appropriate images and messages that can engage the public, the pressure of brand identity, fundraising and stories that demonstrate the work of the organisation tends to dominate. This means that debates around the value of aid and development are rarely, if ever, referred to in the material produced by NGOs.

What NGOs can and do provide, however, is the opportunity for direct connection and dialogue with communities in the Global South. As Weber (2012) has noted with Save the Children, one of the leading international NGOs, this has been an important approach to their educational work. The NGO can provide spaces and opportunities for their partners in the Global South to outline the issues that concern them, above all giving space for the promotion of voices that are not always heard. Weber, in her study on the work of Save the Children in Canada and UK, states: 'through their educational programming, NGOs with their connections to people and organisations from the Global South, have been able to facilitate learning relationships between people living in different global contexts' (2011: 1).

For example, resources that NGOs produce are often based on examples of projects, interviews with people from the Global South and stories about change in communities as a result of people taking action themselves. But all too often these resources do not take a critical view of development or aid because it is in the interests of the organisation to promote positive stories about the value of their activities (Tallon, 2013; Bryan and Bracken, 2011). Even an NGO such as ActionAid, which has focused much more in recent years on seeking change in education around the world through initiatives such as 'Send My Friend to School', starts from an uncritical approach to the issue of access to schooling.

The evidence therefore suggests that whilst NGOs can and do provide valuable data, information and, in some cases, access to a range of voices, wider questions about what is meant by development and how global poverty is best tackled are rarely addressed.

Values – behaviour and change

As suggested earlier in this chapter, central to the visions of NGOs is a strong values base related to themes such as social justice and a more equitable world. Recent research in the UK reflecting on the strengths and weaknesses of the 2005 Make Poverty History campaign demonstrated that the message of 'justice not charity' went largely unheard (Darnton, 2006). This led to the publication in 2010 of an influential report by a consortium of organisations in the UK entitled *Finding Frames* that suggested that a stronger values-based approach could be a popular and successful way of engaging the public in development (Darnton and Kirk, 2011).

This values base has been central to the rationale for the engagement of many NGOs in development education. Worldvision, an organisation with a Christian ethos, refers to 'standing in solidarity (with the poor) in a common search for justice'. CAFOD, another Christian-based non-governmental development organisation, states that it works with partners across the world, to bring hope, compassion and solidarity to poor communities, standing side by side with them to end poverty and injustice. Christian Aid states its values as including fighting 'injustice and inequality with courage, hope and determination, challenging the structures and systems that prevent people from rising out of poverty'. Oxfam, on the other hand, emphasises the importance of 'empowering young people to be active global citizens, to understand the issues that affect their lives and take action to secure a more just and sustainable world'. UNICEF is guided in its educational work by the UN Convention on the Rights of the Child and 'strives to establish children's rights and enduring ethical principles and international standards of behaviour towards children'.

What all of these perspectives demonstrate is an assumption of a relationship between values and a desire to see change in the world. As Weber (2011) states, within NGO programmes there seems 'to be a core value, a kind of moral/ethical/value laden glue that bonds people together to challenge the injustices of the world' through their educational programmes. But she goes on to note that this approach poses two questions: if their educational programmes identify inequitable solutions, 'is one morally obliged to take action?' and if the answer is yes, 'what are the ethical positionings that underpin the type of programming or action taken?' (Weber, 2011: 17).

This assumed values base is therefore seen as central, not only to the motivation but also the approach many NGOs take towards their involvement in development education. This is why many of them in their educational work make an assumption of a causal linkage between learning, empowerment and social action. The role development agencies have therefore played has been to raise awareness with the assumption that this will lead to changes in behaviour, and result in engagement in activities based on support for the values of the NGO.

Thus, one comment often made about NGOs is that their engagement in education has been too heavily determined by campaigning or fundraising agendas (see Cameron and Fairbrass, 2004). For many NGOs, the logic of education work is based on raising their profile, and developing a long-term strong supporter base, using education as a means of securing support for their work.

What has not perhaps been discussed to any degree of detail is that an NGO's ethical and values base will be closely related to a blurring of these educational, fundraising and campaigning agendas. A theme and desire of many NGOs in their educational work is to secure behaviour change in their learners, to get them involved in their campaigns as a result of being more informed about the issues. But as earlier chapters in this volume have demonstrated, this approach can be in conflict with the pedagogical approaches implicit within development education practice (Krause, 2010: 130).

Responses to these tensions have tended to lead to an acceptance that there are two lenses through which these issues can be addressed. Asbrand and Scheunpflug (2006) refer to these as two discourses, one based on action theory grounded in a holistic view about the world where normative views such as tolerance and empathy are aimed for; and secondly a systems theory where the aim is to support the learners' development in terms of acquiring competencies for living in a world society.

An example of the tensions in this area can be seen if one looks at the FairTrade Foundation Award scheme in the UK. Fair trade has considerable public support in the UK and as a result it is not surprising that the Foundation, with support from other NGOs, has introduced a scheme for schools based on an awards process. Whilst fair trade may be an obvious development education theme within schools, there is a danger that simply promoting fair trade as a good thing or as the only answer to inequalities in global trade may offer too simplistic a solution (Asbrand, 2004). Vare and Scott (2008), echoing observations from Asbrand and Scheunpflug (2006), note that whilst there is one approach of promoting positive behaviour posed by experts, there also can be another approach that goes beyond what experts are saying, to look critically at the issues, different options and encouraging the learner to seek their own solution.

Weber, from her research with Save the Children in the UK and Canada, devised a potentially useful framework as a way of understanding these tensions and different positions within an organisation. She suggests, referring to the work of Askew and Carnell (1998), that the relationship between educational goals, values and the purpose of education could be seen in four different ways:

> liberatory (educating for social change emphasising the individual), social justice (educating for social change emphasising the collective), client-centred (educating to maintain status quo emphasising individual achievement), and functionalist (educating to maintain status quo through reinforcement of social and cultural norms).
>
> *(Askew and Carnell, 1998: 83–96, quoted in Weber, 2011)*

These were then located alongside Barnett and Weiss's four humanitarian ethical positionings: deontological (duty-based), consequential (the end justifies the means), virtue (the internal motivation, heroic journey), and situated (dialogical, long-term, contextualised) (Barnett and Weiss, 2008: 43–48).

Weber suggests that the way in which an NGO sees its engagement in development education reflects the role it seeks to play, whether in terms of promoting a specific narrative, or of dialogical collaboration. This means that an NGO's educational programme would be related to its global objective, which could be short-term and seeking solutions, with a likely emphasis on a behavioural model of learning. Alternatively the NGO could be more open-ended in its approach, without a clear result as a motivation for engagement. This latter approach is more likely to have a closer relationship with the social justice-based approach promoted in this volume (Weber, 2011).

Changing influences and roles: Save the Children and Plan International

In reviewing the activities of Save the Children's educational materials in Canada and the UK, Weber's research noted the changes in approach over a period of time in both countries (2011: 230–235).

Before 2005, she noticed, learning materials had a clear learning, dialogical and reflective focus. After then, the materials produced were much more related to the NGO's own development work. For example, she noted that resources for schools produced in response to the 2005 tsunami focused more on the stories of the work of humanitarian aid workers than on connections to curriculum subjects. She did note however that whilst there was a strong emphasis on the Save the Children brand, there was also evidence of critical thinking; for example students were asked to question and compare Canada's contribution to relief efforts with that of other areas in the world; and to question or compare Canada's media coverage of disasters with other areas of the world (ibid.: 187–192).

In 2007 in the UK, NGO educational materials moved towards encouraging children to take part in campaigns by sending messages to politicians. Other materials such as 'Welcome to My World, exploring the lives of children in Ethiopia, India, Peru and Vietnam' were distinctly branded, with frequent references in this case to Save the Children UK projects. Weber notes that:

> The UK children moved from being equal partners in inquiry 'with' children from poor communities around the world, to being learners 'about' children in poverty in order to support campaigns, fundraising, and possibly to have a future as humanitarian aid workers. The new short-term, didactic programming provided limited opportunity to engage in situated learning.
>
> *(ibid.: 178)*

Plan UK provides another example of changing approaches towards development education. Up to 2001, this NGO, part of the Plan International family of organisations, had made a small contribution to development education through production of some materials, but did not directly engage with schools. From 2001 to 2011, Plan UK became a major contributor to development education practice through a range of initiatives including school linking, resource production, and activities directly involving young people. Underpinning many of its activities was the promotion of participatory learning processes in which children and young people in the UK and the Global South engaged with each other to gain knowledge and understanding of the global issues that affect them and how their lives are interconnected (Bourn and Kybird, 2012).

In taking its work forward, Plan UK wanted to give a clearer focus for its development education, related to its Building Relationships work around 'child-centred development' and its belief in the value of direct human-to-human contact. This strategy would 'reduce feelings of alienation and powerlessness, and foster an experience of shared goals and aspirations' (Bourn and Kybird, 2012: 54). Plan's role was seen to be 'linking people together whose common goal is to enable children to reach their potential'. 'Linking people', it suggested, 'helps build an understanding and respect for different communities and cultures' (ibid.). This was seen as providing a distinctive role in what at that time was becoming a crowded marketplace.

The development education team in Plan wanted to position learning as more central to the strategy:

> development education is learning about the world around us; the issues and opportunities that affect people, the systems and structures that affect people's lives and the influence and impact we all have on the world. Development education is also an active learning experience; using that learning to make positive and informed change happen for ourselves and others.
>
> *(Plan UK, 2011: 2)*

Whilst this strategy still had a change element within it, the focus was much more on developing the skills and opportunities young people needed, to make change. There was above all a critical pedagogical approach being proposed: 'We want to help young people look more closely at diverse global situations, to understand, question and have ideas about how to get involved' (ibid.).

This evolution within Plan UK from a series of forms of engagement on development education to a coherent strategy, however, came to a full stop in 2011 when the organisation decided to close its development education department. It continued to engage in a number of projects with young people but these had a distinctly NGO promotional and advocacy focus. Whilst a number of reasons were given for the decision to close the department, including changing political climate and removal of funding from the UK government explicitly for development education, in practice the change in policy was a result of an NGO not being prepared to give its educational programme a distinctive and separate life of its own, one that put an open-ended approach to learning at its heart.

Conclusion

Development NGOs have played, and continue to play, an important role in development education. They have shaped the practice and the focus of much of the engagement in schools on development issues and themes. It can be argued that without their involvement and support for raising awareness and understanding of development issues in education, development education may never have emerged in some countries.

Their influence with the wider public in many industrialised countries is very important. They have on the whole a very positive brand identity, are listened to and respected. What they say is often taken as the 'real voice'. This has had consequences for education because, as Tallon (2013) has noted, educators and young people have felt it was not appropriate to question or criticise their (NGOs') positions because of being seen to be disrespectful.

Standish (2012) has been one of the most vocal critics of NGO engagement in development education and their narrow and campaign-focused approach. Whilst there may be some basis for his position with some organisations, it is all too easy to lump them all together: Oxfam's role in the UK, for example, is very different from that of an organisation like WorldVision.

Yet as the two examples given here from Save the Children and Plan International demonstrate, the independent role of education within an NGO has become increasingly difficult to secure. Having an educational programme that is rooted in an open-ended learning process that can incorporate critical thinking, reflection and dialogue, seems to be perceived as a luxury that can no longer be afforded or tolerated. Perhaps one of the few NGOs that does still approach its development education in this way is Oxfam, whose work in the UK does have a clear critical thinking perspective.

Oxfam's educational work is based on three principles:

> Learn: Exploring the issue, considering it from different viewpoints and trying to understand causes and consequences.
> Think: Considering critically what can be done about the issue, and relating this to values and worldviews and trying to understand the nature of power and action.
> Act: Thinking about and taking action on the issue as an active global citizen, both individually and collectively.[2]

But this approach is by no means the norm today. Whilst NGOs would typically have a distinctive values base and an emphasis on social justice, the purpose and role of education for many has become increasingly determined by the corporate needs of the organisation. They may all have a strong global outlook and would encourage learners to act in a globally socially responsible way, yet they tend not to promote learning that problematises notions of development and poverty. This is perhaps not surprising; their focus tends to be much more about promoting positive stories about their organisation, and most notably over the past decade, with a closer connection to the practices of the NGO.

Notes

1   www.bond.org.uk/about-us/charter
2   www.oxfam.org.uk/education/global-citizenship

References

Arnold, S. (1988) 'Constrained crusaders? British charities and development education', *Development Policy Review*, 6(Summer): 183–209.

Asbrand, B. (2004) 'Competencies to deal with complexity: Fair Trade as a learning possibility in global education', *The Development Education Journal*, 11: 1.

Asbrand, B. and Scheunpflug, A. (2006) 'Global education and education for sustainability', *Environmental Education Research*, 12(1): 33–46.

Askew, S. and Carnell, E. (1998) *Transforming Learning: Individual and Global Change*. London: Cassell.

Barnett, M. and Weiss, T.G. (2008) 'Humanitarianism: a brief history of the present', in M. Barnett and T.G. Weiss (eds) *Humanitarianism in Question: Politics, Power, Ethics*. Ithaca, NY: Cornell University Press, pp. 1–48.

Bond, G. (2013) 'The certainty of change: community engagement and global citizenship for international non-government organisations', in A. Wierenga and J.R. Guevera (eds) *Education for Global Citizenship: A Youth Led Approach to Learning Through Partnership*. Melbourne: Melbourne University Press, pp. 36–55.

Bourn, D. and Kybird, M. (2012) 'Plan UK and Development Education – the contribution of an international development organisation to learning and understanding about global and development issues', *International Journal of Development Education and Global Learning*, 4(2): 45–62.

Bryan, A. and Bracken, M. (2011) *Learning to Read the World? Teaching and Learning about Global Citizenship and International Development in Post-Primary Schools*. Dublin: Irish Aid.

Cameron, J. and Fairbrass, S. (2004) 'From development awareness to enabling effective support: the changing profile of development education in England', *Journal of International Development*, 16: 729–740.

Darnton, A. (2006) 'Mass action and mass education: Make Poverty History in 2005', *Development Education Journal*, 12(2): 3–5.

Darnton, A. and Kirk, M. (2011) *Finding Frames: New Ways to Engage the UK Public in Global Poverty*. London: BOND.

Dogra, N. (2012) *Representations of Global Poverty, Aid, Development and INGOs*. London: I.B. Taurus.

Gearon, L. (2006) 'NGDOs and education: some tentative considerations', *Reflecting Education*, 2(2), available online at http://reflectingeducation.net

Harrison, D. (2008) 'Oxfam and the rise of development education in England from 1959 to 1979', unpublished PhD thesis, Institute of Education, University of London.

Krause, J. (2010) *European Development Education Monitoring Report – Development Education Watch*. Brussels: European Multi-Stakeholder Forum.

Marshall, H. (2005) 'Developing the global gaze in citizenship education: exploring the perspectives of global education NGO workers in England', *International Journal of Citizenship and Teacher Education*, 1(2): 76–92.

Osler, A. (1994) *Development Education*. London: Cassell.

Plan UK (2011) 'Learning from innovative partnerships: exploring the Plan School Linking programme', unpublished report. London: Plan UK.

Rajacic, A., Surian, A., Fricke, H.-J., Krause, J. and Davis, P. (2010) *Study on the Experience and Actions of the Main European Actors Active in the Field of Development Education and Awareness Raising – Interim Report*. Brussels: European Commission.

Rugendyke, B. (2007) 'Making Poverty History', in B. Rugendyke (ed.) *NGOs as Advocates for Development in a Globalising World*. Abingdon: Routledge, pp. 223–234.

Standish, A. (2012) *The False Promise of Global Learning*. London: Continuum.

Tallon, R. (2012) 'Emotion and agency within NGO development education: what is at work and what is at stake in the classroom?', *International Journal of Development Education and Global Learning*, 4(2): 5–22.

Tallon, R. (2013) 'What do young people think of development?' unpublished PhD thesis, Victoria University of Wellington, New Zealand.

Vare, P. and Scott, W. (2008) 'Education for sustainable development: two sides and an edge', DEA Thinkpiece, available at www.tidec.org/Visuals/Bill%20Scott%20 Challenge/dea_thinkpiece_vare_scott.pdf

Weber, N. (2012) 'A comparative study of the shifting nature of international non-government organisation global education programming in Canada and the United Kingdom', unpublished PhD thesis, University of Toronto.

10

IMPACT AND EVALUATION

A major theme of this volume has been that despite its history, political support and excellent examples of practice, the status of development education has suffered from a lack of evidence to demonstrate its contribution to learning and education in general. This is particularly challenging for an approach to education that relies heavily on external funding, for which evidence of impact is an obvious require-ment. Reviews of funding programmes in development education have repeatedly shown this lack of evidence as a major obstacle to continued funding (Verulam Associates, 2009; Rajacic et al., 2010a, 2010b).

This chapter explores why this is the case, and suggests that in too many instances, the measuring of impact has been based on criteria not directly relevant to development education; and moreover that the focus has been on changing behaviour rather than deepening learning. This chapter suggests a more appropriate approach would be to learn from research, and to look at impact and evaluation within the framework of learning.

Whose agenda?

Development education has always suffered from trying to address two competing agendas in terms of impact: its contribution to development goals; and its contribution to education objectives. Most funders of development education are governments, international bodies and NGOs, whose interests are in development and aid and who see development education in terms of how it contributes to building support for development.

For example, in the UK, a review of funding and support for development awareness and education stated:

> We are confident that raising awareness of development issues in the UK has contributed to reducing poverty overseas. However, the evidence is

circumstantial and consequently we have been unable to prove conclusively
that this is the case. We can make the argument that it does, but there are
simply too many causal connections to be able to prove it.

Similarly we have been unable to prove that DFID-funded awareness raising
projects have made a direct contribution to reducing poverty. In part, this is
because DFID's historic approach to funding projects in this area has been
unstrategic, and individual projects have not been properly evaluated.

(COI, 2011: 4)

The relationship of development education to combatting global poverty
presents a major challenge; and whilst it is explored in this chapter, it will be
suggested that the focus of impact should be primarily in the context of learning
and educational outputs. As development education usually operates within educational arenas, would it not be more appropriate to frame any measurement of
impact in terms of its contribution to broader learning goals?

Impact is often seen in terms of numbers of publications sold, people attending
events, hits on websites, etc. You can get thousands, if not millions, of people to
be aware of development issues – for example through the Make Poverty History
campaign in 2005; but this is not necessarily development education, as this volume
has suggested. In the same way, people purchasing resources and attending events,
whilst giving you useful data, tells you very little about what people have learnt
and what they have done with that learning.

This theme was noted in a review of funding of development awareness projects
in the UK, in that 'some projects became overly concerned with reaching large
numbers of the target group and in achieving indicator targets. This resulted in a
shallow effect on the project participants, which probably resulted in low overall
impact' (Tripleline Consulting, 2013: 25).

Linked to the whole area of impact is evaluation, which is often used as the
mechanism employed by NGOs to measure impact and effectiveness. Evaluation
however can take many forms, formative and summative for example. It can also
be seen not only in terms of gathering and assessing evidence, but making judgements from the data gathered about impact. For example, development education
projects can be evaluated in technical terms, by the numbers of people attending
events or the number of resources sold, or even by analysing data about learning;
but it could also require judgements that take account of links to areas such as social
justice, equity and human rights.

In the field of development education, evaluation and impact studies have
also been drawn into identifying evidence of changes in behaviour as a result of
the learning and engagement. As this volume has suggested, this whole area is
problematic as it makes major assumptions about what people do with their
learning; but also it implies a particular approach that is behavioural and posi-
tivistic in nature, and takes no account of context and wider social and cultural
influences.

The trap that development education often falls into is that, because it has a strong political and ideological agenda, evaluation and sometimes even research can be related to justifying progress against pre-determined outcomes. An example is that a lot of development education practice is based around promoting different images of Africa from those portrayed in the media. This often gets reduced, in evaluating projects, to the extent to which the learner now has a positive as opposed to a negative image. But this approach does not address who decides what is positive and what is negative. Surely a more appropriate methodology would be to explore what the different perceptions were, and then assess what they were based on. It is all too easy for development education practice to be seen in terms of promoting right and wrong answers.

Development education: impact, evaluation and research

The challenges as to what constitutes impact and evaluation within development education have been recognised by policy-makers in a number of European countries and have become an increasingly popular topic of debate, research, conferences and publications (see Ongevalle et al., 2013; O'Loughlin and Wegimont, 2008).

In the UK from 1999 to 2002 there was a major project in this area funded by DFID and led by the DEA. Its main focus was on measuring effectiveness and it proposed a threefold framework based on three questions: why, what and how: 'Why is an organisation embarking on a development education programme; what is the programme trying to achieve; and how are they going to achieve their targets and goals' (McCollum and Bourn, 2001: 27).

Whilst this project perhaps put too much emphasis on trying to make connections to development agendas, it did at least pose the importance of educational goals:

> A development education programme does not, and in most cases will not, have as its main objective changing attitudes and understanding of global poverty and international development. This is likely to be much more specific, such as improving the capacity of teachers to deliver effective programmes, or giving educators the tools and resources to engage with development issues.
>
> *(ibid.)*

But perhaps most importantly, this project began to raise the bigger 'what' question of development education: what is the relationship between having the skills to deliver development education and increased learning and understanding?

Elsewhere in Europe, a range of initiatives looked at different approaches to evaluation which resulted in a number of case studies, examples of good practice and toolkits on how NGOs could more effectively undertake evaluation (see O'Loughlin, 2013). A summary and review of these initiatives by the Global Education Network Europe (GENE) identified the following:

- The importance of differentiating 'between the aims of an evaluation and the aims of the process that is being evaluated'.
- 'Not to measure the change of consciousness or attitudes, but to define aims around this and to make them operational in order to assess changes in knowledge and skills' (O'Loughlin and Wegimont, 2008: 29).

Asbrand and Lang-Wojtasik (2003) had in 2002 identified that it was 'difficult to identify a long-term change of attitudes by simple interviews or by observing learning'. They noted that:

> Learning as a complex process is not possible to be put down to a single reason. It means that one never can be sure that the results of global learning, like awareness of global issues, are only due to the impact of the evaluated program. There's no causal connection between intentions and the outcome.
>
> (quoting Luhmann/Schorr, 1999)

Asbrand and Lang-Wojtasik suggested instead that 'evaluation can reflect the concrete results of a measure. For example, has the target group been reached? How many people bought the educational material? Have the visitors been content with the seminar?' They further noted that most important of all it is impossible to measure the impact of global education. They suggest that:

> It is difficult to evaluate change of attitudes or awareness-raising. As the long term change of prejudices, of development awareness or attitudes towards world-wide justice and the possibility to influence world politics are very complex and linked to each other, the specific contribution of a given activity in Global Education can mostly not be identified.
>
> (ibid.)

Too often, they suggest, because of the influence of external funding, evaluation can all too easily become 'an instrument of control, pressure and power' and therefore not an open and transparent process (ibid.).

There have also been a number of international initiatives such as the GENE Peer Evaluation process (O'Loughlin, 2013), where international experts evaluate progress and trends in global education in a particular country; and ongoing working groups, conferences and seminars organised by NGOs (see O'Loughlin and Wegimont, 2008: 40–44).

One publication that took a broader focus was a briefing paper produced by Scheunpflug and McDonnell (2008) for OECD that looked at the relationships between information and communication, advocacy and development education, in terms of evaluation. It noted that development and global education had as its key focus 'learning', and this was not the focus of communications or advocacy strategies. This brought into wider debate the tension between the objectives of a funder, whose indicator of success may be 'increased public support for aid', and those of an educationalist, whose success indicator will be different: 'successful learning does not necessarily result in more public support . . . Success must be a learner who becomes more critical of the aid budget' (ibid.: 11).

One trend in a number of the publications and initiatives on evaluation has been to make connections between evaluation, impact and quality (DEEEP, 2013; IDEA, 2012). The European Development Education Forum, in promoting links between evaluation, impact and quality, produced a toolkit that included what they term an 'impact chain', which can be summarised as follows:

- Intention – what you planned to achieve or change
- Input – the resources available for the work
- Process – the activities carried out using the available resources
- Output – the physical products that the activities lead to
- Outcome – results of the work for your participants (i.e. change created amongst participants)
- Impact – the consequences of the work, what the participants do with the results and output and how beneficiaries benefit (DEEEP, 2013).

The whole area of impact, as suggested in this chapter, brings with it a lot of 'baggage' that goes beyond the learning and educational environment. Not only would it include the contribution to development, but also the organisational goals, overall efficiency and effectiveness. Bergmueller suggests that one way of looking at impact would be to see it in three ways:

- the widespread impact through a project or activity, e.g. the number of people reached, the number of materials distributed, the number and type of media coverage;
- the impact at institutional level, e.g. the strengthening of a field of activity or the extension of projects in development education within an NGO;
- the impact on the target groups; in this case, another distinction can be made between the effects on the level of satisfaction statements, self-mentioned/ reported learning and real learning effects (Bergmueller, 2009).

This framework has some value. It reflects a lot of the discussion on evaluation in development education that tends to focus on debates on impact within institutions or impact of a specific project in terms of funding objectives, rather than impact on pedagogical approaches.

A theme throughout this volume is that learning is complex. There is no simple linear process of teaching and learning. Changes in behaviour are not always logical, nor can they be directly related to learning from a specific activity or series of activities. The relationship between learning and attitudinal change is also very complex. People learn in different ways and the influences on an individual will vary, depending on their own capabilities, their social and cultural background and the quality of education being provided. But this does not mean that the impact of learning on changes in viewpoints, perceptions and follow-up action should not be investigated; rather that it requires clear focus and direction and an understanding of the processes of learning.

Bergmueller provides some valuable insights, and notes that learning has different dimensions:

- Knowledge
- Competencies concerning values and judgement
- Competencies/strategies concerning communication and action.

She suggests that any analysis of a specific activity or programme needs to consider to what extent it creates the necessary learning conditions for any intended changes in values and judgements to be probable (ibid.).

This means there is a need to contextualise the process of learning, compare it with other known data, and examine whether the conditions exist for change to take place within the learner. Evaluations in development education should therefore focus much more on the learning process and the results of that learning in terms of depth of understanding.

Moving from evaluation to research

If evaluation is usually deemed to be a 'systematic activity' that aims to collect data about the 'activities, characteristics and outcomes of programmes, to make judgements about the programme, improve programme effectiveness and/or inform decisions about future programming' (Patton, 2002: 23), then research, whilst also following systematic activity and working with the possible help of hypotheses, aims to arrive at generalised statements but does not aim to make judgements. Research above all aims to generate knowledge based on verifiable data.

However there has been a tendency to use the terms interchangeably. Whilst both are about asking questions, they pose different kinds of questions, have different purposes, and the evidence would normally be used in different ways. Wegimont notes a trend of a

> growing recognition of the need for a more solid research base for global and development education. It becomes clear that clarity of criteria and strengthened evaluation frameworks need to be based on a more solid research and theoretical framework than heretofore.
>
> (O'Loughlin and Wegimont, 2008: 49)

It is this move from a technical form of evaluation to an approach that is more research-based, open-ended and that explores evidence in the light of learning within the aims of development education that would be more beneficial to the organisation and to practitioners and researchers more widely.

Three very different examples from the UK are now taken as the basis for this research-based approach, one from an NGO which has devised a methodology for measuring changes in learning with pupils in a classroom; another a research-based dissertation looking at methods for evaluating the impact of a training course; and finally a summative evaluation of a European Union-funded project for NGOs.

How do we know it's working?

One example that has become very popular within the development education community in Europe has been that developed by a Development Education Centre in England, Reading International Solidarity Centre (RISC). Their *How Do We Know It's Working* programme was based on a rigorous research-based approach. It identified that assumptions were being made about attitudinal changes in pupils to learning about global and development issues; and that many pupils revealed a lack of awareness of the wider world and how they could make a difference, and stereotypical perceptions about children in the Global South.

RISC identified that learning about global and development issues may increase knowledge but not necessarily change attitudes. They defined this as 'increasing understanding of diversity, a more balanced view of people and places, and awareness of how we can make a difference' (Lowe, 2008: 60). A methodology was developed by the Centre that started from establishing what the pupils already knew and thought about a range of global issues. This baseline activity was undertaken with a range of classes and age groups (Allum et al., 2008).

The activities conducted in this initial audit included asking children 'what would you expect to find if you visited a country in Africa?' Many of the visual images that came out of these activities presented negative and stereotypical images of the continent (Charities Evaluation Service/Think Global, 2010).

Following discussion of the outcomes of the audit with the teachers, RISC provided a programme of professional development and support for a two-year period, after which a follow-up audit was undertaken with the same group of pupils and schools.

The outcomes of the second audit revealed in some cases evidence of progress and movement in pupils' understanding and perceptions, but this was not universal. For example, in two schools that were part of the pilot there was less evidence of attitudinal change. There were a number of reasons for this but what appears evident is that these schools had not embedded global themes across the school; rather, they were seen as bolt-on extras and not integral to the ethos of the school (Lowe, 2008: 64).

This project demonstrates a number of things. First, to measure impact and change requires a lot of preparation, time and space for effective gathering and measuring of data. Secondly, despite the best efforts of the NGO, no one can guarantee full engagement from partner schools or that the results will be what one is expecting or hoping. Thirdly, and perhaps most important of all, measuring development education approaches is likely to mean challenging dominant methods for reviewing evidence. For example, there may be no right or wrong answers or simple solutions, and the results may not always satisfy funders. But if there is an open and transparent process and the focus is on learning, then much more can be learnt and used in the future, rather than data which simply tells you that several thousand resources have been issued and that people enjoyed a training session.

Evaluating a training programme in development education

A good example of evaluating development education practice would be to measure the impact of a specific event or activity; one of the most common is training events. A development education training event, like any training event, should be evaluated in terms of whether it helped learners to learn. The challenge is therefore to identify whether learning has taken place, and whether that learning is relevant to the learners beyond the specific training session.

Alcock (2010), in her study of an evaluation of a training workshop with teachers, suggested that Kilpatrick's four levels of evaluation (Winfrey, 1999) could be a useful tool. Level one measures reactions that can be seen as to whether the participants 'liked the training or not. It is more likely, although not guaranteed, that some learning will have occurred if participants have a positive, as opposed to negative, reaction to training.' The second level of learning, Alcock notes, is the extent to which 'participants have developed their knowledge, skills and attitudes as a result of training . . . Within the session on global learning this could relate to how the teachers begin to understand how they can incorporate this dimension within their own practice.' The third level is that of transfer and whether the learning gained is used 'in their everyday environment'. Alcock suggests that this level of transfer 'could be observed through the actual lessons that the teachers are planning and delivering'. Finally at level four, which is seen as results, in terms of a training session on development education, evidence of its effectiveness could be 'in the form of an increase in levels of pupil understanding, effective dissemination of the training session to other teachers including senior managers, with the result of more sustainable change through changes to school ethos, and modifications to policy and longer term curriculum plans'.

Alcock's evaluation of a training session was based on a follow-up questionnaire to participants. She asked them to consider whether the course, based on the stated intended learning outcomes for the day, had helped them significantly, partially, or not at all, in respect of:

- understanding of what the global dimension in the curriculum means;
- practical teaching strategies for global learning;
- making connections between global learning and national curriculum/ educational policy initiatives;
- developing your ability to plan for global learning with your pupils;
- helping you to help others in planning for global learning;
- providing useful follow-up resources and references (ibid.: 69).

The results showed evidence of level one and two responses in terms of enjoying the course and increased learning for themselves. In terms of level three, transferring the learning gained to others, all of the participants gave practical examples of how they intended to do this. Finally in terms of level four, the participants were asked to reflect on the learning gained, and recommend improvements and changes to their experience. Responses included suggesting a learning needs analysis prior to the training. The evidence was that the training event was successful and valuable at all levels. The trainees learnt new skills to apply, they reflected on their understanding of issues, and recognised the importance of multiple perspectives (ibid.: 70–74).

Alcock's research showed that the training had impacted on teachers by providing examples of teaching methodologies that gave them an increased contextual understanding of the relevance of particular approaches and styles of teaching and learning, which they could then share with their colleagues.

This example shows that if there is a clear framework for measuring the impact of the learning related to development education, valuable evidence and data can be secured. Above all this approach demonstrates that if learning theory is applied to evaluation approaches, then a much more rigorous body of evidence will emerge.

Evaluation of a school linking project

School linking has become, as this volume has identified, an increasingly important feature of development education and global learning practice. In countries such as the UK and Ireland it has become well funded by national governments. Also a number of NGOs have seen linking as an area where they can make a distinctive contribution to development education through their own partnerships and activities in the Global South.

Edge has undertaken a number of evaluation studies on school linking (Edge et al., 2010; Edge et al., 2011) and from this work devised a framework for evaluating school linking.[1] This toolkit and her other publications provide an invaluable resource to assist researchers in evaluating school links. Key themes in this toolkit are the impact of links on the Global South, what is meant by high momentum partnerships, and how to initiate and support links.

A specific example of an evaluation of an international partnership that poses many of the issues addressed in this chapter regarding evaluation and development education is the Partners in Development project, which ran from 2009 to 2012 and was coordinated by an international NGO, Link Community Development.

Link Community Development is based in the UK but with offices in six other countries. Its development education programme has been primarily focused on promoting links between schools in the UK and Ireland and schools in sub-Saharan Africa. Part of its programme of activity in this area between 2009 and 2012 was a European Union-funded project. The project had to demonstrate its contribution to building awareness of development issues, mobilise greater public support for actions against poverty, and 'change attitudes to the issues and difficulties the developing countries and their people are facing' (Bourn and Cara, 2013).

A key tension in this project was that any linking project can only be evaluated in terms of impact in both the European and partner schools in sub-Saharan Africa. For example the project had as one of its aims, to 'improve the quality of education for an estimated 800,000 pupils in 750 linked African schools', because this was key to the NGO. However, as the evaluation by Bourn and Cara noted, the benefits to the European and African schools were very different. Having a common evaluation framework was therefore problematic in terms of evaluating the project.

Therefore whilst some common tools were used, such as interviews and questionnaires, to assess the impact of the link, the results were qualitatively different. Specific tools were used to measure the impact in the UK, including detailed case studies to look specifically at the process of learning.

The project had the aim of reaching 700 school partnerships, and because of the pressure to reach quantifiable targets, too little attention was paid to the nature of learning and understanding of development in the European schools. Although the project had hoped to promote a culture of mutual learning through linking, because of funding pressures it became determined by the goals of the European funder and the schools. This meant that perceptions of the lives of the partner schools' pupils and the dangers of reproducing colonial relationships, and sharing examples of mutual learning, were not fully addressed. As a consequence for the UK and Ireland schools, the learning gained varied according to the quality of the teaching and the support available from Link staff.

This does not mean that the project in itself was not valuable. There was some noticeable data identified from both European and African schools in terms of the skills and knowledge needed to engage with learning about global and development issues. For example, the impact of the project on schools in Africa was clearly much more on the skills pupils and teachers had gained, alongside access to resources; whereas in the UK and Ireland, the impact was more noticeable in terms of the knowledge the pupils and teachers had gained.

Conclusion

This chapter has shown that evaluation and impact are important but challenging for development education. They are also not the same thing. Evidence from a range of projects and reviews of funding initiatives suggests that too much emphasis has been placed on measuring impact against the aims of the funder, with a particular focus on the contribution to and support for development, and measurement of behavioural change.

Where measuring processes of learning are central, the results will be more valuable in terms of understanding of what has been learnt, but also in providing evidence of how practice can be improved. The three examples shown in this chapter demonstrate that if development education approaches are central to the evaluation process, then evidence related to increased learning and changes in perceptions and attitudes will emerge. However all too often evaluation is seen in terms of measurement against targets identified; and what these target groups have done with the learning. The process of learning itself is what needs to be at the heart of practices in evaluation and impact in development education.

Note

1   http://internationalschoolpartnerships.ioe.ac.uk/Research.html

References

Alcock, H.L. (2010) 'What is the impact of training and development within North-South educational partnerships?' unpublished MA dissertation, Institute of Education.

Allum, E., Lowe, B. and Robinson, L. (2008) *How Do You Know It's Working?* Reading: RISC.

Asbrand, B. and Lang-Wojtasik, G. (2003) 'Evaluation in global education: improving quality, assuring effectiveness', in *Global Education in Europe to 2015: Strategy, Policies and Perspectives*. Lisbon: North-South Centre of the Council of Europe. www.coe.int/t/dg4/nscentre/Resources/Publications/GE_Maastricht_Nov2002.pdf

Bergmueller, C. (2009) 'From evaluation to research in the continuum of global education' (presentation). www.nuigalway.ie/dern/conf_criticaldeved.html

Bourn, D. and Cara, O. (2013) *School Linking – What Next?* DERC Research Report no. 10. London: IOE/DERC.

Central Office of Information (COI) (2011) 'Review of using aid funds in the UK to promote awareness of global poverty', available at www.gov.uk/government/uploads/system/uploads/attachment_data/file/213991/rev-using-fnds-prom-aware-glob-pov.pdf

Charities Evaluation Service/Think Global (2010) *Evaluating Outcomes of Work to Promote Global Understanding*. London: Think Global.

DEEEP (2013) *A Journey to Quality Development Education: Starting Points that Help You to Be Clear about What You Do and Why You Do It*. Brussels: DEEEP/CONCORD.

Edge, K., Higham, R. and Frayman, K. (2010) *Evidence from Schools Involved in Connecting Classrooms Sub-Saharan Africa: A Study of Successful Partnerships*. London: Institute of Education and British Council.

Edge, K., Creese, B., Frew, E. and Descours, K. (2011) *Learning from Innovative Partnerships: Exploring the PLAN School Linking Programme – 3rd Year Report*. London: Institute of Education and Plan UK.

IDEA (2012) *Quality and Measuring Impact in Development Education*. Dublin: IDEA.

Lowe, B. (2008) 'Research Report: Embedding global citizenship education in primary and secondary schools', *International Journal of Development Education and Global Learning*, 1(1): 59–65.

McCollum, A. and Bourn, D. (2001) *Measuring Effectiveness in Development Education*. London: DEA.

O'Loughlin, E. and Wegimont, L. (ed.) (2008) *Quality in Global Education: An Overview of Evaluation Policy and Practice*. Amsterdam: GENE.

Ongevalle, J.V., Huyse, H. and Petergem, P.V. (2013) 'Learning about the effects of development education programmes: strengthening monitoring and evaluation through reflective practice', *International Journal of Development Education and Global Learning*, 5(2): 47–70.

Patton, M. (2002) *Qualitative Research and Evaluation Methods*, 3rd edn. London: Sage.

Rajacic, A., Surian, A., Fricke, H.-J., Krause, J. and Davis, P. (2010a) *Study on the Experience and Actions of the Main European Actors Active in the Field of Development Education and Awareness Raising – Interim Report*. Brussels: European Commission.

Rajacic, A., Surian, A., Fricke, H.-J., Krause, J. and Davis, P. (2010b) *DEAR in Europe – Recommendations for Future Interventions by the European Commission: Final Report of the Study on the Experience and Actions of the Main European Actors Active in the Field of Development Education and Awareness Raising*. Brussels: European Commission.

Scheunpflug, A. and McDonnell, I. (2008) *OECD Policy Brief No. 35, Building Public Awareness of Development: Communicators, Educators and Evaluation*. Paris: OECD Development Centre.

Tripleline Consulting (2013) *Development Awareness Fund Final Report, 2006–2013*. London: Tripleline for DFID.

Verulam Associates (2009) *Review of Building Support for Development*. London: DFID.

Winfrey, E.C. (1999) 'Kirkpatrick's four levels of evaluation', in B. Hoffman (ed.) *Encyclopaedia of Educational Technology*, available at www.4cleanair.org/Kirkpatrick.pdf (accessed 6 April 2014).

PART IV

Pedagogy for global learning

11

PUTTING LEARNING AT THE HEART OF DEVELOPMENT EDUCATION

This volume has summarised the history, key components and theoretical framework for development education. It has also outlined examples of practice through lenses of development, globalisation and the activities of international NGOs. This chapter aims to present other examples of good practice in development education that reflect the aspirations in this volume. Central to the examples of practice outlined are the role of learning, of critical thinking, and the promotion of different perspectives and voices with a social justice values base.

Development education in practice

Examples of development education practice can be found in most spheres of education. However, in most industrialised countries, the main focus has been in schools, or in areas that directly influence what happens in a school classroom such as the training of teachers or the professional development of NGO practitioners. Whilst examples of practice can be found in areas such as youth work, adult education, work with trade unions and higher education, the tendency in most of these areas has been to focus either on knowledge content or campaigning skills.

Chapter 3 of this volume summarised elements of development education practice in the classroom as follows:

- evidence of moving beyond a traditional view of seeing the Global South as being 'just about poor people who were helpless and needed aid and charity', that challenged assumptions and stereotypes, and located poverty within an understanding of the causes of inequality;
- giving space to stories and perspectives from people from the Global South;
- encouragement of taking forward the learning through further activity based on a sense of 'moral outrage';

- a sense of empowerment and global social responsibility;
- encouragement of participatory learning methodologies;
- enhancing the competences of the learner, enabling them to reflect on their sense of place in a globalised world.

Chapter 6 took these elements of practice forward into a new pedagogical framework based on the following concepts:

- A global outlook
- Recognition of power and inequality in the world
- Belief in social justice and equity
- Commitment to reflection, dialogue and transformation.

In recognising these elements and this pedagogical framework, good examples of development education practice should not only include the elements outlined above but also demonstrate within them processes of learning that recognise different starting points and experiences. Above all they should include questioning of assumptions, challenge to dominant modes of thinking, and options for further engagement and action.

The examples summarised below are therefore more about pedagogical approaches, methodologies and approaches to learning, than descriptive summaries of activity in a school classroom.

Open Space for Dialogue and Enquiry and Through Other Eyes

The work of Vanessa Andreotti has been referred to throughout this volume. An important feature of her work is that it has grown out of practice. Her two most influential initiatives have been web-based educational materials that offer tools to engage educators through a process of dialogue and learning about global and development themes. These are:

- Open Space for Dialogue and Enquiry Methodology (OSDE) (Andreotti, Barker and Newell-Jones, n.d.)
- Through Other Eyes (TOE).

Both resources focus on a series of processes of learning that can be adapted and used with a range of professional educators. The teams responsible for producing the materials, led by Vanessa Andreotti, came from the UK, Brazil, Canada, India, Peru, Singapore, New Zealand and Ireland.

OSDE is influenced by the thinking of Freire, critical literacy and post-colonialism. Its main focus is to create 'learning spaces where participants can engage critically with a range of global issues and perspectives' (Andreotti et al., n.d.: 3). The starting point for the material is to ask: what are the challenges in an interdependent, diverse and unequal world? The response proposed is to build the life skills to deal with the complex, uncertain and insecure world of today, with critical literacy and independent thinking at the heart, helping learners:

- to engage with complex local/global processes and diverse perspectives;
- to examine the origins and implications of their own and other people's assumptions;
- to negotiate change, to transform relationships, to think independently and to make responsible and conscious choices about their own lives and how they affect the lives of others;
- to live with and learn from difference and conflict, and to prevent conflict from escalating to aggression and violence;
- to establish ethical, responsible and caring relationships beyond their identity groups.

OSDE aims to offer safe spaces for dialogue and enquiry; thus an essential part of its approach is ensuring every individual's views are recognised and listened to. The approach also encourages critical engagement with different perspectives, and dialogic questioning, such as 'what do other people think?', and taking responsibility: 'what does it have to do with me?' What is distinctive about OSDE is its focus on knowledge about development and global themes. So, for example, one of the activities is looking at different notions of poverty, and questions for discussion include commenting on different assumptions and perspectives on development, what they are based on, and how the knowledge that informs them is constructed. Each of the activities ends with a debriefing based on what the learner has learned about themselves, about others, and about learning itself, as well as the topic under discussion.

This methodology and approach is popular and well used amongst development educationalists in the UK and elsewhere in Europe, and has also been picked up in Brazil in an English conversation course, examining how the construction of the open space for critical engagement with different perspectives in the world took place. This example noted that it is essential that participants and mediators be willing to engage critically with knowledges, in order for the collaborative construction of an open space to take place (Martins, 2011).

The 'Through Other Eyes' initiative takes a similar approach to OSDE but goes one step further by reflecting more on knowledge systems, and different lenses through which to look at notions such as development, equality, poverty and education, with a focus on an individual learning journey. The resource, particularly influenced by Andreotti's experience in New Zealand, looks at systems of meanings and representations from different indigenous and cultural groups.

This emphasis on culturalism is an important dimension to development education practice that is often assumed but rarely discussed. Building on the work of Bhana and Battiste, the TOE initiative calls for a third and fluid space where notions of cultural hierarchy, power and knowledge are re-negotiated (Andreotti and De Souza, 2008: 26). Influenced also by the work of Spivak, TOE poses a conceptual framework based on the following:

- Learning to unlearn – recognising that what one considers as neutral and objective is a perspective, and is socially, historically and culturally constructed.
- Learning to listen – recognising the effects and limitations of one's own perspective and being open to acquiring new conceptual models.
- Learning to learn – situating oneself alongside others, to compare and contrast different models of learning.
- Learning to reach out – applying the learning to one's own context and putting it into practice (ibid.).

Following a similar model to OSDE, TOE identifies themes on which the learner goes through a process of reflection, a learning journey, looking at different perspectives and reflections. Questions posed for discussion based on the material available include:

> Can you think of different perspectives on what development means?

> Should all countries be aiming for one (universal) ideal of development?

> What are the reasons for and implications of trying to impose one notion of development or progress as universal?
>
> *(ibid.: 8–9)*

Students on the Masters course in Development Education at the Institute of Education, University of London were asked, as one of their assignments, to comment on OSDE and TOE. Here are some of their observations:

> As a learner, I felt the benefits of being accompanied by OSDE principles throughout the TOE process. OSDE promotes appreciation and respect of each other. TOE draws on both reflection and reflexion and that dual learning process is very fulfilling.

> TOE brings a new kind of knowledge, a term from now on used 'as a verb, not a noun, as a process rather than as a product'.

> The main strength of TOE is its use of theory to inform practice. Each component of the course is linked to or influenced by a particular theory, with the intention to induce a reflexive response while dealing with complex issues.

> TOE enables the learner to see the limitations of their perceptions and 'makes them aware of how identities and stories are constructed and gives them the

opportunity to think about entering into dialogue with others in their local community who previously may have been marginalised by stereotypical attitudes'.

What these comments from students show is that both OSDE and TOE demonstrate effectively what good development education should be about: challenging, questioning assumptions, deepening learning, yet at the same time empowering the learner to move forward and take ownership of what they have learned.

What is also significant about both methodologies is the impact they have had around the world, as models of professional development, with a range of educational groups from Canada to the UK, New Zealand to Brazil and Ireland to Finland.

Global citizenship in practice – an example from Hong Kong

Amongst the main international NGOs, Oxfam has one of the best reputations for embedding development education principles in its practice. This is in part because of its long history and tradition of involvement in this work (see Harrison, 2008) but also because its focus has been much more on learning and empowerment than seeing education as a means towards a campaign objective. This can be seen in the practice in many countries around the world.

Common to development education practice in many countries is the concept of global citizenship, discussed in Chapter 2. An example of practice that blends NGO global themes with wider development education, yet is adapted to specific national conditions, is Oxfam Hong Kong's educational materials, notably its *Global Citizenship Education School Guide*.

This publication is in many ways typical of educational publications on a development education theme; but it also brings together in a clear and coherent form many of the themes outlined in this chapter, as an example of good practice. Oxfam Hong Kong's approach to Global Citizenship Education is 'to help young people to observe carefully, think critically, reflect conscientiously and act responsibly about local and global poverty issues'. Its approach emphasises 'interdependence' and aims to help the learner 'to gain the skills to discern, in everyday life, the linkages between the world, one's nation, one's community and oneself'. It further 'enables the learner to think critically and to respond proactively to issues of global poverty and injustice'. Finally the approach aims to promote learning through action that 'emphasises participatory and empowering processes' (Oxfam Hong Kong, 2012: 2).

The Guide outlines the objectives and content of its programme with schools, which focuses on three teaching elements: belief and willingness; understanding; and ability. These three could perhaps be seen as specific examples of values, knowledge and skills, in that order. The content is then located within a range of learning concepts such as poverty, interdependence, diversity, peace and conflict, justice, sustainable development, rights.

Whilst the concepts and methodologies are similar to Oxfam's global citizenship materials in other countries (Oxfam, 2006), what the Hong Kong Guide demonstrates is the necessity of adapting to specific national and cultural contexts. For example the 'teaching elements' section makes reference to 'being humble' and to 'be thankful' alongside empathy and social justice, reflecting specific Chinese cultural traditions.

Good quality materials should be based on evidence, should include engagement with teachers, and emerge from the practice of teachers. This Guide makes reference to research on youth participation and civic engagement and to a focus group with teachers on the theme of visualising a future world. What is significant is that in response to the research, Oxfam Hong Kong identified the value of Global Citizenship Education; and provided opportunities to develop 'alternative knowledges', and from this, to be able to respond to 'challenges of today and tomorrow' (Oxfam Hong Kong, 2012: 8).

The Guide is also prepared to tackle difficult questions such as: 'Why global, when young people have enough local problems to deal with?' 'There is no space in the curriculum for such areas!' 'Doesn't the NGO have a fundraising agenda?' and 'Aren't global issues too difficult for children to understand?'

As suggested in the previous chapter, NGOs can often rightly be accused of simply promoting their own viewpoints and perspectives, and seeing activities in schools as a vehicle for promoting their own campaigns and securing positive support for their activities. What is noticeable is that nowhere in this Guide are activities based around Oxfam campaigns. The focus of the activities is on the professional development of teachers through the development of skills, increased knowledge and a social justice basis which they can apply to classroom environments. Examples of activities include:

- looking at the world thirty years from now in terms of implications for curriculum planning;
- pooling and sharing ideas on what students need in terms of knowledge, skills and values;
- supporting teachers in a school to reach consensus on the objectives and values of Global Citizenship Education;
- identifying how to evaluate students' learning.

The Guide concludes with some specific examples of practice and comments from teachers, with lists of further resources.

A feature of this resource is that it values the contribution of teachers to the development of resources and curriculum materials. This approach is central to the way of working of the NGO and the team behind this resource. One member of the team responsible for this publication, for example, noted in her research on 'global teachers in Hong Kong' the importance of 'creating a participatory learning community for global teachers' (Lee, 2012: 85).

This example demonstrates that NGOs can and do produce educational materials that are not about them as an organisation, but that make a contribution from a civil society body of a type that would perhaps not emerge from mainstream public education sources. Secondly, it demonstrates a pedagogical approach based on learning, questioning, critical thinking and opening up the minds of the learners. Finally, it builds on current educational practice and is produced in a format that is user-friendly and adaptable to specific needs.

The Global School – Sweden

A challenge for development education practice in many industrialised countries has been that despite the best endeavours of NGOs and the support of foreign aid ministries, it has remained on the 'margins' of mainstream educational practice. Activities have been perceived as an 'add on' to an already overcrowded curriculum.

Sweden is one of the countries which has consciously tried to mainstream global themes. It is well known for integrating global and sustainability themes within the life of its schools, and all teachers have the opportunity for professional development in education for sustainable development. This is the framework within which global and development themes are promoted in Sweden.

This initiative is called 'The Global School' and is coordinated by the International Programme Office for Education and Training (IPO), with support from the Ministry of Education and the Swedish International Development Cooperation Agency. The programme is coordinated by a staff of ten, eight of whom are regionally based advisers who are also practising teachers (Nordahl, 2013: 118). Although the programme was introduced in 2001 it is only since 2007 that it has been coordinated by the IPO (Knutsson, 2011).

The overall objective of The Global School has been to:

> stimulate school improvement and support the pedagogical development work on learning about global issues for sustainable development. The goal is that, by the end of their studies, pupils will have developed knowledge and attitudes that will enable them to consciously adopt a position on global issues for sustainable development and to actively participate in the work of achieving a sustainable society.
>
> *(P. Sandahl, 2008, quoted in Knutsson, 2011: 207)*

The focus of the programme is on professional development seminars for practising teachers. The themes of these seminars are based on current or popular topics, responding to needs and demands from teachers as well as identified national priorities. NGOs are involved in supporting these seminars and providing back-up resources for teachers.

Partnerships with local authorities are also important to ensure the effective delivery of the programme. An example of this can be seen in a series of seminars held in the city of Haparanda where the local authority worked closely with The Global School programme to tailor a series of seminars specifically for all teachers in the area's school district. The seminars included a combination of lectures and practical workshops on how to apply sustainable development methods within a classroom.

Another feature of The Global School programme is the opportunity for teachers from clusters of schools to visit partner countries in Sweden's international development cooperation activities. These visits enable teachers to see firsthand examples of projects in practice. All teachers involved in these visits have to prepare a strategy with follow-up activities which they will use in their classrooms as a result of their experience (ibid.: 121).

There have been mixed views about the value of such personal experience visits, as noted in Chapter 6, echoing other literature and evidence that all too often such activities do not necessarily increase understanding of development and can reinforce existing views. One teacher commented that it was like a form of 'tourism' (ibid.: 208).

However if one looks at the broader picture of this programme, its importance is much more at the level of providing opportunities and spaces for curriculum development. Knutsson, in commenting on global education practices in Sweden, identified five approaches including those that reproduced dominant colonial and charitable mentalities as well as those fostering radical solidarity, critical reflexivity and transdisciplinary academic thinking (ibid.: 256).

It is this range of responses that makes The Global School programme so important: it is an example of engaging schools at their starting point, and helping them on an educational journey. Where the programme has perhaps faced greater problems is in framing it within education for sustainable development. Whilst this has had clear advantages, as it is a prominent theme in Swedish education, it is a concept that can be perceived as being vague. As Lund states, there is a danger that 'anyone can call almost anything sustainable development, thereby reaching a meaningless consensus from which no actual change will come'. She also notes that the use of such a concept could become 'overly moralising or dogmatic' (Lund, 2012).

The challenge for the organisers of this programme is therefore to ensure that an open, critically reflective and pedagogical approach remains dominant. As Lund states: 'An important part of the work of The Global School is to ensure that teachers have access to professional development of a high standard that takes account of potentially conflicting views about sustainability challenges and their solutions' (Lund, 2012).

Just Children – global citizenship education for 3 to 6 year olds – Ireland

Themes such as global poverty, social justice and global citizenship could be argued to be appropriate only for approaches to learning with upper primary or secondary school children. This assumption that childhood is framed within dominant and universalised truths has been recently challenged by postmodernist and post-structuralist theories (Kelly and Brooks, 2009).

It is within this context that Oberman, Waldron and Dillon conducted a major programme entitled Just Children, within a global citizenship education context for 3 to 6 year olds in Ireland (Oberman et al., 2012). This programme was a partnership between a development NGO, Trocaire, and the Centre for Human Rights and Citizenship Education at St Patrick's College, Drumcondra, Dublin.

The approach the team took for their programme was framed within a lens of education for global justice, moving beyond notions of fairness to approaches that look at inequality.

The programme was developed through an extensive research process that had three phases:

- exploring young children's engagement with issues of global justice;
- exploring strategies for introducing early childhood global citizenship education;
- piloting the draft programme.

The outcome of the programme was the publication of a Just Children Story Sack containing a teacher's handbook, storybooks, photographs, hand puppets, a CD and posters.

There are four elements to the modular programme for teachers:

- Near and Far, which uses a poem to travel from Ireland to Kenya with puppets and props;
- Another Perspective, which looks at life in Kenya through stories of children;
- Living with Poverty, which looks at how food is produced and daily life;
- Exploring Fairness and Interdependence, which discusses fairness and responses to justice scenarios (Oberman et al., 2012: 60).

This programme demonstrates the value of research and engagement with teachers testing out ideas, building up a picture of what works and why. The finding from the first phase of the research was that young children's understanding of poverty and justice was emerging: for younger children there was a 'conceptual understanding of people not having enough', with the older children showing a tendency to use terms such as 'poor' and 'rich'. Another finding was that any previous experience on the part of children was an 'important factor in their engagement with ideas of poverty and need' (ibid.: 44). The research also showed that children were able to empathise with others who were in need. But it also found evidence that even at a young age media influences on perspectives of poverty in Africa were evident.

The second phase of the programme was to test out the storybooks and reflect on the experiences of teachers as to the extent to which the children engaged with global justice themes. The research identified a range of responses from teachers. One example was the tendency for some teachers to take the easy option. For example, rather than exploring what justice meant, teachers focused on making pancakes because this was one of the activities in the story. What also emerged however was the issue of fairness: but there was a danger of this leading to re-affirming a deficit model of development (ibid.: 47).

The third phase asked the participating teachers and schools to test out the materials and report on their experiences. What emerged was the value of developing materials that enabled children to make connections with their own personal experiences. There was also evidence of 'emotional connection between the children and the characters in the storybooks'. The materials also addressed a deficit model of poverty through an approach that showed the similarities of daily life in Kenya to that in Ireland.

An observation on the programme by Oberman et al. was that by using stories and puppets it was more possible to promote alternative perspectives, because of the participatory methods being employed. Above all, what the research showed was that 'connecting young children emotionally, geographically and intellectually with people and places in developing countries supports a more critical, complex and engaged approach to global learning' (ibid.: 51).

This research highlighted the 'importance of providing open-ended challenges for children'. Oberman et al. noted that rather than posing fairness against unfairness, the value lay in children working through 'justice-related scenarios where the resolutions are multiple' (ibid.: 52).

The Just Children programme demonstrates three important themes that are relevant to the discourses on development education raised in this volume:

- the importance of grounding practice in research and evidence, relevant to contemporary educational needs;
- concepts of social justice are challenging and require support and professional development for teachers to implement;
- the value of encouraging learning that promotes different perspectives and openings for children to explore the relationship of their own life experiences to those they are learning about.

Poverty and Development – empowerment for a better life – Japan

Japan has a strong tradition of engagement in development education through NGOs, universities and the umbrella network association, Development Education Association and Resource Centre (DEAR). An example of its practice that reinforces an emphasis on pedagogical approaches and deepening knowledge and understanding from a range of perspectives, can be seen in 'Poverty and Development' (2005). This is a study kit for teachers produced jointly by DEAR and the Education for Sustainable Development Research Centre (ESDRC) at Rikkyo University.

The aim of the study kit is to promote understanding of poverty and development from 'comprehensive and multilateral perspectives'. It aims to address and challenge dominant assumptions about poverty and development and to suggest that 'poverty' is not a Southern problem but a global question that needs to be understood from different standpoints.

The study kit includes activities that can be undertaken with 14–18 year olds but may well be more appropriate for use in professional development workshops for teachers. The activities include sessions on 'what is poverty?' and two sessions on life in Bangladesh, including one addressing comparisons with Japan. Photographs are used to question and challenge assumptions about who are rich and who are poor, and in which countries. A feature of the study kit is a play on life in Bangladesh including a script that can be performed. The value of such a script is that it gives the learner the opportunity to become immersed in a particular family lifestyle. The activity ends with a debrief and discussion of the play.

Development education has often been criticised for lack of attention to knowledge and content (Marshall, 2005). It is therefore noticeable that this study kit includes material for discussion on what constitutes development, processes of learning about poverty and development, and relating this to principles of development education. The kit does not restrict itself to knowledge: it relates understanding to empowerment, 'facing and addressing power and inequality in the world'. The influence of the work of Amartya Sen can be seen here, particularly through his work on rights and empowerment. For example, the kit talks about empowerment in three stages: Knowing (What is the problem?), Thinking (What should be done?), and Action (What can be done?) (DEAR and ESDRC, 2005: 53).

Whilst study kits like this can be found in many industrialised countries, what makes this publication important and distinctive is the connection it makes between theory and practice, promoting different perspectives but also having a clear pedagogical framework.

Reflections on the examples

All these examples taken from formal education settings show that engagement in global and development themes can benefit from some form of external support and involvement. Such support can encourage teachers and learners to think 'out of the box' and secure evidence of how best to promote development education learning. They all show evidence of the need to deepen understanding of different viewpoints on development and poverty, including where these viewpoints come from and what they are based on. The role of these external organisations has been to work in partnership with the educational group, and to jointly identify ways of working.

For development education practice to 'move from the margins to the mainstream' it needs to secure the engagement and ownership of the deliverers of education. In the case of formal education, this means that teachers need to play a major role in curriculum making and not just be recipients of resources to deliver in an uncritical manner in the classroom. The educational programme also needs to be relevant, and tailored to the needs of the specific national situation.

The examples given here also promote participatory methods and approaches that build on learners' experiences and encourage a sense of global interdependence. What makes the examples distinctive is the recognition of critical pedagogical approaches, with a focus on social justice, in a form that encourages reflection, dialogue and transformation.

This chapter has identified, through examples in Ireland, Hong Kong, Sweden, Japan and the UK, that development education practice can have an influence within formal education if it engages the practitioners in the development of the materials. This practice, if it is based on evidence gained from research, tested and piloted and carefully managed and supported, can be successful.

The next chapter will apply these elements of good practice in the new pedagogical framework for development education.

References

Andreotti, V. and De Souza, L.M. (2008) *Through Other Eyes*. Derby: Global Education Derby.

Andreotti, V., Barker, L. and Newell-Jones, K. (n.d.) *Open Space for Dialogue and Enquiry Methodology – Critical Literacy in a Global Citizenship Education – Professional Development Resource Pack*. Nottingham: Centre for Study of Social and Global Justice and Global Education Derby.

Development Education Association and Resource Centre (DEAR) and Education for Sustainable Development Research Centre, Rikkyo University (ESDRC) (2005) *Poverty and Development*. Tokyo: DEAR.

Harrison, D. (2008) 'Oxfam and the rise of development education in England from 1959 to 1979', unpublished PhD thesis, Institute of Education, University of London.

Kelly, D.M. and Brooks, M. (2009) 'How young is too young? Exploring beginning teachers' assumptions about young children and teaching for social justice', *Equity and Excellence in Education*, 42(2): 202–216.

Knutsson, B. (2011) *Curriculum in the Era of Global Development, Gothenburg Studies in Educational Sciences, 315*. Gothenburg: Gothenburg University.

Lee, K.M. (2012) 'What creates active global citizenship in teachers? Exploring the life journeys of five global teachers in Hong Kong', unpublished MA dissertation, Institute of Education, University of London.

Lund, J. (2012) 'The Global School', *Learning Teaching Magazine*, pp. 4–5, available at www.learningteacher.eu/sites/learningteacher.eu/files/flipbook/389/Web/index.html

Marshall, H. (2005) 'Developing the global gaze in citizenship education', *Citized, International Journal of Citizenship and Teacher Education*, 1(2): 76–92.

Martins, L. (2011) 'Open spaces: an investigation on the OSDE methodology in an advanced English conversation course in Brazil', *Critical Literacy: Theories & Practices*, 5(2): 68–78.

Nordahl, L. (2013) 'The Global School', in N. Forghani-Arani, E.H. O'Loughlin and L. Wegimont (eds) *Global Education in Europe – Policy Practice and Theoretical Challenges*. Munster: Waxmann, pp. 119–122.

Oberman, R., Waldron, F. and Dillon, S. (2012) 'Developing a global citizenship education programme for three to six year olds', *International Journal of Development Education and Global Learning*, 4(1): 37–60.

Oxfam (2006) *A Curriculum for Global Citizenship*. Oxford: Oxfam.

Oxfam Hong Kong (2012) *Global Citizenship Education School Guide*. Hong Kong: Oxfam.

12

A PEDAGOGY FOR GLOBAL LEARNING

The importance of pedagogy

This volume has shown that development education and its various interpretations such as global education, global learning, global citizenship and global perspectives have been part of the landscape of educational practice in many industrialised countries for many years.

The main theme of this volume has been a consideration of the importance of pedagogy: of moving beyond seeing learning about development and global themes as the mere imparting of knowledge, development of specific skills or even promotion of a particular value base. It means going beyond seeing pedagogy, as policy-makers have stated, as being about the methods of teaching (see Ferretti, 2013). This volume has suggested that pedagogy needs to include not only subject and curriculum knowledge, teaching skills, and styles of learning, but also reviews and reflections on issues and their relevance within the classroom, including wider social and cultural factors. Central to the approach taken towards pedagogy in this volume has been the thinking of Henry Giroux and his concept of 'critical pedagogy'. He suggests:

> Critical pedagogy is not about an a priori method that simply can be applied regardless of context. It is . . . always related to the specificity of particular contexts, students, communities and available resources. It draws attention to the ways in which knowledge, power, desire, and experience are produced under specific base conditions of learning and illuminates the role that pedagogy plays as part of a struggle over assigned meanings, modes of expression and directions of desire . . .

> *(Giroux, 2011: 4)*

A constant theme throughout this volume has been that development education should be seen as a process of learning; and that from a critical pedagogical perspective this means recognising that learners and educators come to this area of practice from a wide range of personal experiences and starting points. It also means that learners interpret and engage in debates on development that make reference to their personal experiences and wider social and cultural influences.

Alexander refers to pedagogy as involving 'what one needs to know and the skills one needs to command, in order to make and justify the many different kinds of decisions of which teaching is constituted' (2004: 11). Whilst he further notes that this pedagogy needs to take account of culture, self and identity, there is a danger that this interpretation could lead to a lack of recognition of the influence of power and a critical understanding of the world.

A pedagogy of development education is therefore seen as a process of learning within which learners will interpret and engage in debates on development and make reference to their personal experiences, wider social and cultural influences, and their viewpoints on the wider world.

Illeris refers to processes of learning in terms of three dimensions: 'content, incentive and interaction' (2007: 29). The content dimension includes knowledge, understanding and skills. The incentive dimension includes 'motivation, emotion and volition'. The interaction dimension includes 'action, communication and co-operation' (ibid.). These dimensions are reflected throughout the pedagogy, recognising the interaction of these areas and the impact they have on a learner's own process of personal and social development.

With reference to development education, this process of learning may come about from exposure to different approaches, personal experience, further learning and study. Development education is proposed here therefore as an approach to learning that:

- is framed within an understanding of development and global themes;
- is located within a values base of social justice;
- promotes critical and reflective thinking;
- encourages the learner to make connections between their own life and those of others throughout the world;
- provides opportunities for the learner to have positive and active engagements in society that contribute to their own perspective of what a better world could look like.

This means that, whilst recognising the importance of increasing knowledge of developing countries and of elements of globalisation within schools, it is how this knowledge is presented, perceived, interpreted and promoted that makes it a pedagogy of development education. It means recognising learners' engagement with this knowledge and encouraging them in constructing their own interpretations. Learners will have different starting points and will be influenced by a range of external factors. For the learning to have lasting impact, links need to be made to the learners' own sense of place and identity in the world.

Global learning as the application of this pedagogy

The term Global Learning, as has been outlined in this volume, has gained increased currency as a way of communicating in a user-friendly way what development education can mean in practice. It is suggested therefore that this term, seen as the application of this pedagogy of development education, could be an appropriate approach to secure wider engagement in the discourses around this area. In promoting the term global learning, this should be seen specifically in relationship to formal education and schools; other terms such as global youth work, or global perspectives, may well be more appropriate for taking forward development education in other sectors of education.

Themes underpinning a global learning approach within a pedagogy of development education could be:

- deepening an understanding of different viewpoints and perspectives on development and global poverty;
- encouraging a critical reflection on teachers' and pupils' own perceptions of development, aid and poverty;
- promoting an emphasis on learning that contextualises development and poverty themes within historical, cultural and social traditions and frameworks of social justice.

The emphasis of these particular themes in different subjects (and with pupils of different ages) would clearly vary considerably.

If global learning is to be built around a pedagogy of development education, its practice needs to reflect the different starting points of the learner and be located within a process of learning that 'opens up minds' to see a broader global vision, to deepen knowledge and understanding, to encourage critical thinking and reflection, and encourage dialogue around a values base of social justice and challenging inequality.

The learning process therefore needs to address the following:

- how the term development is perceived;
- the Millennium Development Goals and what they mean in practical terms;
- why there are inequalities in the world;
- how the different lifestyles people have around the world relate to perceptions of wealth and poverty; and what is perceived to be a 'good life';
- the links between global issues and our own lives;
- the impact of globalisation on areas such as personal and political identity, migration and movements of people; and the particular impact on poorer countries and peoples.

These areas relate to deepening knowledge, and need to be approached through a process of learning that also encourages a range of skills. These include:

- ability to communicate and participate in discussions on development themes and topics;
- ability to question viewpoints and perspectives and to challenge stereotypes;
- ability to listen to, understand and respect different voices and perspectives;
- ability to be self-reflective and self-critical, and willing to change views and perspectives;
- ability to co-operate and work with others;
- ability to deal with the emotional impact of poverty and development on the lives of individual learners;
- skills that enable learners to take forward their learning into informed action.

Finally, learning about development and global themes inevitably brings with it a values base. To ensure there is continual reflection and dialogue in addressing learning about development themes, there is a need to recognise or include the following:

- the value of exploring one's own values and their wider social relevance;
- consideration of the values of others and the impact on one's own values;
- the relevance of themes such as rights, equality, and social justice to learning and understanding about development;
- the need to respect and value diversity.

Putting global learning into practice within schools

In many schools there are examples of learning about development issues or some activity or project about global issues. What would first distinguish such activity as having an overt 'global learning' approach would be the extent to which it went beyond a traditional view of seeing the Global South as 'just about poor people' who were helpless and in need of aid and charity. This would mean, for example, including in Geography or History lessons examples of the similarities and differences in people's lives, showing the efforts people make to get themselves out of poverty.

Learning about development issues and themes directly located within a curriculum subject can encourage deepening of understanding, and increased knowledge about the causes of poverty and inequality. This increased knowledge and understanding can be taken a step further if poverty and development themes are located within a historical, economic and political context.

Global learning practice can provide opportunities for giving space to stories and perspectives from peoples from the Global South that demonstrate the impact of inequality on their lives and how this relates to wider social, economic and political forces.

For global learning to be effective there needs to be recognition that for many schools and teachers, their engagement with development themes comes from a wide range of influences and experiences. The initial engagement with development education for some schools might derive from a history of working with a specific international development organisation. The school might also have a strong link with a partner school elsewhere in the world. There may also be children and teachers in the school whose families and cultural heritages are from a large number of different countries around the world, with staff working to celebrate and promote this diversity. Fundraising activities might be seen as a particular focus for a school.

A global learning approach would recognise these starting points and look for ways to move forward from them, addressing the values base from which the learner views a particular country or community, for example whether as a 'helpless victim' or 'agent for change'.

Learning about themes such as poverty and inequality poses challenges to the learner about their own viewpoints, sense of place in the world and how they should respond.

A common feature of development education organisations' materials is the use of visual images as a way of encouraging questioning of perceptions of poverty and inequality. Photographs that show images of life that challenge dominant assumptions are particularly popular. This approach necessitates critical thinking, questioning of views and re-thinking them.

Dialogue and engagement could question and challenge assumptions in the learner about how they see their relationship to the wider world. An important component of global learning practice therefore has to be how to take learners forward, to show them options and alternatives for change, whether in combating global poverty or taking action on climate change. This is where the discussion on 'transformative learning' comes into play, although the relevance of this concept may be more at the educator level than with children and young people.

Professional development initiatives may have a number of starting points for implementing global learning. For example, development is discussed as more than economic growth or progress, 'doing good' and 'aid to rescue'; it would include looking at the structural causes of inequality and poverty around the world. Also more than one perspective on development would be promoted; and use of materials from NGOs would be considered in a critical fashion.

Topics and issues would be looked at through different lenses as part of this practice. This could include how images of other countries are presented; challenging assumptions about 'how poor people live'; and looking at the causes of inequality, exploring questions such as who has power, who is voiceless and who benefits. Visual images play an important role here: images are powerful tools in global learning but they can reinforce stereotypes that portray simplistic messages, the typical 'good and bad'.

Development and global themes can often be seen as remote and not directly relevant to the learner. A challenging and important component of good global learning is to identify and demonstrate relevance and connection, to show that living in a global society means living in an interdependent and interconnected world. This means understanding the starting points, experiences and influences on the views and thinking of the learner.

The process of learning thus needs to be carefully handled. All too often emotional approaches can dominate. There is evidence (Tallon, 2012) of the influence of emotions and feelings as motivators for engagement in development education. But this emotional approach can all too easily be manipulated. A key challenge for teachers and educators is to ensure that feelings and emotions are connected to knowledge and skills, and lead to reflection and debate. In summary, engagement in development and poverty needs to be more than an emotional reaction.

Learning about development and global issues can be morally challenging, leading to questioning the assumptions pupils may have. Teachers need to be sensitive in how topics are introduced and discussed in the classroom, so that engaging with these moral questions supports young people's values development.

Learning about themes such as global poverty may lead to a number of pupils wishing to take the knowledge and understanding they have gained further. The teacher therefore has an important role in promoting skills that enable pupils to engage critically, as well as actively, with the various ways of responding to development and global issues.

Engaging with these debates requires time and space for the teacher to reflect on this pedagogy of development education, in order to put global learning successfully into practice. It means above all locating what might be a personal passion or enthusiasm for global themes into a learning context; and recognising that fellow educators as well as pupils are likely to have a range of experiences, views and perceptions that will influence their outlook.

References

Alexander, R. (2004) 'Still no pedagogy? Principle, pragmatism and compliance in primary education', *Cambridge Journal of Education*, 34(1): 7–33.

Ferretti, J. (2013) 'Whatever happened to the enquiry approach in geography?', in D. Lambert and M. Jones (eds) *Debates in Geography Education*. Abingdon: Routledge, pp. 103–115.

Giroux, H. (2011) *On Critical Pedagogy*. New York: Continuum.

Illeris, K. (2007) *How We Learn*. London: Routledge.

Tallon, R. (2012) 'Emotion and agency within NGO development education: what is at work and what is at stake in the classroom?' *International Journal of Development Education and Global Learning*, 4(2): 5–22.

13

CONCLUSION

In the introduction to this volume, I outlined my personal journey to development education and the rationale for the themes addressed in this volume. I still prefer to use the term development education to summarise the pedagogy outlined here, as this is still the dominant term, at least in Europe, to identify organisations and approaches that promote a pedagogy for global social justice. I do however recognise that in applying the pedagogy in education, other terms such as global learning may well be more appropriate in engaging practising educationalists.

As this volume has suggested, there is a wealth of practice taking place in many countries that could be called development education. However this practice has all too often been constrained by external factors, whether in the form of political and ideological opposition, narrow agendas of funders, or lack of clarity as to the purpose of particular projects and activities.

A response to these challenges is outlined in this volume: seeing development education not as a goal based on changing behaviour and engagement in global and development issues, but as a process of learning.

Development education and its related themes, whilst not always central to mainstream educational practice, have clearly had influence in many industrialised countries. These themes and approaches to learning are also potentially relevant to education in the Global South.

What is also evident is that themes such as learning in a global society, global citizenship, sustainable development and understanding the causes of poverty are not going to go away. Indeed they are likely to become more important in the years to come, as education becomes more and more globalised, and employment patterns are more determined by global forces. In an increasingly interconnected world, cultures, communities and societies will come into even greater daily contact, so understanding different viewpoints and interpretations is an important element in ensuring cohesion, tolerance and mutual respect within all societies.

Above all, living in a globalised society threatened with extinction because of climate change will increasingly require a greater sense of global social responsibility.

This volume has suggested that the discourses and practices in development education can make an important contribution. However those engaged in this area of practice need to recognise the necessity for greater rigour, conceptualisation and clarity of thought. The loose use of language and the ways in which both policy-makers and practitioners have used concepts for their own ends remain a major barrier.

The introductory chapter to this volume summarised the rationale, setting out why there is a need for a new conceptualisation of development education, but recognising and building upon the practice that has been evident in a number of countries for over thirty years.

Chapter 2 outlined the chequered history of development education and its relationship to areas such as global education and global citizenship. It showed that, whilst there is evidence of increased recognition of the importance of this area of learning, it has been too open to political and ideological influences that have diverted practice away from a primary educational purpose.

Chapter 3 reflected on the different interpretations of the term development education, and its relationship and contribution to broader debates in education and development. It also showed that despite the concept being a construction from policy-makers and practitioners in the Global North, it is an approach to learning that has global relevance.

Chapter 4 addressed the challenge that development education has tended to be an educational movement that speaks only to itself. By looking through the lenses of communities of practice, social movements and networks, there is evidence to suggest that in too many countries and practices, development education has been seen as linked to organisations that have tried from the outside to influence educational practice. Development education has thus not been embedded in mainstream education.

Chapters 5 and 6 took the themes that have influenced this practice and suggested that they could have greater clarity and rigour if they were more grounded in academic theories related to postcolonialism, globalisation, development, cosmopolitanism, critical pedagogy and transformative learning. From these theoretical influences, a conceptual pedagogic framework is proposed, based on the following themes: promoting a global outlook, a recognition of power and inequality in the world, a belief in social justice, and a commitment to reflection and dialogue.

Chapter 7 reviewed examples of practice that focus on learning about development, and how they relate to the pedagogic framework outlined in this volume. Examples were given based on research in the UK and Ireland, covering not only learning in the classroom but also personal experience such as international volunteering and school linking. A key theme to emerge from the research was the different ways in which knowledge and understanding about development are constructed, and the impact this has on the values base and world viewpoint of the learner.

Chapter 8 took a similar approach by reviewing practice that has globalisation as its theme. Here examples of research and practice are referred to from youth work, schools, further education and universities. These examples show the popularity of the use of the term 'global' over 'development', how it opens up opportunities for making connections between the individual's own lifestyle and issues elsewhere in the world. The evidence also shows however that the use of the term 'global' can also lead to a process of learning that emphasises a more economic and uncritical approach to understanding globalisation, of developing the skills to adapt to, rather than to challenge, the inequalities that exist in the world.

Chapter 9 looked at the practices of NGOs in relation to the pedagogical framework, particularly the work of two organisations, Save the Children and Plan UK. The evidence from research on the development education activities of these two NGOs suggests that whilst they both offered a wealth of expertise, resources and contacts that could help the learner understand global issues, organisational constraints meant that all too often creative and open-ended learning lost out to the need for evidence of impact, to secure support for their aims.

Chapter 10 reviewed through examples how development education has addressed the challenges of impact and evaluation. As development education has been heavily reliant on public funding, there has been a need to demonstrate value for money, and that, as a result of grants being allocated, changes have taken place within individuals and communities towards understanding of development. This has led to a form of development education in many instances resulting in an uncritical approach towards aid and international development, with a focus on measuring impact in terms of changes in behaviour. If approaches are taken that focus more on processes of learning, and adopt a more open-ended and research-based methodology, then evidence can be identified that shows the impact of development education in terms of questioning assumptions, challenging view-points, and deepening knowledge about development issues. Examples are taken from evaluating a training course, a project on international school partnerships, and a series of activities with teachers and pupils to assess how to know whether development education approaches are having an impact.

Chapter 11 gives examples that show the value of putting learning at the heart of development education practice. These examples are taken from Japan, Hong Kong, the UK and Sweden. They show the value and importance of involving external organisations in enabling educators and learners to understand different viewpoints and deepen their understanding of development issues.

Chapter 12 summarises the importance of pedagogy in the framework outlined in the volume and how it is applied within formal education. This application is called global learning and can be summarised as: deepening an understanding of different viewpoints and perspectives of development; encouraging a critical reflection on one's own viewpoints; contextualising learning within historical, cultural and social traditions; and promoting a sense of social justice.

A recurring theme throughout has been that development education should be seen as a pedagogy, an approach to learning. The proposed pedagogical framework starts from recognising that educators will engage in learning about global and development themes from a wide range of starting points, perspectives and experiences. They will construct their own interpretations as to what is meant by development and poverty.

The pedagogy of development education and its application through global learning need further debate and discussion. What is certainly needed is greater clarity and a better understanding of how best to promote learning about development and global themes in the classroom, in ways that are meaningful to children and young people, and that help them make sense of the globalised world in which they play so great a part.

Global learning needs to be relevant to the curriculum. It needs to have a clear knowledge base that is located within discourses around international development. It needs to recognise the importance of critical thinking. A belief in social justice should have a prominent role. It needs above all not to be seen as the simple application of a specific series of topics, but rather as an approach to learning that necessitates reflection on the part of the educator and the learner.

INDEX

Note: Page numbers followed by 't' refer to tables.